The Hart Sisters

The Hart Sisters

*Early African Caribbean Writers,
Evangelicals, and Radicals*

Edited and with
an Introduction by
Moira Ferguson

University of Nebraska Press
Lincoln and London

© 1993 by the University of
Nebraska Press. All rights reserved.
Manufactured in the United States of
America. The paper in this book meets
the minimum requirements of
American National Standard
for Information Sciences – Perma-
nence of Paper for Printed Library
Materials, ANSI Z39.48–1984.
Library of Congress Cataloging-
in-Publication Data The Hart sisters :
early African Caribbean writers,
evangelicals, and radicals / edited and
with an introduction by Moira
Ferguson. p. cm. Includes various
works by Anne Hart Gilbert and
Elizabeth Hart Thwaites. Includes
index. ISBN 0-8032-1984-9 (alk.
paper) 1. Caribbean poetry (English) –
Black authors. 2. Gilbert, Anne
Hart, 1773–1833 – Correspondence.
3. Thwaites, Elizabeth Hart, 1772–
1833 – Correspondence. 4. Authors,
Caribbean – 19th century – Correspondence. 5. Christian biography –
Caribbean Area. 6. Radicalism –
Caribbean Area – History. 7. Women –
Caribbean Area – Biography.
8. Methodism – Antigua – History.
9. Antigua – Biography. I. Ferguson,
Moira. II. Gilbert, Anne Hart, 1773–
1833. III. Thwaites, Elizabeth
Hart, 1772–1833. PR9205.6.H37 1993
811 – dc20 92-33056 CIP

Contents

Acknowledgments

In the course of researching this book I have incurred a number of debts that I am happy to have an opportunity to acknowledge.

I want first to thank the very helpful staff at the National Archives, St. Johns, Antigua, especially the curator, Mrs. Bridget Harris, who answered all my inquiries promptly and efficiently, facilitated my access to primary and secondary sources, and generously opened the collections to me. I also thank most appreciatively Mrs. Maudrey Gonzales, assistant archivist at the National Archives, for invaluable assistance and for putting me in touch with other sources. I thank, too, staff person Louise Hector for her warm welcome and Hubert Henry for his helpfulness with an inquiry.

I am also delighted to have this occasion to thank numerous staff members of the Museum of Antigua and Barbuda, St. Johns, Antigua, for making my stay pleasant and productive. I am especially indebted to curator Desmond V. Nicholson, who over the years speedily answered all my queries painstakingly and meticulously. An ardent vote of thanks also to assistant curator Kitz Rickert. I thank Brenda Lee Browne, Michele Henry, and Bernard Jones for their helpfulness and assistance.

At the London Methodist Missionary Archives, School of Oriental and African Studies, University of London, I am deeply indebted to Rosemary Seton, archivist, Jane Partington, library assistant, and Brian Scott, assistant librarian, from Reader Services, and Gail Miller, reading room supervisor, all of whom aided me in tracking down and obtaining documents and liberally opened their collections to me.

For helpful responses to queries, I thank Angela Whitelegge, chief librarian, University of London; Jack Smith, Principal Archives Office, Liverpool Record Office, Liverpool; Horace Lewis, assistant to the curator, National Library of Jamaica; the archivist of the Moravian Archives, Bethlehem, Pennsylvania; Mrs. Joy Fox, archivist, Methodist Missionary Society; David Way, publishing manager of the British Library, as well as the general staff of the library; and John Tuck, head of administration, The John Rylands University Library of Manchester.

Last, at my home institution, I extend grateful thanks to the circulation department, especially supervisor Debra Pearson, and to staff members at the Interlibrary Loan Office, particularly supervisor Brian Zillig, for their prompt and courteous assistance in obtaining books and documentation. I also thank the Department of English for a Faculty Development Fellowship and the Research Council for a Maude Hammond Fling Fellowship, both of which enabled me to visit the Antiguan archives.

For indispensable research assistance, I thank Kate Flaherty, Nicolle French, Lisa Toay, and especially Steven Hayes. I thank Thomas Bestul for assistance in interpreting and deciphering difficult handwriting and Robert Haller for help with biblical allusions. Cora Kaplan's incisive reading of the manuscript in its final draft was invaluable.

Finally, I warmly thank Roma Rector and LeAnn Messing for a proficient job of typing the text and appendixes.

Notes on the sources of the texts are found at the foot of the first page of each selection. I have used holographs for all texts where they were available. Occasionally, as with some of Elizabeth Hart Thwaites's works, I had available only a published version.

I have not retained italics or underlining unless they were intended for emphasis, and I have deleted superfluous quotation marks at the beginning of lines. Square brackets enclose words added for clarification. A question mark means the original was unclear. Obvious typographical or spelling errors and inconsistencies have been silently corrected, and I have emended subject-verb agreement.

There seems to be no consistency of spelling for Anne Hart Gilbert's first name. I have used the final *e* as it is the spelling most generally used.

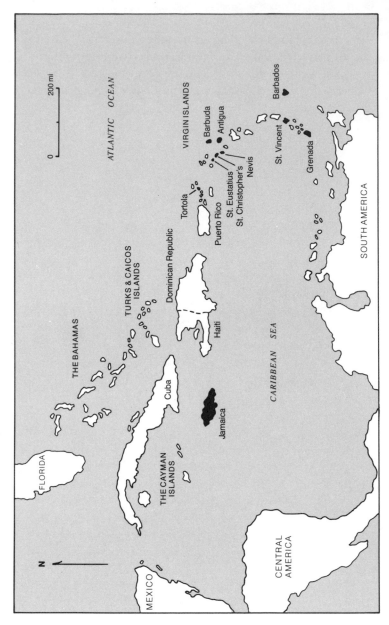

Caribbean Region

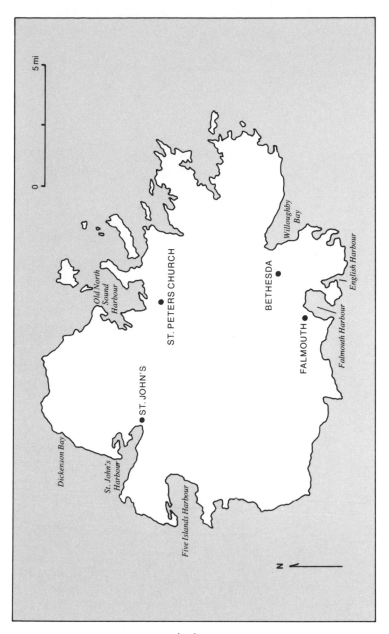

Antigua

Introduction

HISTORICAL EVENTS

Sisters born a year apart to a black slaveholder father, Anne Hart Gilbert (1773–1833) and Elizabeth Hart Thwaites (1772–1833) were the first educators of slaves and free blacks in Antigua and among the first African Caribbean female writers.[1] Elizabeth Hart, moreover, was one of the first women in the Caribbean to agitate and write against slavery. Related to distinguished Methodist families, they were prominent members of the religious and cultural intelligentsia in Antigua during the late slave period there, when the institution was under attack and the character of society was changing.[2] Between them the sisters tackled a wide range of genres, from biography and religious history to poetry and letters. Several texts doubled as political manifestos and antislavery polemics. Anne Hart Gilbert wrote a short solicited history of Antiguan Methodism and a biography of her husband, John Gilbert, and Elizabeth Hart Thwaites wrote a similarly solicited history, poems, hymns, letters, and an antislavery letter-tract.

In her detailed study of late eighteenth-century slave society in the British Leeward Islands, where Antigua held an important historical and political position, Elsa Goveia defines slave society as "the whole community based on slavery, including masters and freedmen as well as slaves."[3]

For the most part whites viewed the free colored, as the population of African Caribbean former slaves was known, as too insignificant numerically to make trouble; or perhaps whites downplayed their concern, since race and shade of complexion were decisive factors in sociopolitical life. In 1788, for example, William Hutchinson stated that "their whole number at Antigua amounts to only a few Hundred."[4] Out of proportion to their numbers, however, was the political influence of free colored communities. For one thing, their numbers were growing, which meant they would gradually acquire private property, and for another, they functioned as a critical buffer between the whites and the slaves. In Antigua particularly, free colored men and women had obtained rights of citizenship. This voting freedom angered many whites, who tried to perpetuate ideas about racial superiority and maintain political hegemony. Voting rights, moreover, suggested how much the power of free coloreds was on the increase.[5]

For African Caribbeans in a slave society, becoming free men and women was a difficult process and usually came about through reward or purchase. In some cases it began by whites' hiring out slaves as porters and boatmen. The slaves were able to keep part of their cash income and eventually purchased their freedom.

Important consequences followed from the fact that half the adult slave population was not cultivating fields and hence living in very poor conditions but, instead, worked as domestic servants or in trade, jobs that afforded a greater opportunity for gaining manumission. A slave who was a good servant could receive a grant of freedom as a reward. Some black female concubines, moreover, were able to buy freedom, often because of the children they bore white men.[6] Nonetheless, the account of how black women gained freedom is not always straightforward. Mary Prince, a former slave living in Antigua who chronicled her experiences, is another case in point. When her owners were on holiday, Mary Prince narrates, she would go down to the docks and sell provisions. White male friends, moreover, offered to purchase her from her owners, the Woods.[7]

Another factor in the anxiety the plantocracy manifested about the ascendancy of free colored men and women was the dilution of their own power. Members of the white professional class in Antigua,

> merchants, lawyers, doctors, government officials, and even clergymen made up some part of the membership of the Assemblies. This group was well represented in the Assembly at

Antigua. At the general election of 1788, for instance, 12 professionals were returned out of a total of 25 members of the Assembly. St. Johns, the capital town, returned as its four representatives an attorney and three merchants; and the new Assembly also counted among its members five doctors and three lawyers—one of them the Solicitor-General of the Leeward Islands. At least some of this group were proprietors of land; most were probably substantial men of property. They combined with the planters to give the political system of Antigua its reputation for superiority to the other governments of the Leeward Islands, which lacked Antigua's advantages of settled population and property.[8]

The more slaves were freed, the more whites worried about control and sought ways to keep society divided. The subjugation of the free colored community guaranteed white supremacy. During the Napoleonic wars, which offered opportunities for freedom, the plantocracy was very much afraid for its power. Yet slaveowners, caught in their own political contradictions, granted civil rights even to white men of little property and ceased excluding Roman Catholics from jury service. Primarily, they wanted as many white representatives as possible among the ruling class.[9]

The gap that separated lower-class from upper-class whites was much greater than that separating the free colored from lower-class whites. Owning property did not entitle free colored people to an automatic status change. Bryan Edwards, a notoriously ethnocentric historian, put it this way: "The courts of law interpreted the act of manumission by the owner, as nothing more than an abandonment or release of his own proper authority over the person of the slave, which did not, and could not, convey to the object of his bounty, the civil and political rights of a natural-born subject; and the same principle was applied to the issue of freed mothers, until after the third generation from the Negro ancestor."[10] In their own words in a petition of the Antiguan free colored to the Legislative Assembly, that population considered themselves "a distinct and degraded class. . . . Let the distresses of a Coloured Person be ever so great, in this Country, there is no Parochial Relief for such a one!" More specifically, they could not hold public, parochial, or commissioned offices or be jurors. They could prosecute cases only if they could produce white witnesses, since their evidence in courts was accepted only against other blacks. Indigent "illegitimate" children of color—their number far greater than white ones—could not receive money from public funds, although the black population was taxed at the same rate as whites.[11]

The number of Methodists reported for Antigua in 1797 by the Leeds Connection was 25 whites and 2,379 colored people.[12] A decade later the Reverend John Baxter of Antigua informed the Reverend Joseph Benson in Antigua that "Our numbers are Whites 22, black and colored 3,516. Many have died this year. I believe more than three hundred."[13] This increase in the Methodist population further alarmed the mostly Anglican island's elite. Slaveowners feared conversion as much as if not more than African religious traditions.[14]

Not surprisingly, becoming as "white" as possible was a goal, because only by crossing the racial line (passing) could free coloreds achieve upward mobility. Increasing fairness of complexion through miscegenous relations was an almost guaranteed way of moving up the social ladder.[15] Free colored men thus sought free colored women; for social advantages, however, free colored women often sought out white men. Free colored men, then, often ended up marrying slaves, in turn augmenting the potential size of the free colored population.

The discrimination against free colored people provoked such acrimony that in 1823 they presented a petition of their grievances;[16] hence the desire of many African Caribbean women to associate with or (a much less common occurrence) marry white men. This vigorous system of racial disparity meant that the most poverty-stricken and subjugated group consisted of black slaves. Clement Caines encapsulates the abominable condition of field slaves as opposed even to house slaves: "They are also the most miserable creatures that we own, the most corrupt and the most dangerous."[17]

In such a society, Anne Hart Gilbert and Elizabeth Hart Thwaites occupied a special niche, first, because they were respectable members of the free colored community and, second, because as members of a Methodist family their religion and by extension their political values were oppositional to nominally Anglican ruling-class values.

The Antiguan Methodist church to which the sisters' family belonged was dominated in its early days by several households: the Clearkleys, the Cables, the Lynches, and the Gilberts, the last related to Nathaniel Gilbert, who introduced Methodism to the West Indies.[18] The Hart sisters were connected to all four families.

Their maternal grandmother, for example, was Frances Clearkley, an African Caribbean convert to Methodism under the ministry of Francis Gilbert, Nathaniel Gilbert's brother. "My grandmother," states Anne Hart Gilbert, "reserv'd her first [admission] Ticket [to a Methodist meeting] pinned in the rules of the Society."[19] Frances Clearkley must have been a free colored; otherwise her daughter would have been a slave, because in slave society the mother's status determined the children's. The original membership of the Hart family within the free colored community may, then, have come from this marriage. Their maternal grandfather was Timothy Clearkley, and their mother was Frances Clearkley's daughter Anne, acclaimed for her piety and virtue. She married Barry Conyers Hart, an African Caribbean plantation owner, a trouble shooter and poet who wrote for the local newspaper. He owned an estate in Popeshead, near St. Johns. Known as a man who agonized over punishments and tried to act humanely toward his slaves, Hart took seriously his conflictual role as a planter. Possibly his religious convictions made a difference to his attitudes, since black slaveowners were notoriously hard taskmasters.[20] On one occasion he spent a weekend in the homes of work-gang members to have a better sense of the slaves' way of life. Before traveling missionaries ministered regularly, his home was used for public worship. Unconventionally for these virulently pro-slavery times—and especially for a member of the plantocratic class—Hart helped slaves execute their affairs by preparing their manumission papers without charge and by offering general advice.

Hart's position as a black slaveholder reflected how complex such a role had become within Antiguan society as a whole. Free colored communities occupied a complicated space in Antiguan society; their demands overlapped with those of the slaves—they abhorred subordination. Like slaves, they were buried in a separate cemetery with criminals and suicides: William Green reported, "Even the bell used to toll the death of a colored person was inferior in size and quality to that which announced the death of a white colonist."[21] Yet like the entrenched white ruling class, they too owned slaves. Politically, then, they found themselves in a critical intersecting zone between the two groups. To a limited extent the social structure favored them, or at least occasionally accommodated certain of their legal demands. As a result of a diverse but all-round opposition, the white oligarchy could never sever its ties with the metropolis even when the emancipation movement reached its height. Ultimately, the imperial military forces were all that stood between the colonial ruling class and any coalition of slaves and the free colored population. Colonial insularity inevitably bred forced alliances.

Still, despite their political connections to slaves, in attitude free people of color were considered harsh masters: "Instead of strengthening the relationship between the free people of color and the Negro slaves, their common origin served only to embitter it," Goveia comments.[22] Bryan Edwards wrote that the free colored were "objects of envy and hatred, for the same or a greater degree of superiority which the Whites assume over them, the free Mulattoes lay claim to over the Blacks. These again, abhor the idea of being slaves to the descendants of slaves."[23]

About the turn of the century, Barry Conyers Hart's finances collapsed, and he moved to Trinidad to rebuild his career. As a free man of color who was also a planter, Hart faced severe disadvantages. In the first place, major white landowners traditionally squeezed out small planters, black and white alike. With even less access to credit than his white counterparts and no social status, a man like Barry Hart would have to work extraordinarily hard to succeed. His difficulty in earning a decent living probably spurred his decision to leave Antigua. Possibly he followed the "common Practice, if they [free colored] have any Land of their own, to hire poor Negroes at leisure Hours to cultivate it." Hart's subsistence farming lost out even to the activities of slaves eager to sell vegetables at Sunday market. His overhead was high, his profit margin lower, and by the end of the eighteenth century men like him scarcely participated in local markets. Given the condition of free colored farmers, Hart had little incentive to remain at Popeshead. To what extent Hart's financial failure was due to his politically complicated, even self-contradictory status can only be a subject of speculation. As a black slaveowner, he might well have had considerable difficulty maintaining the number of white servants mandated by law. Also, obviously, he would have found mercantile credit less easily accessible and social and commercial connections less likely.[24] Certainly he and his daughter Elizabeth must have talked over the clash between his slaveholding and her abolitionist principles.

The Methodist presence on Antigua took hold just after the mid-eighteenth century. In the early 1760s, Methodists made spiritual inroads in New York and Philadelphia. On his travels to England before 1760, the Honorable Nathaniel Gilbert met the founder and spiritual father of Methodism, John Wesley, and was astounded when Wesley baptized two of his slaves. Lawyer, planter, speaker of the Antiguan Assembly in 1764, and a major slaveholder, Gilbert was influenced by Wesley's teaching and brought his spiritual mentor's religious message back to Antigua as the Caribbean's first self-appointed missionary. The first Methodist chapel in North America was established in New York at that time. (Wesley sent out several missionaries to capitalize on early successes. A decade later, the Methodists in North America boasted about a thousand members. By 1794 their numbers had increased to 51,416 whites and 16,227 blacks; in 1807 membership had climbed to 114,727 whites, with "coloured people and blacks" numbering 29,863).[25]

Female-administered religious instruction at home greatly contributed to the increasing presence of African Caribbean converts to Methodism. In the words of a contemporary ethnocentric Methodist historian, the Reverend John Horsford:

> In most cases, however, a mother, or sometimes a grandmother, and that maternal ancestor perfectly black, or nearly so, was a devotee of Methodism, sang its hymns with rapture, loved its Class-Meetings, delighted in its Lovefeasts, heard its tenets from the lips of its Ministers with avidity. . . . These females have each led with them to the Wesleyan chapel a little boy or girl, initiating them into the habit of attending the church of the coloured people, since the "big church"— so called—was, in those days, intended for greater folk; and,

more than this, they conducted such boys and girls to the Sunday-school.[26]

As an evangelical household that benefited from an informed matrilineal religious descent, the Hart, Clearkley, and Cable family members undertook such charitable deeds as visiting the sick and distributing Bibles. Because of their political marginality and the propaganda implied by their spiritual labors, many of these activities were objectionable to the Antiguan ruling class: the governor, the council, the magistracy, and numerous Assembly House members all subscribed to the Anglican church.[27]

In John Wesley's journal for February 17, 1758, the following entry appears: "I preached at Wandsworth [England]. A gentleman come from America has again opened a door in this desolate spot. In the morning I preached in Mr. Gilbert's house. Two negro servants of his, and a mulatto, appear to be much awakened. Shall not His saving health be made known unto all nations?" On November 29 of the same year, Wesley further states: "I rode to Wandsworth, and baptized two Negroes belonging to Mr. Gilbert, a gentleman lately come from Antigua. One of them is deeply convinced of sin; the other rejoices in God her Savior, and is the first African Christian I have known. But shall not our Lord, in due time, have these heathens also for His inheritance?"[28] Ultimately Antiguan ruling class scion Gilbert became the first Antiguan to promote religious instruction and conversion among slaves and the "humbler free classes of society." The method was simple. Wesleyan missionaries directed their efforts almost exclusively to what one evangelical historian calls "the upper and lower classes of that description of society which [Methodism] was intended to reach, namely, the black and coloured people."[29] Additionally, white Methodists sought to convert well-connected black people, who could aid in the conversion of a predominantly black constituency. Nonetheless, although John Wesley championed abolition and although Antigua was the "mother-island of West Indian Methodism" from the start of evangelizing missions, Methodist missionaries shied away from advocating emancipation overtly, since they were already regarded suspiciously as outsiders.[30]

Not surprisingly, two of the daughters of Anne Clearkley Hart and Barry Conyers Hart responded positively to missionaries, who aimed primarily to convert "heathen" African Caribbeans. During the first year of the ministry of the Reverend Thomas Coke, a renowned Methodist missionary who arrived in Antigua in 1786, Anne and Elizabeth Hart were received into the Methodist church and baptized. Following Wesley, Coke did not mention emancipation as a principle.[31] Elizabeth Hart's aunt, her mother's sister Grace Clearkley Cable, had attracted her to Moravianism from a young age and influenced her religious conversion. That familiarity with the Moravians may account for her early espousal of abolitionist principles.[32] After their Methodist conversion, the sisters changed their habits, dressed plainly, and renounced what they considered worldly pursuits. Elizabeth Hart stopped playing the piano because music, she felt, "drew her heart from better things."[33]

After the death of her mother in 1785, twelve-year-old Anne Hart had staunchly acted as surrogate mother to her many siblings. When Anne married in 1798, her sister Elizabeth took over the responsibility for the next three years. Not content with instructing their siblings, both sisters also offered religious instruction to slaves and taught them to read, a courageous and conspicuous decision for any woman to make when slavery was being attacked transatlantically and societal values were shifting. Having been raised in homes where religion and culture—Methodist principles as well as the writings of John Milton, Edward Young, and William Cowper—were prized, they habitually involved themselves in philanthropic work.

Such remarkable pursuits, especially in women so young, discomfited the white Antiguan population, who politically feared the spread of nonconformity.[34] Successful conversions not only flouted religious hegemony but suggested manipulation of the vulnerable that could lead to social unrest, if not rebellion. Besides, at a social level non-Methodists looked down on the Methodist Society for its orientation toward the disadvantaged. Even more critically for the island elite, Elizabeth Hart's forthright views on abolition were repugnant. The idea that marginalized members of society were to be embraced as spiritual equals was deemed scandalous as well as injurious to white safety.

Any instruction of blacks challenged traditional views and indirectly undermined white authority. Thomas Coke, for example, was unequivocal in his view of African Caribbeans as people in a state of "heathenish and savage darkness," living in "all manner of uncleanness with greediness." [35] Black Antiguans had to be converted before they could be "civilized" and hence moral. In Coke's own words:

> To contemplate the spread of the everlasting gospel; to see its benign and sacred influences diffused through the barbarous departments of human nature, and illuminating the benighted regions of the globe, must be a scene of the most exquisite delight to the sincere followers of Jesus Christ. To view myriads of our fellow-creatures rescued from the vices of the most odious nature, and from ignorance the most consummate; from crimes which it would be even hateful to name, and which almost exceed belief; to survey these, now rejoicing in the God of their salvation, with a joy that is unspeakable and full of glory, must be a new source of joy even to angels; and must tend to enhance even the felicities of heaven. [36]

Coke goes on to answer the obvious question why, if God is a universal good father, Africans were not converted in Africa. Pontificating from a Eurocentric perspective and attributing bestiality to African Caribbeans, he somewhat illogically answers that the conditions of Africans were such that light could not at all enter:

> Lost in an abyss of iniquity, the feelings by which these negroes were governed, were little more than mere animal sensations. The violence of their passions, and their habitual indulgence of them, must have nearly smothered the internal dictates of their consciences, and reduced every emotion of the soul to one common level, and melted all into one general mass. Unable to discriminate between perceptions which through their habits of iniquity were apparently allied, though in themselves distant and remote, they were incapable of analyzing their thoughts. Their ideas were few, and bounded by narrow confines; the gratifying of their inclinations seemed to encircle all. Thus circumscribed in their views, and acting under the impulses of those affections which were the only incentives to action; ignorance, the inseparable concomitant of

savage life, seemed to shut up every avenue of the soul, and fixed a barrier, which prohibited all access. Their reasoning faculties having never been called into action, were in a torpid state. Of the truths of the gospel they had never heard; and on its excellencies or defects, they were incompetent to decide. Their passions were enthroned; and, reigning with absolute dominion, would submit to no control. Thus shielded by ignorance, and impelled by their desires, influenced by that carnal mind which is enmity against the things of God, and acting with views that were bounded by contiguous objects, with distracted notions of a *First Cause*, too confused to admit of any regard, or to procure reverence; and with prospects of an hereafter too much obscured to incite to action, or to keep alive any adequate conceptions of rewards and punishments beyond the grave, Christianity had before it no prospect that could promise any success; or justify any attempt to introduce it into these benighted regions of the globe.[37]

The Hart sisters had their work cut out with "fallen" slaves because the social order—let alone the much bandied assertion of slave polygamy—made monogamy almost impossible. Husbands had no legal rights as family men. Males vastly outnumbered females. White men in diverse positions of power kept black women as concubines.[38]

Thus black women in a sense could not win. Those who favored slavery branded them harlots or temptresses who sexually indulged themselves at will; emancipationists saw black women as innocent, morally degraded victims. Abusive sexual practices (at the hands of white men) were used, too, as evidence of the alleged instability of the black family.[39] In the British Parliament, in deference to an avowed moral sensibility toward women in general, Foreign Secretary George Canning introduced separate legislation to stop female flogging and uphold the modesty of black women. In the last era of slavery, in Barbara Bush's words, "religious abolitionists preached that the duties and joys of monogamous Christian marriage would greatly benefit the moral and material welfare of the slaves."[40]

By the time the Hart sisters began teaching, the slave system was expensive and becoming even more so as slaves got wind of efforts in

London to pass an emancipation law. Sugar production had become much less beneficial to planters and required a large slave population to ensure adequate profits. Antigua had one of the highest population densities, with three hundred slaves to the square mile. The upkeep of such a huge population was enormous, especially after 1807, when no more slaves could legally be imported. Contrary to William Wilberforce's expectations, this led not to improved but to deteriorating conditions, a psychological as well as financial consequence of abolition. Publicized atrocities intensified, helped by the establishment of the *Anti-Slavery Reporter* in 1816. One argument goes that only the sugar boom of the 1790s saved the plantocracy from financial disaster. But the writing was on the wall.[41]

Despite white ruling class opposition and unacknowledged internal prejudice from Methodists themselves, in 1798 Anne Hart Gilbert married John Gilbert, cousin of Nathaniel Gilbert. This contract instantly raised her social status.[42] Born in St. Johns, Antigua, in 1767, Gilbert was apprenticed at fourteen to a naval storekeeper. Seriously ill in 1784, he was nursed back to health by the wife of John Baxter, a shipwright and influential Wesleyan preacher. Having married a Miss Lorin in 1789, Gilbert joined the Methodists in 1794 and became a class leader and preacher by 1797. His wife died soon afterward. As a white lay preacher, he was criticized by fellow officers in the militia for referring to slaves in his congregation as "brothers." Any such familiarity imperiled white control within the plantocracy. The threatened court-martial that Gilbert pointedly ridiculed was never convened.[43]

When Gilbert, in 1798, decided to ask Anne Hart to marry him, a startling act in slave society, the same fellow officers again disavowed Gilbert and attempted to court-martial him, whereupon he resigned his commission. After he proposed, both Anne Hart and her father tried to dissuade him from such a socially proscribed alliance. Possibly they feared physical violence. They suggested he travel to England, but since Gilbert, in his own words, "had not the means of paying the expense of travelling . . . I therefore persisted."[44] One week later, Anne Hart accepted his offer.

In the governor's absence, the president of the council as well as the superintendent of the Wesleyan mission, John Baxter, advised him against the match. So rare were miscegenous alliances that Baxter warned Gilbert he would be "committed to jail as a madman."[45] As a further mark of public censure, he was deprived of his commission as a notary public. Even the painted sign outside his business office was thrown into the sea. After he was refused a marriage license, he published the banns in church, despite the fact that one of his relatives requested all Antiguan clergymen not to marry the couple. A sad, wry, realistic Gilbert comments on this protracted persecution in his autobiography:

> I was informed that he [this relative] also wrote to the naval Commander-in-Chief, requesting him to forbid all the Chaplains of His Majesty's ships on the station to perform the office.
>
> It is proper to observe, that if I had determined upon seducing and degrading the object of my regard and esteem, I should have been considered by the ungodly aristocracy of the country as having acted quite properly, and incurred no reproach from them, as she was a woman of colour.[46]

The expansive Antiguan commentator Frances Lanaghan, in *Antigua and the Antiguans*, puts it this way: "Slaves and free black females were often expected to become the mistresses of white men" or, in West Indian terminology, *"housekeeper."* [47]

Having provoked public outrage, John Gilbert and Anne Hart returned from their honeymoon to find the door of his office painted a symbolic half white, half yellow. Who married them remains a mystery. Elizabeth Hart's subsequent marriage to a white evangelical educator, Charles Thwaites, not to mention her abolitionist views, probably clinched the sisters' unpopularity and the threat they represented to traditionally minded whites in the community.

In 1801, after her father's financial setback, Elizabeth Hart moved from the Popeshead estate to St. Johns to be near her sister Anne. She then founded a private school. Two years later Anne Hart Gilbert and her husband moved to English Harbour, a neighboring town a few miles south, where John Gilbert was promoted as first clerk to the storekeeper in the royal naval yard.

About this time, it seems, both Anne Hart Gilbert and Elizabeth

Hart were separately invited by a Methodist missionary, the Reverend Richard Pattison, to write a history of Methodism. In 1804 they both complied. Then in 1805, after Elizabeth Hart's marriage to Charles Thwaites in St. Johns, where he was an instructor, the couple moved to English Harbour to join the Gilberts.

From an evangelical viewpoint, English Harbour was a "deplorably wicked" place,[48] with military barracks and warships an everyday presence that engendered immorality and confounded God's work. To add insult to religious injury, not only was Sunday observance ignored, but people were tolled to work on Sundays by the same naval yard bell that summoned them on weekdays.

In an effort to offset what evangelicals considered corrupt living, Methodist ministers from the time of John Baxter had preached on a weekday evening once every two weeks in Porter's Row, where black Antiguans lived in thatched huts. John Gilbert maintained this tradition. When the congregation outgrew the available open space, however, the Thwaiteses' more spacious home became the site for preaching. After numerous conversions and Gilbert's promotion to naval storekeeper, preaching resumed at the Gilberts' home. Anne Hart Gilbert presumably also continued to work informally, in addition to her other chosen tasks, as John Gilbert's principal clerk and assistant.[49]

Concurrently, Beilby Porteus, bishop of London and a leading evangelical Anglican, issued a prospectus in favor of Sunday schools for slaves. The Society for the Conversion and Religious Instruction and Education of the Negro Slaves in the British West India Islands had been established in 1794. With Bishop Porteus as president, the Anglican charter specifically forbade any interference in Caribbean commerce or political affairs.[50] If anything, it suggested that mission teaching would transform slaves into more malleable workers. Charter signatories stressed the importance of obedience, piety, and marital fidelity. This goal did not markedly differ from that of the Methodists, especially as Wesley's emancipationist "commandment" was gradually eroded. The Reverend Thomas Coke, principal founder of Methodist foreign missions, intended "to complete the work of [Bryan] Edwards by supplying a narrative of the spread of Christianity in the Caribbean islands. . . . Coke asserted 'it is to the gospel, that Great Britain in all probability, stands indebted for the preservation of many of her richest colonial possessions, even to the present day: that her swarthy subjects have not revolted like those of a neighbouring island; and committed those depredations on the white inhabitants, which humanity shudders to name.'"[51]

Responding in September 1809, Anne Hart Gilbert and Elizabeth Hart Thwaites opened the first Caribbean Sunday school for boys and girls, without regard to class or race: "Many [slave children] came from neighbouring estates; it was the first institution of the kind formed in the West Indies, and was formed at a time, too, when teaching slaves to read was so unpopular and suspicious a measure, that the missionaries were instructed [by the London hierarchy] to avoid it, lest it should prevent their admission into places where they might otherwise be allowed to preach the Gospel."[52]

This defiant commitment of the Hart sisters to the education of slaves suggests how unprecedented a space they were creating for themselves as educators in Antiguan society. Their actions also stressed both the necessity and the importance of educating all black Antiguans. The commitment of Charles and Elizabeth Thwaites to education far exceeded the establishment of Sunday schools. At some point Elizabeth Hart Thwaites visited Montserrat to observe how the Lancastrian system of education worked.[53] In England Joseph Lancaster and Andrew Bell had "mapped out factory methods of teaching. . . . By division of labour, student monitors were to funnel instruction from a single teacher to the pupils."[54] The Thwaiteses introduced that innovative system to English Harbour.[55] At an important historical gathering in 1813, Elizabeth Hart Thwaites and her husband met with teachers and five hundred children from neighboring plantations on the estate belonging to the Lyon family and instituted a plan to teach the children to read. Halfway between English Harbour, where the Thwaiteses lived, and the Lyons' estate, slave volunteers built a schoolroom within six weeks to house this project. Elizabeth Hart Thwaites named it Bethesda and daily taught some two to three hundred children and adults there. Her occasional writings in favor of emancipation suggest another motivation for her philanthropic work. Possibly discussions about freedom subtly entered into her instruction and raised the chance of

slaves more openly contesting their situation. She also rode around
neighborhood estates ministering to the infirm. After these visits,
she and her husband had to extract numerous "chigoes" (chiggers)
that burrowed into their legs and toes.[56] As a further mark of personal asceticism and devotion, Elizabeth Hart Thwaites ate bread
and vegetables almost exclusively and gave the needy some of what
she could have eaten herself. Frances Lanaghan chronicles a fascinating vignette of Charles and Elizabeth Thwaites at work and of their
intention to educate not for education's own sake or only for the sake
of religion, but with a view to former slaves finding employment.

> As regards the population of this town . . . [Bridgetown or
> Willoughby Bay, Antigua] I can give but little information.
> With the exception of the very kind-hearted superintendent
> of the Wesleyan schools, Mr. Charles Thwaites, and his equally
> amiable wife, their very pretty little boy, one or two domes-
> tics, and their scholars of every shade, the only inhabitants I
> saw were flocks of black-headed gulls, busily employed in fol-
> lowing their piscatory avocations; a few half-starved looking
> sheep . . . and three or four long-necked, screaming birds. . . .
> After resting for a short time at the superintendent's dwell-
> ing, we proceeded to the school-room, a most commodious
> apartment, measuring 50 ft. by 48 ft., and capable of contain-
> ing 50 persons. The whole of this establishment, including the
> superintendent's house, which is detached, was erected by the
> Church Missionary Society; but after being used by them for
> a short time, it was turned over to the "Ladies Society," to
> whom it still belongs, although the Wesleyan Mission holds
> its school there.
>
> The school-room was but thinly attended upon the day of
> our visit, there not being more than 40 children—the usual
> number is about 100. Upon our entrance, they all rose up
> with "We'll make our obeisance together, as children ought to
> do," and then, quitting their raised seats, formed into double
> lines, their teacher at their head, and marched round the apart-
> ment to the tune of one of their infant rhymes. After perform-
> ing many martial-like evolutions, they finally arranged them-
> selves into a deep phalanx, and thus sang another of their little

songs. . . . I was much pleased to learn from Mr. Thwaites that, in almost every instance, the pupils who have left the schools under his charge have followed agricultural employments. To a country whose grand resource, and, indeed, entire dependence, is placed upon the cultivation of the sugar-cane, this conduct upon the part of its rising generation must be very important; and if the lower classes continue to do so, and not, because they are free, despise the hoe, Antigua may stand forth as pre-eminently flourishing among the other West Indian colonies.[57]

In letters to her cousin Elizabeth Lynch, Elizabeth Hart Thwaites expressed evangelical preoccupations and values, such as those concerning two of the children, referred to only by their initials, P. O. and M. M. Indirectly she also assails white discriminatory attitudes and values:

Many of the children are truly benefitted by religious instruction. I will give you an instance in P. O., the white orphan, who has to beg at the grog-shops, &c. I asked her, a few days ago, how her "mother," as she calls her, was: she answered with tears in her eyes, "She is very poorly, Ma'am, getting worse; but she don't pray; and when I beg her to pray to God, she swears at me."—M. M. is about eleven or twelve years old; you would hardly think, from the modesty and rectitude of her behavior, that she lived in a house of ill-fame, the resort of the basest characters. Her mother, at present having no rest to the soles of her feet, and being miserably poor withal, sends every day to get her meal from a wealthy woman, of the most vulgar manners, who lives with Commissary D.[58]

After subsisting on nominal remuneration, Charles Thwaites was finally appointed by the Anglican Church Missionary Society in 1817 as catechist and superintendent of Antiguan Sunday schools at English Harbour. In accordance with Elizabeth's Methodist commitment to chastity before marriage, the Thwaiteses condemned the practice of concubinage that had inevitably developed owing to the legal prohibition against slave marriages. But as well acquainted with Antiguan history as they were, they also understood the historical reasons why the numbers of black single mothers and "illegitimate" babies would be disproportionately high. Charles peppers his journal with tales of their philanthropic work regarding "fallen" women, backsliding, and young people's conversion. In all, the Thwaiteses ministered to sixty estates in addition to conducting a night school in their own house for eighty to one hundred children.

This intense commitment to domestic missionary work that did not include any explicit advocacy of emancipation followed the Society's new post-Wesley political direction. In this respect, it seems likely that the Thwaiteses disagreed with Methodist principles but self-protectively chose to manifest their opposition to slavery obliquely. Unlike John Wesley, Coke was not an emancipationist, although he did view enslavement as an evil practice. He saw Methodism as a stable social force. Coke's mystical view of history explains this seeming contradiction. Worldly disasters counted for very little beside the glory God conferred on a loving soul. Coke believed that God's ways were impenetrable and always good.[59]

Coke's primary goal was religious conversion. Hence he does not seem to have disapproved of the government's response to antislavery insurrections; he quarreled with the government only over religious toleration. In the sense that he urged inculcating Christian virtue in slaves to "civilize" them, his message did not differ qualitatively—and certainly not ideologically—from that of the Anglicans. Missionaries were men who saved the spiritual day. On this reading, Coke clearly saw missionaries through a Eurocentric lens as superior beings and slaves as people who were basically wild and needed spiritual taming:

> Defiled and polluted without a title to heaven, or a qualification for the enjoyment of it, they represented man as being naturally depraved, and on that account exposed to punishment; and as having added his actual transgressions to that original depravity; and by that means riveted his doom, and rendered his condemnation sure. Debilitated through sin, which held dominion over him, they held him forth as utterly unable to return to God without supernatural aid; to recover himself from that condition in which he was involved; or to

escape that misery to which he lay exposed. In fine, they described him as dead in trespasses, and dead in sins, destitute of all power to retrieve himself; and without an inclination to "flee from the wrath to come."

From these views in which they represented both God and man, they inferred the necessity of a Saviour; through whom man might have access to God, and be reconciled unto him, notwithstanding his past offenses. From the relation in which man stood to God, they inferred the necessity of an expiation; of a vicarious sacrifice which should be equal to the claims of justice; and from hence they led them to "behold the Lamb of God who taketh away the sins of the world."

By pointing out the Saviour in all his glorious offices, the affections of the poor negroes through accompanying grace became enkindled, their native ferocity was softened through the efficacy of dying love; and from a full conviction of the excellencies of this Saviour, and of the absolute necessity of obtaining an interest in him, they were led to call upon God for mercy; and to venture by faith on that sacrifice which the adorable Jesus had made: By this venturing on him, they soon knew in whom they had believed; and by feeling in their own souls the witness of his Holy Spirit, they were enabled to set to their seal that God is true.[60]

Somewhat surprisingly given the tenor of the times, this state of affairs, in which abolitionist Methodists administered the education of all Antiguan children, lasted over a decade. In 1825, however, the Anglican bishop of the diocese visited—possibly as a result of complaints and of growing divisions between metropolitan slaveowning Anglicans and antislavery nonconformists. Between 1826 and 1830–31, for example, the proportion of antislavery petitions that were filed by English Dissenters rose from 6 to 70 percent; the percentage filed by Anglicans dropped from 5 to 3.[61] The bishop chided Charles Thwaites for being a catechist of the Anglican Church Missionary Society, since he was still a Methodist and persistently "refused to disavow his membership." Even though Charles's position was terminated in 1827, the Thwaiteses continued the same work for some time without remuneration.[62] Both the Ladies' Negro Edu-

cation Society and a Mrs. Bethune of New York assisted Charles
Thwaites after his termination, with money and books, respectively.
Fifteen months later the Wesleyan Missionary Society formally em-
ployed him.

Meanwhile, in 1816 Anne Gilbert and Elizabeth Thwaites
planned and founded a society for the orphans and children of
"fallen and depraved relatives." Their cousin Elizabeth Lynch was
also involved. The organization was afterward designated the Female
Refuge Society. As a result of petitioning, evangelical British women
sent money and clothes to support this cause.[63] Anne Gilbert's philanthropic enterprises continued to expand. As Box reported,

> The English Harbour Sunday School and the Female Refuge
> Society were not the only charitable institutions which Mrs.
> Gilbert was engaged in—there were several others. She kept
> a weekly school, to teach writing and arithmetic. She superin-
> tended, and had the direction of, a large Infant School, sup-
> ported by the Ladies' Society in London. She was the dis-
> penser of blessings through the poor's fund for many years;
> visiting the sick, comforting the afflicted, clothing the naked,
> and feeding the hungry. She devised and organized a Juvenile
> Association, which has been more useful than could have been
> imagined in prospect. She presided also over other modes of
> charity.[64]

Joseph Sturge, a well-known British antislavery activist who traveled
to Antigua in 1837 to see how former slaves were being treated after
emancipation, stated that Anne Hart Gilbert held meetings in the
dark so that those who had only one set of clothes (usually soiled)
could attend meetings without shame.[65]

Teaching ceased at the Gilberts' house in 1817 at the end of the
Napoleonic wars, when the royal navy reduced its base in English
Harbour—and hence eliminated John Gilbert's position. The Gilberts moved their work to St. Johns but returned to English Harbour in 1821 when John Gilbert was appointed naval storekeeper. By
this time the Honorable Lady Grey, patroness of the English Harbour Sunday School Society, had been providing Methodist schoolroom space for four years. She appointed Anne Hart Gilbert super-

intendent of the girls' section of the school.[66] The Gilberts also took over from Elizabeth Hart Thwaites the responsibility of supervising Sunday schools.

Back in Britain, abolitionists' concerns about the conditions of Antiguan slaves culminated in a subscription campaign for "diseased and destitute" slaves. An infuriated Antiguan legislature convened a committee of the House of Assembly to investigate the matter. Along with Moravian missionaries and Joseph Phillips, secretary to the Moravians and the only white member of the Moravians in Antigua, Elizabeth Hart Thwaites was called to testify before the committee, since she had disbursed funds to those in need. Like Elizabeth Hart Thwaites, Joseph Phillips was a staunch and much hated abolitionist, the subject of great censure for his marriage to an African Caribbean woman. He refused to release certain papers to the committee and was sent to jail for over a year. Among British evangelicals he became a cause célèbre. This same Joseph Phillips would later testify on behalf of Mary Prince, the former slave whose memoirs caused a tremendous uproar in Britain in 1831.[67] Elizabeth Thwaites in turn gave general answers to whatever the Committee of the House asked her and mentioned all the cases she had occasionally relieved. True to her principles, however, she apparently refused to "name the estates, the proprietors, the slaves, the kind of relief, whether money, clothes, or food." In her journal she records her reaction to the end of the proceedings: "We came home very late and tired, and committed ourselves to Him who judgeth righteously, and in confidence that He will be with us and deliver us. Our sleep was refreshing. As I awoke, the path of duty in this matter seemed to open before me, and Mr. Thwaites and I had one view on the subject; and it is comfortable to think that we were under the Divine direction."[68] After the case was tacitly adjourned, she pursued her work without hindrance from planters, although she became the target of pro-slavery ire in the British press. James Macqueen, editor of the *Glasgow Courier* and notoriously pro-slavery, cast serious aspersions on both Joseph Phillips and Elizabeth Thwaites in the famous *Blackwoods Magazine*. Macqueen's attack shows that Elizabeth Thwaites's opposition to slavery scandalized those favoring slavery on both sides of the Atlantic:

In his [Joseph Phillips's] capacity as second secretary to the deluding society entitled, "The Society for the Relief of Old Worn-out and Diseased Slaves," the Assembly of Antigua, in the name of the colony he had unjustly attacked and basely calumniated, thus speak of him in the Report of their Committee appointed to examine into his charges against the colony:—"Previously to dismissing his evidence, your committee cannot help remarking upon the character of this *second* secretary of the Society, which unfortunately ranks equally low with that of the former one, so much so, *as scarcely to leave a worse in the whole community!!*"

Time, space, and circumstances, compel me to quit this miserable tool of anti-colonial faction and rancor, and his bosom crony, *Mrs. Thwaites.* . . .

By tools like *Mary Prince*, and *Joseph Phillips*, Pringle, and the band of which Pringle is the tool and the organ, mislead and irritate this country, browbeat the Government, and trample upon, as they are permitted to trample upon, our most important transmarine possessions, the value and importance of which I am bound to shew to your Lordship and the public.[69]

In fact, Elizabeth Thwaites's vigorous antislavery perspective was no longer championed in Methodist circles as it had been when Wesley was alive. Hence her interrogation in the House of Assembly amounted to punishment for suspected pro-emancipation talk and actions, however concealed. The economic situation in North America figured large in this policy shift against emancipation in Methodist circles, which further marginalized Elizabeth Thwaites and her views.

Let me retrace some history. The North American Methodists' position on slavery—conceived in energetic and deliberate opposition to the establishment—was gradually, in one critic's words, "effaced by compromise."[70] John Wesley, of course, was responsible for the fact that the Society's philanthropic activities had included emancipation from the start; it needs to be stressed, however, that Methodist missionaries were not expected to preach emancipation, for fear of angering the white ruling class. In 1743 Wesley indicted the slave trade in the General Rules, and thirty-one years later he wrote *Thoughts upon Slavery*, a vigorous pro-emancipation document.

In North America, British Methodist missionaries Francis Asbury and Thomas Coke similarly condemned slavery, though again, notably, Coke did not do so in the Caribbean. By 1780, in Baltimore, Asbury had supervised the passage of a statement supporting gradual emancipation as well as religious instruction for slaves. But always on that continent the power of any emancipationist statement was undercut by clauses that excluded such actions in states where slavery was legal, and slavery was legal in all thirteen colonies throughout the colonial period. Eventually this justification in civil law became the defense for a pro-slavery ethic.

By 1784 Methodists at the Christmas conference in Baltimore had declared themselves independent from the Church of England. In the organization of the newly formed church, at Thomas Coke's instigation, antislavery became a church law, with certain rules:

> Every slaveholding member must within a year execute a legal instrument, agreeing to free his slaves, and the preachers were required to keep a record of all such transactions in their circuits. Those who had not complied with this rule within the year were to withdraw from the church. Exceptions, however, had to be made at once for those residing in states where manumission was prohibited by law, and a special exception was made for the Virginia brethren, because of their special situation, and they were given two years to accept or reject the provision.[71]

Since Methodist revivalism meant a continuing, appreciable increase in membership—it doubled between 1780 and 1785—Methodists could not systematically instruct the membership on political issues in the manner of, say, Quakers. Coke had to admit, in fact, that the Society was "in too infantile a state to push things to extremity."[72] Just as much to the point, if not more, time was changing the face of profit and hence of politics. New British inventions for spinning and weaving and the invention of the cotton gin in North America in 1792 had created an enormous demand for cotton, which rapidly became North America's most valuable single crop. The general price of slaves increased accordingly; a slave sold for $300 in 1790 sold for $1,200 in 1830.[73] Slavery was big business.

Consequently, by 1796 Methodist policymakers had thoroughly watered down Wesley's original position. To compound the situation, annual conferences and states themselves began to ignore the Society's recommendation and injunctions. By the turn of the century, Methodists had repudiated their original antislavery position. They encoded the rationale for this retreat as spiritual; what mattered was bringing souls to God, physical bondage being a worldly affair, nothing more. By 1804 Asbury had to admit defeat when the Section of Slavery was suspended for all states south of Virginia. At that point, two Disciplines were printed that crystallized the fierce ideological division within the Society. (Dating from 1784, such Disciplines set forth the official acts and proceedings of conferences.)

Nevertheless, when the insurrection led by Denmark Vesey erupted in 1822 in Charleston, Methodists were among those condemned for helping to foment rebellion. Methodist clergy were subsequently at pains to dissociate themselves from antislavery intentions; at this point many Methodists were slaveholders and wanted to rid themselves of outsider status.[74] This categorical about-face in 1822 from Wesley's emancipationist ideal followed directly from entrenched negrophobic attitudes that had not altered qualitatively since the mid-eighteenth century. Black Methodists, long aware of social prejudice and political discrimination within the Society and used to sparring with the pro-slavery leadership, finally decided to secede.

Joined by other secessionists, Daniel Coker, Richard Allen, and Absalom Jones established the African Methodist Episcopal church. By the year of the Vesey conspiracy,

> the independent church movement among Wesleyan Negroes extended from New York to Charleston. In reaction to the schisms, and to petitions from other Negroes requesting their own conferences under the bishops, the General Conference of 1824 decided to employ Negroes as itinerants wherever necessary. They also were prepared to allow Negro preachers and

members to have "all the privileges in the district and quarterly conferences which the usages of the country in different
sections [would] justify.[75]

In Antigua, therefore, the persistence of the Thwaiteses in cham-
pioning emancipation was remarkable. So too, probably, was the
decision to hire African Caribbeans as instructors, in accordance
with the principles established by the African Methodist Episcopal
church. Although no evidence is available, Elizabeth and Charles
Thwaites were possibly secessionists too. When he visited Antigua in
1837, four years after Elizabeth Hart Thwaites died, Joseph Sturge
commented on the situation. Specifically, he reported on the effects
of the apprenticeship system (Sturge's pro-Moravian bias should be
taken into account):

> We called at Willoughby Bay upon Charles Thwaites, the ven-
> erable father of education in Antigua. He has lived thirty-nine
> years in the island, the last twenty of which have been devoted
> to this work. We visited with him a large school of one hun-
> dred and twenty children, of whom only twenty are in the
> alphabet class. The rest can read in one or two syllables, and
> some of them in any part of the Bible. The principal teacher,
> a negro young man, governed the school, we were told, suc-
> cessfully, and in the spirit of love, yet it appeared to us that he
> taught the children rather by rote than intelligently. The chil-
> dren spelt correctly; and were quick to reply to the Scripture
> questions proposed by ourselves, or C. Thwaites.[76]

Elizabeth Hart Thwaites, then, with her enterprising and active
commitment to emancipation, emerged as a member of the political vanguard, unafraid of controversy and personal calumny. When
she died in 1833 at Willoughby Bay on the eve of emancipation,
which she had steadfastly championed since her youth, that commitment was warmly recognized. (Her letter to a friend, included
here, testifies to this fact.) The following obituary reproduced from
the "public press" by the Reverend John Horsford, which deserves
quoting at length, speaks to the reverence with which the evangelical
community regarded her:

Of Mrs. Thwaites it may with truth be said, although she filled
no elevated station in society, that she was eminently useful in
her day and generation, and a blessing to the community in
which she lived. Distinguished by an excellent understanding,
a cultivated mind, a sweet and amiable disposition, possessing
fervent and enlightened piety, she was peculiarly formed for
conveying instruction with considerable effect to the youthful mind; and it is strikingly illustrative of this fact, that of
those young persons who enjoyed the benefits of being under
her care, while she was engaged in private tuition, there is
scarcely one, if any, to be found, who did not form a personal attachment to her. She had been from early life engaged
with an elder sister in educating a numerous family of younger
brothers and sisters; and, not satisfied with communicating
knowledge to these primary objects of their attention, they extended it to the slaves of their father's household and estate,
by teaching them to read, and inculcating the principles of
revealed religion. Mrs. Thwaites afterwards assisted this sister in forming and conducting the first Sunday-school ever
established in these Colonies, since it was established more
than twenty-four years ago. Not long after, in conjunction
with him who now survives to lament her loss, a system of
instruction was begun on estates in the country, which afterwards became extensive under the auspices of the Church Missionary Society, by which they were at length employed, so
much so that sixty-one estates had teaching regularly established on them, and two thousand children and youths were
brought under instruction at one period. When circumstances
not necessary to be here detailed compelled the Church Missionary Society to withdraw from this useful field of labour,
Mr. and Mrs. Thwaites were engaged in the service of the Wesleyan Missionary Society and lately, under the kind and liberal patronage of the Ladies' Negro Education Society, commenced a new and delightful branch of instruction,—that of
training infants in the way they should go. Mrs. Thwaites' influence, and its beneficial effects on the young females of her
charge, can never, when considered in connexion with eter-

nity, be sufficiently appreciated in this delusive world. Suffice it to say, that, being defamed, she endured it; and that her record is on high, and her reward with her God.[77]

After the death of John Gilbert, also in 1833, Anne Hart Gilbert suffered erysipelas in her hand following an accident, and the infection became general. Committed to good works and moral authority to the last, she wrote the continuation of her husband's memoirs in this last year of her life, probably while in severe pain. She died the next year.[78] Her eulogist stated that with her death the Methodist Society had lost "a member, a leader, a shepherdess, a pattern, a pillar, a star of the first magnitude."[79]

TEXTS

As free colored Methodist educators married to white men, Anne Hart Gilbert and Elizabeth Hart Thwaites occupied a special position within Antiguan society. The texts they wrote elaborated on their roles in the community as well as on their ideas and how they transformed what many considered scandalous marriages into a means of serving their neighbors spiritually and politically.

Looking at voice, imagery, perspective, and the sense of subjectivity, we witness the conflicts in what was historically at stake for them. The way they set up most of their texts and how they temporized about what they wrote tell much about the level of their sociopolitical, as well as their cultural, acceptance. Both sisters were asked to write their histories, and Anne Hart Gilbert was invited to finish her husband's memoir after he died. The hymns and letters that Elizabeth Hart Thwaites wrote were two of the few acceptable forms for women at the time.

What makes the texts stand out, then, is not so much their generic range as how the authors couch what they are saying, always being careful to represent themselves as spiritual mothers while subtly introducing their own independent thoughts and actions. Their texts are skillful expositions of the kind of life they had to lead, superficially conformist and spiritually impeccable, yet marked with their own perspectives and desires.

The texts—as well as their obituaries—testify to their evangelical work and their Christlike compassion toward "lost souls," despite their disquiet about ungodliness. Put slightly differently, their texts spell out a strong sense of identification with African Caribbean men, women, and children and a recognition of inequities. These works represent the conscious chronicling of a heritage while revealing a clash of epistemologies and the array of interpretive strategies with which the authors respond to complex situations.

Both sisters were asked by the Reverend Richard Pattison to write a history of Methodism in Antigua, and both complied with his request. The minister may have wanted to be filled in on their version of the island's Methodist history. Pattison had been sent out from England in 1792 as a missionary to Nevis.[80]

Anne Hart Gilbert

In the *History of Methodism* (1804) that Anne Hart Gilbert wrote, she occasionally addresses Pattison and painstakingly stresses black women's contributions from the time of Nathaniel and Francis Gilbert in the 1760s.[81] She makes a point of spotlighting the work of Mary Alley and Sophia Campbel, two black women who from 1774 to 1778 maintained a Methodist base—a "praying remnant"—after the Gilberts left Antigua. Anne Hart Gilbert stresses African Caribbean women's contributions—the importance of the black female signature—her own as well as those of her compatriots.

Anne Hart Gilbert's unusual foregrounding of herself suggests, too, that these testimonies of the Hart sisters were meant to double as conversion narratives. John Wesley advocated rigorous self-examination as part of recording and maintaining the conversion experience.[82] Such conversion narratives and religious histories, moreover, validate the sisters as important Methodists and as authors in their own right. Unobtrusively and indirectly, Anne Gilbert sets herself up as a black Methodist female paradigm. In representing herself this way, she marks and affirms black women as upholders of the faith and mothers of spirituality, legitimate public authorities. In a word, she refuses to erase the story of black women, as the following excerpt from her *History of Methodism* illustrates:[83]

. . . tho' it cannot be said, that they abounded in knowledge, brightness of reason or soundness of speech, yet I say would to God there was the same simplicity, purity & love of the cross in only one half of our greatly increased Society now. The leaders of them were Mary Alley a Mulatto Woman & Sophia Campbel a black. The former after wading thro many trials & temptations is still alive & steady in the good cause. The latter went to her eternal rest in the year 1799. They met together for reading, singing & prayers & with many prayers watered the seed sown by their fathers in the Gospel.

Alley and Campbel "ventured in faith to agree for a spot of land to build a chapel upon," although other church members discouraged their project:

The most decent, and creditable of the black women did not think it a labour too servile to carry stones and marl, to help with their own hands to clear the Land of the rubbish that lay about it, & to bring ready-dressed victuals for the men that were employed in building the House of God. They now re-joiced to sell their Ear-rings & bracelets and to buy Lumber & pay Carpenters, to forward this blessed work; and at last they got a comfortable little Chapel, which soon became too small.

In the *History* Anne Gilbert also emphasizes the role played by Mary Gilbert, widow of Francis Gilbert,[84] another recuperation of female spiritual solidarity. On the other hand, she makes no bones about her disapproval of immorality among allegedly spiritual white people. Sin is a major enemy, though it speaks multiply as a social and political sign as well as a spiritual one and sometimes slides into a secular meaning.[85] Gilbert also states that a certain Mrs. Birken-head opened a meeting for children's religious instruction and music teaching after her arrival, which many young people of color at-tended. She also founded a public prayer meeting conducted by women and intended for the benefit of young women.[86]

Anne Hart proudly relates her own transition from "vilest reptile me" to the ecstasy of conversion. Her modesty, however, precludes her maintaining an undue focus on herself.[87] At the same time, contradictorily, she places herself in the select group of those who record their conversion. Her sense of personal power and exemplary status firm, she punctuates the narrative with direct and indirect references to injustice. In her claim as a black Antiguan who must be accorded equal religious treatment with whites, she clears space for a general argument about social and political equality and implicitly denies any assumption of power wielding over women or slaves. An implication lurks in these silent polemics that human exclusion is as sinful as is missionary wives' immorality. Secular and spiritual transgression slide into each other. As an appointed ecclesiastical historian-cum-autobiographer, her text densely populated with usually silenced voices, she validates the status of all black people; as a church historian, she celebrates in her *History* the triumph of the black community of believers:

> It will swell this Letter to size almost enormous, to tell you all the love and watchful care that has covered my defenceless head; or to particularize those events that have united together all the links in the chain of Providence, which has been working together for my good ever since I came into existence but unnoted by me, 'till the scales of pride, ignorance & unbelief, fell from my eyes, by the light & power which accompanies the Gospel faithfully preached. Let it suffice that I add my feeble testimony to that of innumerable multitudes, that "God is no respecter of persons"—That "He willeth not the death of a Sinner"—That he hath never failed the feeblest nor the most unworthy that ever confided in his promise. He hath been with me, according to his faithful word, "Thro the Water & the Fire." He has upheld me (tho' at times almost sinking) upon the tumultuous sea of life. And in seasons of sore trial & temptation, The floods have lifted up their voice, & the waves seem'd ready to o'er whelm my frighted soul, yet, "The Lord has been mightier than the noise of many waters, Yea than the mighty waves of the Sea." I can indeed adopt the language of the Psalmist & say— "O how great is thy goodness which thou hast laid up for them that fear thee, which thou has wrought for them that trust in thee before the Sons

of men, Thou didst hide me in thy secret presence from the pride of man: Thou didst keep me secretly in a pavillion from the strife of tongues." Blessed be his name, He is indeed my strength & my Son, & is become my Salvation; And by his power I will rest upon his faithfulness while I sojourn in this vale of tears, 'till my last change shall come, & then I trust thro' grace to join the innumerable multitude in ascribing, Blessing, & glory, & wisdom & thanksgiving and honor & power & might unto our God forever and ever. Amen.

Her discussions of social issues complicate the question of her standing—and that of her family—within the Antiguan community. When she and her husband arrive in English Harbour, for example, she explains how immoral whites masquerading as missionaries have scandalized "a small society of black & coloured people, consisting of 28 Members & all but a very few in earnest for Salvation. They have never had one half the advantages of the people of St. Johns, having no place of worship to go to on Sundays, & very few of them able to read the word of God." At one blow, she censures white apostates, applauds the judgment of the community, radiates a certain moral command, and liberates herself and her constituency from corrupt white spiritual authority. She indicts past white leaders with impunity. Suggesting that Methodism will be purified by its black practitioners, she directly refutes old stereotypes not only of pagan slaves but also of licentious black women. She rejoices that conversion not only renders slaves upstanding citizens but makes them a threat to the white community. Implied in her argument, too, is the contention that slavery and social environment alone—the practice of obeah, for instance, which only Christianity can cancel out—separate blacks from whites:

The great civilization of the Slaves, their gradual emergence, from the depths of ignorance & barbarism, has imperceptibly had an over-awing effect upon the System of tyranny & cruel oppression that was formerly exercised over them with little or no restraint when they differed in so few respects from the Beasts that perish; And as a natural consequence, those that

are set over them feel more cautious in dealing with rational creatures than they did with beings imbruted in ev'ry way
both body & mind. The Slaves in general that attend a Gospel ministry, whether they are subject themselves to Church
discipline or not, become more creditable & decent in their
families and manners than those that do not.

Gilbert resolutely vanquishes old designations of Africans as brutes
or as brutalized humans. Philosophically, she rejects the great chain
of being and insists on recognition of human equality. In Anne
Gilbert's discourse, Africans epitomize Wesley's original conception
of a breakaway church, a sectarian splinter group sanctified by God.

Her text is divided against itself but quietly fights its internal
contradictions. While acquiescing to, yet criticizing, a white spiritual
status quo, she adopts a near feminist stance in insisting on women's
right to pursue God's work. Just as politically, this time across gender lines, she also rejects lack of representation for black men and
women, presses their viewpoints in public, and dissolves or at least
deeply questions received opinions about their ontological status.
The black slave community, she realizes, treats her observations differently from those of the white missionaries. In her commentary,
she declares her unity with that community and her counterhege-
monic views regarding status:

> My complexion exempted me from those prejudices & that dis-
> gust which the instability of their white Brethren had planted
> in their hearts & they tremblingly ventured to receive us as
> friends. Mr Baxter desired the women to meet with me; I soon
> found that they were all desirous to have a little Chapel, & to
> have service on Sundays; & at the time Mr Lumb laboured
> here had collected five joes among themselves for that purpose
> but it was never brought into effect. I told them how our Sis-
> ters in St Johns had heartily united together and even labor'd
> with their hands to forward the building of the Chapel, &
> they generally agree to do the same. Previous to our coming
> here they had been in treaty for a house for the purpose of
> preaching, but the situation is so hot, and so low, that both
> Preacher, & hearers, run the risk of getting sick as soon as

they come into the open air. We have therefore petitioned the Commissioner to give us a Grant of Land to build in a more convenient place & he has readily granted the petition.[88]

Connected to her proclaimed alliance with the black community is a related matter: her analysis of prostitution, in which she specifically blames the institution of slavery and immoral whites and reevaluates established plantocratic narratives about "natural" black female depravity and sexual excess. Although diluted versions of such a perspective had circulated in British abolitionist texts, her graphic condemnation of the institution and its white practitioners is unprecedented:

I see with heart-felt joy that prostitution is now esteemed abominable & disgraceful by the greater part of the Colour'd Women in St Johns where the great bulk of them reside; and lawful alliances take place as frequently among them as among the whites. This is one happy effect of seeing the Gospel seed sown in the hearts of their Mothers; and many of them seeing themselves examples, corroborating, those truths that recommend, chastity tho' accompanied with labour & self-denial.

Hence Gilbert's founding of the Female Refuge Society constitutes a counterargument against contentions of black inferiority and recodes assumptions about the sexuality of female slaves. Just as being a spokeswoman is constitutive of her own public identity, she claims a bicultural identity for African Caribbeans: as spiritual beings and as a self-representing though oppressed community. Even memoirist-eulogist William Box, in his seemingly unrelieved hagiographical account of Anne Gilbert's charitable work, leaves room for the notion that environment has degraded black females and gravely impeded their growth:

Mothers, who had promoted the degradation and impurity of their daughters, began to bewail their wickedness, and to wish to screen their yet undebased offspring from the destroyer.[89]

Anne Gilbert is represented as constantly refusing to be inscribed in the patriarchal order or to accept insistent public norms of female silence. Her interventions matter. Box notes:

In the establishment and support of Refuge Societies, for
such of the female sex as were either comparatively or entirely
destitute,—in the formation of Benevolent Institutions, for
feeding the hungry, clothing the naked, and relieving the afflicted—in the extension of Sabbath and other Schools for
the instruction of the young—and in the promotion of every
cause having for its object the general welfare of her undying
fellow creatures, and especially of such as were too long accounted the filth and offscouring of all things, she was "instant
in season and out of season;" nor is it too much to hope that
scores, if not hundreds, of those whom she has nurtured in
domestic and religious life, will be the crown of her rejoicing
in the day of the Lord Jesus.[90]

This is a very important statement, because this contention of
successful intervention has been denied by every British slaveowning
society and the powerful plantocratic lobby in the British Parliament. Gilbert quietly challenges dominant ideology in the voice of
an instructor who desires more for her pupils. She underscores her
subtle but ubiquitous endorsement of black equality by a strategy
that summarizes white abolitionist and plantocratic texts; if fully
heard, these texts that stress slaves' intellectual hunger would dissolve existing arguments on behalf of innate racial differences. In the
History she writes:

> There is in all a thirst for a knowledge. The greater part of
> those that can afford it get themselves taught to read & some
> to write also. There are hundreds of black & coloured children
> sent to school every year in this little Island; and the great
> change wrought in the manners & condition of all people of
> this description is beyond any thing that could have been ex-
> pected and such as nothing could effect but the wisdom &
> power of God.

Simultaneously, as crusader and pioneer, Gilbert centers what
she deems proper conduct (the behavior she herself exemplifies) by
criticizing the sexual conduct of certain missionary wives. As the
following extract from the *History* records, she brilliantly transfers a
traditional focus on black women as preeminently sexual beings by

zeroing in on how white missionary wives, uncharacteristically, act in the sexual realm:

> I have at times been grieved to see some of the Wives of our preachers that have been like works for flatterers and syco-phants to shoot at; Who deceived, by what is falsely called, (and bears a strong resemblance to) kindness & hospitality; & under the idea of doing good, & winning souls to Christ by familiarity with the World, have lost their simplicity, & dead-ness, to the world, been shorn of their spiritual strength & had their affections estranged from the real people of God.

She is not afraid to assign culpability to people either within or outside Methodism. Anne Hart Gilbert's public posture had to be impeccable if her ideas about black and white equality—however gently inflected—were to take hold. In a sense then, her writings not only helped to formulate the ideological strategy for emanci-pation, but also proffered tools for an assault on traditional social hierarchies generally expected to gain ground before emancipation and to be more thoroughly challenged afterward. Gilbert prepared the ground for that critical intervention.

Elizabeth Hart Thwaites

Anne Hart Gilbert's sister Elizabeth argued from the same premises, but she geared her activities in a somewhat different direction. For one thing, she was more vocal about emancipation—she was in a minority in this respect—and suffered public persecution as a result. Before emancipation, Antiguan society was becoming much more politically volatile. In 1831, for example, slaves rioted over the sup-pression of Sunday markets. This resistance attracted support from intrepid women like Elizabeth Hart Thwaites. Along with her hus-band, Charles, Elizabeth Thwaites was renowned as the instigator of an educational system for slaves throughout the eastern Carib-bean islands. The acknowledged "superior condition" of Antiguan slaves in 1833 was later attributed not only to the absence of an ap-prenticeship period following emancipation and the attention of missionaries, but specifically to the work of the Thwaiteses.[91]

A letter written by Elizabeth Hart from her father's estate at

Popeshead to a male friend in another colony in October 1794 reflects at an early age a highly self-conscious emancipationist point of view that she had previously confided to no one but her sister: "I find none disposed to receive such hard sayings; and why? Because they are not disinterested, self is concerned; and as I cannot, to please the best and wisest, lower the standard of right, or bend a straight rule to favour a crooked practice, I am, for the most part, silent." She disagrees with this friend—if he is indeed a friend—that she (and people in general) should "guard our minds against unnecessary solicitude at evils which we cannot remedy." With barely concealed mockery, she ridicules the plantocratic contention that slaves are better off than impoverished Europeans and notes that the latter at least have legal protection unilaterally denied to slaves.[92]

What she does not add is that to be an abolitionist in Antigua in 1794 could be dangerous. An arduous national fight to pass a bill in Britain for the abolition of the slave trade had ground to a standstill after the French Revolution in 1789, Jacobinism, and the successful San Domingan revolution in 1791. That a neighboring island was in the process of becoming independent must have given the Antiguan ruling class pause. The free colored population, buoyed up by these events, nevertheless needed to tread carefully. Some, indeed, were leaving still colonized islands and sailing to freedom.[93]

She remains orthodox in her acceptance of social subordination, "for this is," she claims, "the condition of many." On the other hand, she excoriates anti-emancipation values of the dominant ideology by tendering compassion toward the "black train of ills which I know to be inseparably connected with *this* species of slavery: such as may you never know, if it will give you needless pain,—such as my eyes see, and my ears hear daily, and makes my heart shrink when I write." The controversy over San Domingo silently resounds in this debate, though neither of them names the celebrated revolution, which is still being violently resisted.

Thus Elizabeth Hart Thwaites, like her sister, lays the social and political impediments faced by African Caribbeans at the door of slavery. She adopts a simple version of the argument advanced by Toussaint L'Ouverture and other contemporary African Caribbeans. Silently, any attack on slavery is an attack on British foreign policy and the white Antiguan ruling class's implementation of that policy. In her attack on the severance of family life, and in her copious examples of wives and children wrenched from their families, she further suggests that black families could live in harmony and comparative wealth like the Clearkleys and Harts, for instance, if their beliefs and actions were not frequently subverted. With her sister Anne, she also argues that social conditions alone determine the constitution of the intelligentsia. This argument had become hard to deny. Olaudah Equiano, Ottabah Cuguano, Phillis Wheatley, and Toussaint L'Ouverture himself, among many others, had made irreversible inroads among the cultural and political elite. She identifies an omnipresent consciousness of this oppression among all enslaved Africans and demonstrates a good grasp of the social construction of subjectivity:

> There are likewise others [slaves] who, being [endowed] with good natural understanding, aspire after refinement, useful knowledge, and sweets of social life, &c., &c.: were there a possibility of changing the colour of their skin, and emancipating them, with culture they would become ornaments to society. These are not permitted to emerge; they are bound down by some unenlightened, mercenary mortal, who perhaps has not a thought or wish above scraping money together. You may suppose such slaves find it a galling yoke.

The sharp sarcasm of this passage, rhetorically effective in itself, reveals the resentment she feels toward those who condemn her and her family on the basis of complexion. Like her sister, she alludes to an equation of black women with sexuality, only to refute it. In so doing she marks her intricate status as a triple outsider: as a Methodist, a woman, and an African Caribbean. Rejecting a simple Methodist dualism that pits good people against evil people, she rejects any ascription of alien status to herself and her family and sets herself up literally and figuratively as a spokeswoman. Although she screens herself to some extent behind a mask of historical orthodoxy, she nonetheless constitutes herself as a complex female subject who is obliged to negotiate a certain balance of expectations with personal-political maneuvering.

Beyond that, she advances the radical contention that men and women are equal across any racial lines and that illegitimate force and complexion—the visible signifier of difference—alone separate them. She underscores the constant brutalization that diminishes any individual's natural capacity and refuses to countenance the argument that God intended Africans to be slaves since they are a lesser people. In the process she indicts both white Europeans and creoles:

> It does not suit me to say the worst I know concerning it [the situation of slaves]: only I assure you it comprises a mystery of iniquity, an endless list of complicated ills, which it is not likely you will ever know. You will not, perhaps, find the sufferers disposed to complain of their case. Not many are capable of *explaining*, however keenly they may *feel*, their disadvantages. . . . I agree with you, that there might be some clue to [the existence of slavery] quite unknown to us; but this does not strike me as being the sins of the Africans; for, from all I can learn of them, according to their light, though barbarous and uncivilized, they are not so depraved as the generality of the Europeans, but more especially the West Indians.

In the companion *History of Methodism* that Elizabeth Hart Thwaites was asked to write by the Reverend Richard Pattison, she explicitly states many of her unorthodox political opinions while maintaining the expected posture of rectitude. She elaborates on the virtue of family members, elevating them to the Antiguan Methodist pantheon of holy families and refusing to separate them in any way by race. Quietly she insists on the recognition of racial and spiritual equality.

Her *History*, like her sister Anne's, is also a conversion narrative that helps her construct a firm public identity. Her dramatic account of conversion precedes such North American chronicles as *The Life and Religious Experience of Jarena Lee, a Colored Lady* (1836) and is equally trenchant. Conventional bias generally attributed to the free colored population also erupts in the *History*. She is well aware of the unique position she and her sister hold as outspoken free colored female educators and writers in a society dominated by a white male ruling class. Criticizing her own prejudice against slaves, which she feels she has transcended, she records that

> contrary to my intention, I became a constant hearer. There were no young persons, that I knew of, who were in Society at this time, that were not Slaves; on this, and some other accounts, I proudly held out as long as I could, from wholly joining them, tho' I gain'd admittance to many of the private meetings.

Thus she proclaims herself on a moral par with slaves. Her coupling of antagonism toward slaves with conversion, moreover, powerfully underscores her championship of emancipation. The implication is that hegemonic social views about slaves and slavery are sinful. Still in the conversion mode, she poignantly describes the temptations of "company, conversation, and Books." Especially she mentions the temptation of music, which beguiled her, and points out her double standard (which she now deplores) in exhorting slaves to virtue. She self-critically points out that slaves had lived virtuous lives long before she caught up with them morally:

> I met a Class of young women who were Slaves and to whom I said nothing of my then experience, which, when at the worst, did not prevent my enforcing upon them the necessity of a present Salvation. I abated in nothing my severity against Sin, and continually enjoined upon them to avoid the very appearance of evil. Most of these are still in the good way.

But this vindication of the respectable lives of slaves is later undercut by her insistence that the better-educated free colored are morally sovereign:

> The Blessings which I have experienced by the Ministry of the word, from the coming of Doctor Coke to Antigua, to the present day, and its salutary effects upon others, makes me bold to declare that the Gospel has not visited these Parts in vain; and I know of a truth, that the labours of every Minister who himself adorns the Gospel, and propounds the Truth in the plainest terms, is more or less attended with success. This was evidently the case during Mr. Murdoch's labours

here. The Congregations are principally composed of illiterate People, who are neither interested nor affected by what they cannot understand, and those who are better informed, well know that the Preacher is doing his duty when he seeks rather to Edify the many than please the few.

Internal contradictions or, more simply, overlappings mount when this passage is followed by one that reasserts the spiritual readiness of slaves. By encouraging the expression of affective states, she is also therapeutically affording slaves the opportunity to vent and rechannel frustration and pain, however indirectly:

> Having to meet upwards of 160 in Class, affords me an opportunity of knowing several who have a hearing ear, and understanding heart, two of them are Whites who have a saving knowledge of the truth, the others are Black and Coloured from 13 to 60 years of age.

The sisters construct an identity partly based on their relations with slaves and the spiritually egalitarian ideas that inform them. Slaves cause them to revise their scripts.

> Some of the poor Africans, [she continues] can particularize such parts of a Sermon as they felt most, and one of them told me a few Sundays ago, after Preaching, "Massa open me poor sinner heart. He tell me every thing me do," with many of such expressions. I rejoice in the certainty that there are many real converts in St Johns, both of young and Old. I am inclined to think, that one reason why so many of the poor Slaves upon the Estates, cause you trouble and discouragement is, that they are in general received into the Society, as Catechumens, and not convinced Sinners, and if a genuine work of Grace does not take place, they soon relapse into those Sins, which habit and custom have rendered in their meat and drink, particularly Quarreling and Unchastity.

The pidgin English attributed to the speaker, which reconfirms the author's superiority (though with a possibly embedded or even suppressed sense of cultural bonding), is juxtaposed with an admonition to the white audience: institutionalized discrimination—and

only that—is causing moral strife.[94] Elizabeth Hart Thwaites's ambivalence—her conflictual attitudes concerning the equality of all
African Caribbeans, the preeminence of the free colored population,
and white prejudice—infuses the text. Concurrently, she presents an
affidavit of her religious faith and her political beliefs while enabling
slaves to resist their condition through healthy explosions of pent-up
emotions.

In the elegiac "On the Death of the Rev. Mr. Cook,"[95] she un-
veils her intricate attraction to Methodism. In one of her earlier
hymns, she extravagantly claims that she would prefer death to life
if it meant seeing Jesus:

> Weary world, when will it end,
>   Destined to the purging fire?
> Fain I would to heaven ascend;
>   Thitherward I still aspire.
> Saviour, this is not my place.
> Let me die, to see Thy face.[96]

Yet in the poem on Tortolan missionary Thomas Cook she illumines
the importance she discerns in Methodism's commitment to blacks
and her sense of the equality accorded blacks within this spiritual
framework:

> The Saviour drew him with the cords of love,
> Wean'd him from earth, and raised his heart above;
> Commission'd him to spread the Gospel grace,
> And offer mercy to the fallen race;
> Nor in his native land alone proclaim
> The saving power of Jesu's precious name:
> But distant climes the adventurous youth invite,
> His labour with the faithful few to unite,
> Who, in obedience to the heavenly call,
> And for our sakes, had left their earthly all.[97]

Yet this measure of equality, to which John Wesley himself subscribed, was a controversial matter. Fearful of consequences, very
few of the Caribbean Methodists openly championed emancipation
as Wesley recommended. Elizabeth Hart Thwaites, by contrast, took

Wesley at his word and wrote and acted accordingly. The poem flaunts her radical proposition that African Caribbeans not only deserve legal equality with whites but are equal in all other respects. Almost no whites—Joseph Phillips and perhaps a few others—concurred with this idea.

In fact, Elizabeth Thwaites and her sister were implicitly threatening the Methodist male hegemony with the establishment of a breakaway church. In the United States, by a much popularized religious action, in 1793 Absalom Jones, a former slave who was insulted by bigoted Methodist institutional practices, had established, with other angry black free men and women, the African Methodist Episcopal church. Throughout their writings, the sisters sound an intertextual echo of a potentially comparable religious separatism, as in the following verses:

> With rapture heard the diff'rent tribes converse,
> In Canaan's tongue redeeming love rehearse,
> And Afric's sable sons in stammering accents tell
> of Jesu's love, immense, unspeakable.
> The grace that reach'd his heart, to all it came;
> Their language, as their spirit, was the same.[98]

In Elizabeth Hart's correspondence with her cousin Frances Lynch, she advances the argument about equality one critical step further than white abolitionists would go, into the realm of employment. This articulation is tantamount to an emancipationist statement, since forced labor is the exclusive signifier of a slave:

> We have ten girls learning to write. I ought in course to have observed to you that Mr. Thwaites has for some time past been so concerned about the poor children, that he has begged me, if possible, to get myself taught to make lace or any thing that I could teach the girls; and he has been trying to manufacture the long straw into hats for him to teach them; but he made no hand of it.
>
> We have the happiness to see many bidding fair to be valuable and good women, who would probably by this time have been tending their steps to infamy and woe. But what would

have been the use of schools, books, teachers, lectures, &c., had not a few benevolent hands been stretched out to enable the poor little creatures, as well as those who are growing up to womanhood, to come at these good things?[99]

The Hart sisters' texts answer back to all those who cast aspersions on the intellect of African Caribbeans. Given altered circumstances, all the black children could be literate. But then, how will they survive? Elizabeth Hart Thwaites's texts clarify the difficulties she and her sister faced in deciding on priorities. This letter induced British abolitionists to send money, clothes, and other forms of aid, including patronage and support of the Ladies' Negro Education Society.

Upheld by their spiritual knowledge that the *imago dei* resided in every individual, Anne Hart Gilbert and Elizabeth Hart Thwaites knew the power of the word and the importance of historical precedent. Hence their concerted efforts to educate black adults as well as children and dissolve attempts by whites to distance or to represent as an other—in Edward Said's formulation—the black population—free like themselves or enslaved.[100] All differences among blacks, for them, were grounded in spiritual difference. Through their texts and actions, the sisters performed radical surgery on the Antiguan body politic.

Although they accepted—somewhat questioningly—the concept of social hierarchy, the sisters' values inevitably differed from those of the plantocratic ruling class. They strove to convert young females not simply to eliminate sexual predation and free up their lives, but to give them a chance to be as socially mobile and respected as they themselves were. They saw their social superiors as self-indulgent accomplices in such immorality as prostitution, gambling, and public drunkenness, and they sought to eradicate these practices throughout all levels of society. In some senses, then, they pictured white plantocrats as predators—a minority group who subjugated the majority on the island. John Gilbert, for example, strongly resisted French militarism. Somewhat in accord with her pro-emancipation sister, moreover, Anne Gilbert indirectly affirms the methods of the slave insurrectionists on San Domingo in her *History of Methodism*: she gives thanks that Antiguans can agitate for change peacefully.

Its having been effected by the Un-bloody Sword of truth that
has almost unperceivedly cut its way thro' mountainous obstacles; And not by tumultous distracting revolution, massacre
& bloodshed, is cause of unspeakable thankfulness to God.

Unlike Mary Wollstonecraft, who claimed or implied that Olaudah Equiano could not be as intelligent as middle-class whites, Elizabeth Hart Thwaites and Anne Hart Gilbert regarded African Caribbeans as calculatingly excluded from the body politic, a socially
and culturally deprived community, but not a community of lesser
beings. Quite simply, Africans needed to be saved. Hence, religious
distancing and ethnic bonding are silently yoked in the sisters' prose,
and the contradictions that follow from this ambivalence permeate
their texts. They are black Antiguan religious outsiders, and yet as
lay instructors they are an integral part of a religio-cultural intelligentsia. Thus they constantly and successfully negotiate from different marginal positions. In a sense they even *represent* slaves and
other blacks to the white community while simultaneously seeking
the conversion of pagan others in spite of the censure of plantocratic others. One suspects that after 1800 they felt their independent actions were validated by the work of their North American
black Methodist counterparts. Expressing new human possibilities
for African Caribbeans, their writings disrupted, or at least inter-
sected with, all past and contemporary white texts. Representing
a silenced class of people usually relegated to the borders, these
two women capitulated to no one and introduced cultural scripts
of novel signification that established a new and complex dialogue
with their own society and with posterity.

As free colored women in Antiguan society, Anne Hart Gilbert
and Elizabeth Hart Thwaites stood at the crossroads of social, gendered, racial, and sexual constructions. In the first place, inevitably,
the sisters had to contend with standard discriminatory attitudes
based on gender and race.[101] The following quotations reflect how
free colored women tended to be configured within a misogynous,
ethnocentric economy. The Reverend John Baxter stated his views
on women in 1804, for example, in a letter to Joseph Benson in
London:

As for living a single life property and chastely there is no such thing known among the Blacks after they are eighteen years old I believe. I believe few of the females at sixteen, and their coming together improperly without affection, young women taking old men and young men old women is the cause of constant jealousy and separating from each other in which case we exclude the guilty person and never receive. . . . Some of the coloured women have good gifts in prayer and hold prayer meetings: but the free women in general have no relish for religion.[102]

Thomas Coke's perspective on African Caribbeans has already been noted.

As female members of well-read black Methodist families, the Hart sisters were acutely aware of their sociosexual profiles and their spiritual equality with whites. That doctrinal egalitarianism, however, did not translate into cultural equality. Linked ethnically to heathen Africans—always irredeemably fallen—they occupied a much lower place in the social hierarchy than whites.

Yet concurrently, that spiritual equality afforded them an incomparable outlet for personal and public advancement. As evangelicals, they could represent themselves as Caribbean counterparts of white Methodist women. In a broader context, their work was also linked to the contemporary upsurge of evangelical women's activities in England. Especially by the nineteenth century, when the doctrinal differences that separated Methodists and Anglicans had somewhat abated, good works assumed a high profile as a tool toward salvation.[103] Since evangelical women were traditionally associated with good deeds rather than intellectual pursuits—the heart and not the head—this conflation and partial dissolving of orthodox roles drew them into the male evangelical mainstream. As Wesley had put it: "Whenever you have opportunity, do all the good you can, particularly to your poor, sick neighbour. And every one of you likewise 'shall receive *your* own labour.'"

Psychologically, this religious shift eminently suited wives and mothers, who came to dominate the sphere of philanthropy. Many of them had felt domestically confined for so long that social-spiritual communities answered a deep need for extradomestic pursuits. As members of high-ranking Methodist families, the Hart sisters knew of this recent energetic female intervention, but their motivation to engage in such undertakings had even more complex roots. Not only were religious pursuits liberating in a physical and psychological sense, but they also helped nullify their allegedly inferior status as black Antiguan women.

Thus the sisters declined to be situated in any prescribed colonizing space for free colored women. Instead, they carved out for themselves a politically positive, even self-preservingly ambiguous niche that served several purposes: they elevated their status not only as women but as African Caribbeans. Through their vivid pursuits and social position, they canceled out conventional stigmas attached to free colored status. Most particularly, they helped dilute some of the negative meanings associated with free black women. Their piety, moreover, precluded any potential (and customary) designation as "loose" women. Not only was such colonial coding based on abuse and expropriation of black female bodies, inappropriate to their situation, but their conscious transcendence of such roles unsettled the designations themselves. Anne Hart Gilbert and Elizabeth Hart Thwaites split the usually conflated gendered and colonial spaces reserved for free colored women: as black women, they insisted on an individual and moral status.

Beyond the significance they personally gained from their evangelical activities, their domestic missionary work also connected with an impulse toward black self-determination. In most of their pursuits, they undermined dominant ideology. Presenting slaves as educable and smart, they rebutted centuries-old stereotypes, vindicating codings of both the free colored and the slave population. In that sense they became representatives of slaves and free colored people alike. Instead of catering to the old image of slaves as infantilized human beings—a designation that affirmed and perpetuated the metropolitan as well as Antiguan advance of colonial power—they subverted these centuries-old formulas. They pictured slaves as people like themselves who lacked favorable circumstances and opportunities. And since they were in an organization headed by John Wesley, a distinguished international Anglican as well as a Methodist, slaves in turn were represented as men and women like Wesley, but caught in a historically coerced situation. Thus their texts and activities halted the isolation of free (or enslaved) Africans as people with no rights. Indirectly they "reveal[ed] their political usefulness and . . . len[t] themselves to economic profit."[104] The pivotal presence of those texts effectively altered the material context and its power relations.

In Frantz Fanon's conceptualization, the sisters' tireless domestic missionary work can also be seen in another light. Aware of their constructed inferior status, they channeled repressed anger into counterinsistences, mimicking and otherwise.[105] Since they could not condemn prejudice out loud, could not even name it publicly, they inscribed it in their instruction of black children ("You are literate too"), in their own texts ("We are writers too"), in their silences about a clearly discriminatory condition, and in a deadpan, seemingly unmediated emulation.

The sisters, then, write from the edges as a way of coping with their psychic and cultural fragmentation. But these borders are not visible ones. They are nuanced actions, textual silences, quiet rebuttals that exist simultaneously with maintaining a visible position in the nonconformist mainstream. By thematizing their concerns as black Antiguans while foregrounding the occupiers' religion, they established a specific black Antiguan Methodist cultural identity. In their unity of sorts with indigenous culture, they foreshadowed and even helped precipitate an end to Antiguans' powerlessness vis-à-vis white Europeans. A sense of black self-determination—however inchoate and faint—induced innovation and experimentation disguised as spiritual orthodoxy.

NOTES

1. Oddly enough, except for his son-in-law John Gilbert in his autobiography, no one mentions that Barry Conyers Hart, a man from a politically well known white family, was a "man of colour." Rev. William Box, *Memoir of John Gilbert, Esq. Late Naval Storekeeper at Antigua. To Which are Appended. A Brief Sketch of His Relic, Mrs. Anne Gilbert* (Liverpool: D. Marples, 1835), p. 22.

2. No recent book specifically documents the history of Antigua in the decades before emancipation. In her wide-ranging study, *Slave Society in the British Leeward Islands at the End of the Eighteenth Century* (New Haven: Yale University Press, 1965) Elsa Goveia documents some important history and statistics about slave society. Other important data can be culled from a valuable variety of often religiously based histories and studies of the island mentioned in these notes.

3. Goveia, *Slave Society*, p. vii.

4. Ibid., p. 96. For information about the free colored society, Eurocentrically perceived, see also Frances Lanaghan, *Antigua and the Antiguans: A Full Account of the Colony and Its Inhabitants from the Time of the Caribs to the Present Day, Interspersed with Anecdotes and Legends. Also, an Impartial View of Slavery and the Free Labour Systems; The Statistics of the Island and Biographical Names of the Principal Families*, 2 vols. (London: Saunders and Otley, 1844), 2:170 and passim.

5. Goveia, *Slave Society*, p. 97. See also William A. Green, *British Slave Emancipation: The Sugar Colonies and the Great Experiment, 1830–1865* (Oxford: Clarendon Press, 1976), pp. 17–22.

6. Goveia, *Slave Society*, pp. 146, 141, 147, 217.

7. *The History of Mary Prince, a West Indian Slave, Related by Herself*, edited with an introduction by Moira Ferguson, with a preface by Ziggi Alexander (London: Pandora, 1987; Harper Collins, 1991), pp. 15, 16, 35, 79, and passim. All references will be to this edition.

8. Goveia, *Slave Society*, p. 91.

9. Ibid., pp. 217, 91–92. For an account of slave societies themselves, see B. W. Higman, *Slave Populations of the British Caribbean, 1807–1834* (Baltimore: Johns Hopkins University Press, 1984), pp. 52–53 and passim. For an account of the earliest master-slave relationships in Antigua, see David Barry Gaspar, *Bondsmen and Rebels: A Study of Master-Slave Relations in Antigua, with Implications for Colonial British America* (Baltimore: Johns Hopkins University Press, 1985).

10. Bryan Edwards, *The History, Civil and Commercial, of the British Colonies in the West Indies*, 3 vols. (London, 1801), 2:21; Goveia, *Slave Society*, p. 218.

11. Goveia, *Slave Society*, pp. 219–22.

12. *Extract of the Minutes of Several Conversations Held at Leeds, July 31, 1797, between the Preachers late in Connection with the Rev. Mr. John Wesley* (London: G. Whitfield, 1797). The minutes of the conference are divided into questions: question 11, "What numbers are in Society?" elicited the statistics cited.

13. Letter of John Baxter; see appendix E. See also Green, *British Slave Emancipation*, pp. 12–14.

14. Mary Turner, *Slaves and Missionaries: The Disintegration of Jamaican Slave Society, 1787–1834* (Urbana: University of Illinois Press, 1982), p. 8.

15. Goveia, *Slave Society*, p. 218.

16. Ibid. For a discussion of the free colored sector of San Domingan society, see David Patrick Geggus, *Slavery, War, and Revolution: The British Occupation of Saint Domingue, 1793–1798* (Oxford: Clarendon Press, 1982), pp. 18–23 and passim.

17. Clement Caines, *Letters on the Cultivation of the Otaheite Cane, the manufacture of sugar and rum, the saving of molasses, the care and preservation of stock, with the attention and anxiety which is due to negroes. To these topics are added a few other particulars analogous to the subject of the letters, and also a speech on the slave trade, the most important feature in West Indian culture* (London, 1801), 1:192; Goveia, *Slave Society*, p. 141.

18. G. G. Findlay and W. W. Holdsworth, *The History of the Wesleyan Methodist Society*, vol. 2 (London: Epworth Press, n.d.), p. 140.

19. Anne Hart Gilbert, *History of Methodism*, pp. 6–7.

20. Goveia, *Slave Society*, p. 223.

21. Green, *British Slave Emancipation*, p. 17.

22. Goveia, *Slave Society*, p. 223.

23. Edwards, *History*, 2:34–35.

24. Goveia, *Slave Society*, pp. 225–27.

25. Thomas Coke, *A History of the West Indies containing the Natural, Civil, and Ecclesiastical History of each Island: With an Account of the Missions instituted in those islands, from the commencement of their civilization; but more especially of the Missions which have been established in that Archipelago by the Society Late in Connexion with the Rev. John Wesley*, vol. 1 (Liverpool: Nuttall, Fisher, and Dixon, 1808; reprinted Liverpool: Meneosyne, 1969), p. 212.

26. John Horsford, *A Voice from the West Indies: Being a Review of the Character and Results of Missionary Efforts in the British and Other Colonies in the Charibbean Sea, with Some Remarks on the Usages, Prejudices, etc. of the Inhabitants* (London: Alexander Heylin, 1856), pp. 160–61.

27. Ibid., p. 153; Findlay and Holdsworth, *History*, pp. 30–31.

28. Findlay and Holdsworth, *History*, p. 29.

29. Horsford, *Voice*, pp. 168, 153.

30. Goveia, *Slave Society*, pp. 299–300. See also Findlay and Holdsworth, *History*, p. 135, and Seymour Drescher, *Capitalism and Antislavery: British Mobilization in Comparative Perspective* (London: Macmillan, 1986), pp. 119ff.

31. Drescher, *Capitalism and Antislavery*, p. 120.

32. Goveia, *Slave Society*, p. 280. I note for the record that Moravianism was Methodism's major religious rival in Antigua. When Dr. Coke arrived, he established that five thousand black Antiguans, a sixth of the population, were Moravian converts. Findlay and Holdsworth, *History*, pp. 141, 32.

33. Horsford, *Voice*, p. 195.

34. Drescher, *Capitalism and Antislavery*, p. 114.

35. Coke, *History*, p. 92.

36. Ibid., p. 26.

37. Ibid., p. 30.

38. Goveia, *Slave Society*, p. 235.

39. Barbara Bush, *Slave Women in Caribbean Society, 1650–1838* (Kingston: Heinemann; Bloomington: Indiana University Press, 1990), pp. 17–18.

40. Ibid., p. 101.

41. Goveia, *Slave Society*, pp. 122, 143. For another view of slave society, see Green, *British Slave Emancipation*, pp. 22–32.

42. Findlay and Holdsworth, *History*, p. 140.

43. Box, *Memoir*, pp. 7, 85, 21.

44. Ibid., pp. 23–24.

45. Ibid., p. 23. An Antiguan contemporary popular historian speaks explicitly and at some length about prejudice on the island, including the treatment of the Gilberts. See Lanaghan, *Antigua and the Antiguans*, 1:177–82 and passim. I thank Desmond Nicholson for supplying me with Frances Lanaghan's correct name.

46. Box, *Memoir*, p. 25.

47. Lanaghan, *Antigua and the Antiguans*, 1:179.

48. Horsford, *Voice*, p. 196.

49. Box, *Memoir of John Gilbert*, p. 86. Note also that Mary Gilbert, widow of Francis Gilbert, had much earlier organized women's classes and instructed black Antiguans. This model of female in-laws who were religious instructors might have helped Anne Hart Gilbert flout conventions about female roles in society. See Findlay and Holdsworth, *History*, passim.

50. Goveia, *Slave Society*, pp. 263–66, 287, 284.

51. Elsa Goveia, *A Study on the Historiography of the British West Indies to the End of the Nineteenth Century* (Washington, D.C.: Howard University Press, 1980).

52. Box, *Memoir*, pp. 86–87.

53. Horsford, *Voice*, p. 188.

54. Roy Porter, *English Society in the Eighteenth Century* (New York: Penguin, 1982), p. 305. Note also that the educational organizing undertaken

by the sisters coincided with a time of "moral backsliding" in Antigua, as noted by the missionaries. See Findlay and Holdsworth, *History*, p. 136 and passim.

55. Extract from a letter written by Charles Thwaites, Antigua, August 25 (no year given).

56. Horsford, *Voice*, pp. 203–4.

57. Lanaghan, *Antigua and the Antiguans*, 1:317–19. Although little is said about the status of the children of either Anne Hart Gilbert or Elizabeth Hart Thwaites, there are occasional remarks. A child of Elizabeth Hart Thwaites is mentioned here in Frances Lanaghan's *Antigua and the Antiguans*. Anne Gilbert's children are mentioned once in the "Brief Sketch" by the Reverend William Box (see appendix A).

58. Letter from Elizabeth Hart to Miss Lynch in Horsford, *Voice*, p. 198.

59. Goveia, *Historiography*, p. 93.

60. Coke, *History*, pp. 34–35.

61. Drescher, *Capitalism and Antislavery*, p. 127. For further context, see C. Duncan Rice, "The Missionary Context of the British Anti-slavery Movement," in *Slavery and British Society, 1776–1846*, ed. James Walvin (London: Macmillan, 1982), pp. 150–63.

62. Horsford, *Voice*, p. 209.

63. Box, *Memoir*, pp. 37, 87; Horsford, *Voice*, pp. 197, 200.

64. Box, *Memoir*, p. 89.

65. On his official travels to oversee the implementation of the Emancipation Act, Joseph Sturge offers a Methodist's retrospective view of Anne Hart Gilbert's charitable work: "We went, also, to see the 'Refuge for Female Orphans'; an interesting and most useful institution, which is dependent on the English 'Ladies' Society.' It was declining for want of attention; its chief support had been Mrs. Gilbert, an excellent lady of colour, now dead." Joseph Sturge and Thomas Harvey, *The West Indies in 1837: Being the Journal of a Visit to Antigua, Montserrat, Dominica, St. Lucia, Barbadoes, and Jamaica, Undertaken for the Purpose of Ascertaining the Actual Condition of the Negro Population of Those Islands*, 2d ed. (London: Hamilton, Adams, 1838), p. 36.

66. Horsford, *Voice*, p. 201.

67. *History of Mary Prince*, pp. 19, 35–36. Joseph Phillips was something of a hero among British evangelical emancipationist women. For example, they reported on his tribulations and voted "fifteen pounds to the relief of this much injured man." *The Fifth Report of the Female Society for Birmingham, West Bromwich, Wednesbury, Walsall, and their Respective Neighbourhoods, for the Relief of British Negro Slaves, Established in 1825* (Birmingham: B. Hudson, 1830), p. 21. Joseph Phillips was also a polemicist against slavery in his

own right. See *West India Question: The Outline of a Plan for the Total, Immediate, and Safe Abolition of Slavery throughout the British Colonies* (London: J. and A. Arch, 1833). In short, Elizabeth Hart Thwaites was associated with mainstream British pro-emancipation circles. For Phillips's marriage to a woman of color, see Vere Langford Oliver, *The History of the Island of Antigua, One of the Leeward Caribees in the West Indies, from the First Settlement in 1635 to the Present Time*, vol. 3 (London: Mitchell and Hughes, 1899), p. clii.

68. Horsford, *Voice*, pp. 211–12; quotation on p. 212. The exact details of Elizabeth Hart Thwaites's testimony are unclear, as records somewhat conflict. Aside from Horsford's record that insists she "held out" and kept silence, there is also commentary in Charles Thwaites's journal that suggests she cooperated, since she did not think her answers would harm people. See Charles Thwaites's journal, no. 1, pp. 1–3.

69. James Macqueen, "The Colonial Empire of Great Britain," *Blackwoods Magazine*, November 1831, pp. 744–64. See appendix L.

70. Donald G. Mathews, *Slavery and Methodism: A Chapter in American Morality, 1780–1845* (Princeton, N.J.: Princeton University Press, 1965), pp. 3–4.

71. William Warren Sweet, *Methodism in American History* (New York: Methodist Book Concern, 1933), p. 233.

72. Mathews, *Slavery and Methodism*, p. 13.

73. Sweet, *Methodism*, pp. 235–36.

74. Mathews, *Slavery and Methodism*, pp. 41ff.

75. Ibid., p. 64.

76. Sturge and Harvey, *West Indies in 1837*, p. 33.

77. Horsford, *Voice*, pp. 214–15. The date of Elizabeth Thwaites's death is also recorded in Horsford, p. 213.

78. Box, *Memoir*, p. 92. Vere Langford Oliver throws some light on where Anne Hart Gilbert and Elizabeth Hart Thwaites might have been buried. In his *History of Antigua*, Oliver writes: "1827, Dec. The burial ground at the Point having become unfit for use owing to floods, the glebe land attached to the Rectory to be used as a burial ground for black & coloured people." He follows that entry with: "1832, Sep. 15. The 1st color'd person buried in the churchyard. In future that & the glebe ground to be considered open for all free persons." Oliver, *History of Antigua*, p. 362.

79. Anne Gilbert's eulogist; the eulogy follows Reverend William Box's comments. See appendixes A and B.

80. Elizabeth Hart Thwaites's *History* is addressed to Richard Pattison. See Findlay and Holdsworth, *History*, 55. They add that Pattison was "a

young man of excellent sense and fidelity, who did good service in the West Indies while his health lasted."

81. In the London Methodist Missionary Archives also the Reverend Richard Pattison is mentioned as Anne Gilbert's correspondent in the *History of Methodism*.

82. Felicity A. Nussbaum, *The Autobiographical Subject: Gender and Ideology in Eighteenth-Century England* (Baltimore: Johns Hopkins University Press, 1989), p. 89 and passim.

83. See also Goveia, *Slave Society*, pp. 7–8.

84. Findlay and Holdsworth, *History*, p. 35.

85. Her disapproval of the morals of missionaries' wives may be linked to her expressed fear of "backsliding."

86. Box, *Memoir*, pp. 15–16.

87. Nussbaum, *Autobiographical Subject*, p. x.

88. Propagating orthodox Methodist practices, Mr. Baxter seeks out black spiritual leaders and makes sure that converted people conform to Wesley's desired terminology in using the word "chapel," not meetinghouse or church.

89. Box, *Memoir*, p. 33.

90. Ibid., pp. 78–79 (see appendix A).

91. Findlay and Holdsworth, *History*, pp. 140–41.

92. Letter from Miss Elizabeth Hart to a Friend, Popeshead, October 24, 1794 (included in this volume).

93. *History of Mary Prince*, pp. 8–9.

94. For a discussion of pidgin and its relations to power, see Suzanne Romaine, *Pidgin and Creole Languages* (London and New York: Longman, 1988), pp. 72–75 and passim.

95. Elizabeth Hart, "On the Death of the Rev. Mr. Cook" (this volume).

96. Elizabeth Hart, "Hymn" (this volume); Findlay and Holdsworth, *History*, p. 137.

97. Hart, "On the Death."

98. Ibid.

99. Hart, Letter to Frances Lynch (this volume).

100. Edward Said, *Orientalism* (New York: Vintage, 1979). See particularly the introduction to Said's argument about the production of knowledge and the representation of (often subject) peoples in the interests of the colonial ruling class. Said argues that one group, usually dominant, distances or offensively represents another group, usually thought of as subjugated or "the other."

101. Goveia, *Historiography*, p. 92.

102. Goveia, *Slave Society*, p. 269; letter from John Baxter (appendix E).

103. F. K. Prochaska, *Women and Philanthropy in Nineteenth-Century England* (Oxford: Clarendon Press, 1980), pp. 8–10, 99–100.

104. Michel Foucault, *Power/Knowledge: Selected Interviews and Other Writings, 1972–1977*, trans. Colin Gordon (Brighton: Harvester, 1980), pp. 100–102.

105. Frantz Fanon, *Black Skin, White Masks* (New York, 1967: rpt. London: Pluto Press, 1986), especially chapter 4. See also Frantz Fanon, *The Wretched of the Earth* (New York: Grove Press, 1963), p. 49 and passim.

Chronologies

ANNE HART GILBERT

1773 Born third daughter of Anne Clearkley and Barry Conyers Hart of Antigua

1785 Death of mother

1786 Baptized Methodist along with sister Elizabeth during visit of Dr. Thomas Coke to West Indies

1798 Marries John Gilbert, October 7

1804 Writes *History of Methodism*

1809 First Sunday school established in West Indies (with Elizabeth Hart Thwaites)

1815 Founds Female Refuge Society of Antigua (with Elizabeth Hart Thwaites)

1817 Appointed superintendent of girls' department of English Harbour Sunday school

1833 Death of husband, July 16

1833 Death of sister Elizabeth

1834 Completes John Gilbert's memoirs

1834 Death of Anne Hart Gilbert, July 18

ELIZABETH HART THWAITES

1772 Born second daughter of Anne Clearkley and Barry Conyers Hart of Antigua

1785 Death of mother

1786 Baptized Methodist along with her sister Anne during visit of Dr. Thomas Coke to West Indies

1804 Writes *History of Methodism*

1805 Marries Charles Thwaites of Antigua; couple moves to English
      Harbour the same year to join John Gilbert and Anne Hart
      Gilbert

1809 First Sunday school established in the West Indies (with Anne
      Hart Gilbert)

1813 Organizes, with husband, Sunday-school classes among Anti-
      guan plantation slaves; Bethesda school erected May 29 at the
      Lyons' estate, Antigua

1815 Founds Female Refuge Society of Antigua (with Anne Hart
      Gilbert)

1821 Oversees operation of English Harbour Sunday school in ab-
      sence of Anne Hart Gilbert

1827 Brought before Antigua House of Assembly committee to
      answer questions on expenditure of Quaker-supplied relief
      funds

1833 Death of Elizabeth Hart Thwaites at Willoughby Bay

Anne Hart Gilbert
History of Methodism

Antigua English-Harbor, 1st June 1804

My Dear Sir!

Having seen most of the accounts transmitted to our Brethren in Europe, respecting the rise, progress and present state of Methodism in the West Indies; and having I think matter of fact, and the concurrent opinions of other impartial persons on my side, for differing with some in many, and with others in a few particulars; I feel some reluctance to giving you the information you require of me, lest the testimony of those that have gone before should render my time so employed, uselessly disposed of. I will however venture; hoping at least to profit my own soul by calling to mind the wonders God has wrought in this benighted Land.

In the Year 1790 One of our Preachers who is now in Europe, requested me to inform him by letter of all that I knew respecting the rise and progress of Methodism in Antigua. I endeavor'd at that time, to collect all the information I could get, and having part of a copy of that letter now in my possession, I will give you the substance of it as far as it goes.

The remotest period to which I can trace the Preaching of the Gospel, in these Islands, is in the year 1671: By William Edmundson a Quaker, who with five other friends visited Bermudas, Jamaica, Barbadoes, Antigua, Barbuda, Nevis, and St. Christophers. He made the attempt at Mountserat also but was not suffered to land, Colonel

This letter was probably written to the Reverend Richard Pattison. The holograph copy is now in the Missionary Society Archives, School of Oriental and African Studies, University of London. Reprinted by permission.

Stapleton, the Governor, having heard that by means of their preaching seven hundred of the militia had turned Quakers and that Quakers would not fight. They were obliged to return immediately to
Antigua from whence they came, and were again graciously received.
To give you the paragraph from his own Journal ——— "After we
had laboured sometime in Barbadoes, we were moved in our minds
to visit the Leeward Islands; and Colonel Morris of Barbadoes,
would go with us; so we took ship and in four days we landed in
Antigua, where we had large and heavenly meetings and many were
convinced and turned to the Lord; several Justices of the Peace and
Officers, and Chief men came to the meetings, and confessed the
truth which we declared in the power of God. When we left Antigua
Colonel Windthorpe (who had been Governor, being convinced,
he and his family received the truth; we had several large and heavenly meetings in his house) would go with us to Nevis, and having
a vessel of his own shipped us in it with himself, Colonel Morris,
their waiting men, and Seamen; so we set sail from Antigua, and in
the way we touch'd at a little Island called Barbuda where we made
a little stay and preached the truth."

This Colonel Windthorpe, was I doubt not ancestor of the person
mentioned by W. Nathaniel Gilbert in his letter to Mr. Wesley called
"The Dawn of a Gospel Day" and published in the 3rd Volume of
the Arminian Magazine. He calls her Miss Molly Windthorpe a first
Cousin of his Wifes. In the year 1683 after spending sometime in
America, W. Edmundson returned to Ireland, from whence he came.
To the best of my knowledge the Islands were destitute of a Gospel ministry till the year 1756 when a Moravian Mission began. The
clouds of sin and error began to disperse among the Slaves by their
instrumentality; and while they preached the truth, they laboured
with their hands to forward the Work in which they were engaged.
But yet "darkness covered the Land and gross darkness the hearts of
the people." In the Year 1760, the Lord rais'd up Messrs. Nathaniel
and Francis Gilbert. The Slaves at this time were in a state of incon-
ceivable darkness and diabolical superstition. The torch of Moral
and divine truth was carefully hid from them, lest by it they should
discover that they were Men, and Brethren, and not Beasts, and
Reptiles; or as Doctor Magaw observes "kept back from Knowledge

expressly for this reason lest it should unfit them for beasts of burden." Their Dead were carried to the grave attended by a numerous
concourse, some of them beating upon an instrument they call a
"Shake Shake." (This is a large round hollow Calabash fixed upon
the end of a stick, with a few pebbles in it) and all singing some
heathenish account of the Life & Death of the deceased; invoking a
perpetuation of their friendhsip from the world of Spirits with their
Surviving friends and relations, & praying them to deal destruction
among their enemies; especially if they thought their death had been
occasion'd by the power of Witchcraft; which was commonly trans-
acted among them (in some of [its] effects exactly the same as what
Mr. Baxter relates in his piece called "Baxter's Certainty of the World
of Spirits; fully evinced by unquestionable Histories of Apparitions
& Witchcrafts" and published by Mr. Wesley in the 6th Volume of
the Arminian Magazine) as Debauchery, Drunkenness, Duelling,
& Sabbath-breaking, among the Learned & polished Heathens of
the present day. The Grave yards & burying places, both in Town
& Country, would be crowded on Christmas mornings with the
friends & relatives of deceased persons, strewing quarters of boiled,
and roasted, meat; or fowls & yams, & pouring bottles of Rum,
upon the graves of their departed friends. The Obeah men & women
of that day were very rich people; possessed of large sums of money;
being kept in constant pay, by those that could afford it, to prevent
their enemies from injuring their persons or properties, to procure,
& keep the favor of their owners, to give their children good luck,
and to make them prosperous in every thing. I have heard a very
aged black woman relate many years ago, that she was washer to
a very cruel Manager, who lived upon the estate to which she belonged, and that by some means or other, one of his shirts got stain'd
with the juice of the fruit we call Cashue; That in great distress, from
the apprehension of punishment, she carried it in with the rest of
his clothes, & shewed it to him making a very humble apology: He
returned her the Shirt saying, that by such and such a day (which he
named) if she did not bring him a Shirt free from Stains, & equally
as good as that she had spoil'd, he would give her fifty lashes. She
says being totally ignorant of God; there being no Gospel ministry
in the Island at the time; she immediately resorted to an Obeah-man

& told him her case: After receiving his fee, he made a circle upon the floor with chalk & then repeated his incantations, and invoked the powers of darkness; she says after some minutes had expired, there appeared upon the circle two little beings, about four inches long, quite black, and they moved upon the circle for sometime; The Obeah-man threw the shirt into the circle & said something to the two little Devils which she did not understand. She says they got upon the shirt & appeared very busy indeed, they seem'd to be talking to each other & ran up & down upon the shirt frequently meeting each other; what they said was quite unintelligible to her & only sounded like "whis, whis, whis." After sometime they disappeared. The Obeah-man then returned the shirt to her; and gave her powder wrapt up in paper, with directions to blow it through a quill, into a crevice in the window, at the head of the Managers bed; & she was to blow till he sneezed three times; this she was to do between three & four o'clock in the morning before any body was stirring: She punctually followed the directions given her, & the Manager sneezed three times; she also obey'd further instructions given her; which was to lay the shirt upon his bed after she had made it up & that he would look at & excuse it. & not inflict any punishment upon her for it; all which came to pass. I am sorry to say that too much of this diabolical work still exists in the Westindies and am of opinion that our preachers in general not being aware of it, pass too lightly over the sin of witchcraft. I understand that to this day, the time of Horseracing is time of great imolument to these Ministers of Satan; having to supply Ointments, to rub the Horses, & Riders, & materials to bury under the ground over which the Horses run; and (shame to tell) some of the owners concur, or connive, at it, & furnish money to pay these Factors for the Prince of darkness. There also prevailed great Heathenism among the free people of Colour: They were in general hardly allowed to believe that any of the virtuous, refined, or literary pursuits of the mind, were attainable by them; or that they were beings endued with the same understandings faculties & powers that were in the white people; tho by blood most or many of them, as nearly allied to the whites as to the blacks. Among the upper classes those called white people, excepting a few that had been educated in Europe, there was great ignorance & superstition; Applying to fortune-tellers to know what lot they were to have in life, and for every trivial loss sprinkling grave-dirt & mixing it for the people about the house to drink. This grave-dirt is procured by sending a piece of money which we call a dog* by some faithful hand to a grave, over which the person prays the dead not to be offended; & tells of the loss that has happened in the family, and that in order to discover the offender they are going to give all round a drink of this dirt mix'd thin enough with water to be drunk. They pray that in three days the guilty person may be swell'd to an enormous size, & the innocent preserved in perfect health.

Turning the sifter as they term it, was, & is still a prevailing custom among them, to find out the thief when any thing is stolen. The process of this business is as follows. The sharp points of a pair of scissors are stuck into the circumference of a hair sieve & the handle of the Scissors balanced upon the fingers of two people that stand opposite each other and alternately repeat the following words—"By Saint Peter by Saint Paul Such a one stole such a thing" mentioning the name of some or other of the family, & naming the thing that is stolen; and they say if they call over fifty names the sieve remains unmoved till the name of the guilty person is mention'd & then it swings round & drops off the balance. In respect of religion all were equally, & grossly dark, excepting one family & two or three others. A few, & but a few of white, colour'd & black people had some form of Godliness; so as to go to Church on Week days and partake of the Lord's supper at the four festivals. Perhaps these were the eighth or ninth Spiritual generation from W. Edmundson, who had from one to another degenerated into mere Moralists. But as yet the transporting sound of the Saviors name had never reached their ears, the Souls dead in trespasses & sins had never been quickened by the life-giving word; the Glorious beams of the Sun of righteousness had not shone upon their frozen dispensation. The family alluded to above, are particularly spoken of in that same letter of Mr. N. Gilbert's to Mr. Wesley. The per-

---

*I forgot to mention that this piece of money is left upon the grave to pay for the dirt that is taken away.

son who he calls the other Sister, was Miss Betty Strong; Who tho'
She appear'd to possess all the nonconformity to the world, & lively
interest in the concerns of the Church, & the spiritual prosperity
of mankind, which characterises the real Christian, laboured under
bondage thro' the fear of death for many years; yet at the last she
got the victory and longed to depart & be with Christ. My sister &
myself spent a few solemn moments with her some hours before she
died; by her own desire we sang "Vital Spark," etc, etc with her; She
said her soul fervently breath'd the substance of those words. The
progress of religion under the ministry of these two blessed men is
faithfully transmitted by them in their letters to Mr. Wesley & which
are published in the 3d–5th–6th–& 9th Vols of the Arminian Magazine. They formed a Small, but lively society of persons who obeyed
from their very heart that form of Doctrine delivered unto them;
they inforced Mr. Wesley's rules upon every individual & family that
received the truth. My Grandmother receiv'd her first Ticket pinn'd
in the rules of the Society. Their own families were miniatures of the
Primitive Church. Truly it might be said of them.

> ——— "Their hearts were warm,
> Their hands were pure; Their doctrines and their lives
> Coincident, discover'd lucid proof
> That they were honest in the sacred cause."

But alas! they and their sacred cause were soon in perils from false
pretended Brethren: There were two or three white men who came
to the Island with a flaming profession of Godliness & soon as
they made themselves known as professors, they were patronized
& befriended by these two unsuspecting men, "Whose wisdom
often woke while their suspicion slept and to simplicity resign'd
her charge." The soaring profession and grov'ling practice of these
men soon brought much scandal upon the Gospel; And when it
pleased the Lord to remove his servants (Messr. Nath & Francis
Gilbert) many who before had been staggered by the miscarriages
of these men, now stumbled over the blocks, some almost imperceptibly declined in spirituality became friends with the world &
inwardly enemies to God & his people, others fell into gross scandalous sin. However blessed by God, there were a few who never

forsook the Assembling of themselves together. A praying remnant held fast where unto they had attained; and tho' it cannot be said, that they abounded in knowledge, brightness of reason or soundness of speech, yet I say would to God there was the same simplicity, purity & love of the cross in only one half of our greatly increased Society now. The leaders of them were Mary Alley a Mulatto Woman & Sophia Campbel a black. The former after wading thro many trials & temptations is still alive & steady in the good cause. The latter went to her eternal rest in the year 1799. They met together for reading, singing & prayers & with many prayers watered the seed sown by their fathers in the Gospel. The Lord owned & blessed their labors some brought forth fruit to the praise of God and remain to this day. I have witness'd the happy deaths of many that have died gloriously in the faith & left behind them. Finding that their feeble efforts were attended with a divine blessing, they got a friend to write to Mr. Wesley to send them a Preacher; and were fervent in prayer that the Lord would send them one after his own heart. These remained bright Initials of a Methodist Society 'till the Lord by his providence sent Mr. Baxter. The wisdom of God in the choice of this instrument was greatly displayed: His being in a capacity to give (having a respectable employment in the Shipwrights department in His Majesty's Yard here) and not to receive together with his zeal & disinterestedness greatly contributed to the success of his labours in his master's vineyard. The Lord at this time revived the work in the hearts of many, whose darkened evidences only glimmer'd like a dying taper. Others were in the same state as the disciples that the Apostle Paul found at Ephesus 17th Chapt of Acts 2d verse. "He said unto them have ye received the Holy Ghost since ye believed." And they said unto him, "Nay we have not so much as hear'd whether there be any Holy Ghost." Others who were wallowing in sin were as brands plucked out of the fire; many of these have fallen asleep in Jesus others remain to this day and adorn the Gospel. Mrs. Mary Gilbert Widow of Mr Francis Gilbert, upon her return to the Island, greatly helped to hold up his hands. Their letters to Mr. Wesley in the 14th Volume of the Arminian Magazine speak fully of the state of the Church at this time. Between this & the time of Mr. Baxters visit to America, A Mr Cuff an Old Man a native

of Ireland arrived here driven by contrary winds. He preached to
Mr Baxter's congregations and met the classes; this circumstance is
also related by Mrs Gilbert to Mr Wesley and published in the 14th
Volume of the Magazine. After this we had a Mr Lambert a Methodist preacher from America who supplied Mr Baxter's place during
his absence. He was an excellent man and an awakening preacher;
his labours were bless'd. Some of our members who now adorn the
Gospel were brought to God by his instrumentality. Being seldom
free from bodily pain he had contracted a sort of gloom in his air &
manner that in general rendered him inaccessible to any but believers. How far this may have contributed to the safety of his own mind
he was the best able to judge, and indeed I know that all things do
not happen alike to all men, Yet I say happy are they who can receive
& practice Doctor Watt's excellent advice.

"Let your conversation be grave and manly, yet pleasing and engaging. Remember your station in the Church, that you sink not
into levity and vain trifling, that you indulge not any ridiculous
humour or childish follies, below the dignity of your character, keep
up the honor of your Office by a remarkable sanctity of manners,
by a decent & manly deportment, remember that our station does
not permit any of us to set up for a Buffoon, nor will it be any
glory to us to excel in spreading a laugh round the company" etc.
etc. Mr Lambert left a good report behind him & I believe is now
reaping the reward & sharing the Glory of those that turn many to
righteousness. Our two dear Sisters Mary Alley & Sophia Campbel
mentioned above; ventured in faith to agree for a spot of land to
build a Chapel upon: They were greatly discouraged by all to whom
they mentioned it, as an undertaking too great & expensive so small
a Society to engage in; but being emboldened by faith tho they
knew not the way, they struck for the land & had to pay the cash
down. Sister S. Campbel went herself with James Watkins (another
of our steady old black friends who is now alive & resides in St
Christophers) to the Lumber yard & bought materials for building.
The most decent, and creditable of the black women did not think it
a labour too servile to carry stones and marl, to help with their own
hands to clear the Land of the rubbish that lay about it, & to bring
ready-dressed victuals for the men that were employed in building

the House of God. They now rejoiced to sell their Ear-rings & bracelets and to buy Lumber & pay Carpenters, to forward this blessed
work; and at last they got a comfortable little Chapel, which soon
became too small.

Upon Mr Baxter's return, being free from every other employment his labors were more extensive & the Society particularly in
the country encreased considerably. The events relating to Doctor
Coke's arrival you know are circumstantially published in his journals. This I know respecting his labors & the labors of the missionaries that accompanied him, that they were truly blessed so as
in every possible way to prove beyond dispute that those winds &
waves, which obstinately drove him into St. Johns harbor on the
25th December 1786 were under the peculiar command of an over-
ruling providence. May my heart never cease to adore & praise my
gracious God for this event. I never recall it to my memory without
those emotions of gratitude that warm my heart and constrain me
to cry out.

> "What am I, O thou Glorious God!
>   And what my father's house to thee?
> That thou such mercies hast bestow'd,
>   On me, the vilest reptile me!
> I take the blessing from above
>   And wonder at thy boundless love"!

> "Me in my blood thy love pass'd by,
>   And stop'd my ruin to retrieve.
> Wept o'er my soul thy pitying eye;
>   Thy bowels yearn'd and sounded "Live."
> Dying I heard the welcome sound
>   And pardon in thy mercy found." etc. etc.

It will swell this Letter to size almost enormous, to tell you all the
love and watchful care that has covered my defenceless head; or to
particularize those events that have united together all the links in
the chain of Providence, which has been working together for my
good ever since I came into existence but unnoted by me, 'till the
scales of pride, ignorance & unbelief, fell from my eyes, by the light

& power which accompanies the Gospel faithfully preached. Let it suffice that I add my feeble testimony to that of innumerable multitudes, that "God is no respecter of persons"—That "He willeth not the death of a Sinner"—That he hath never failed the feeblest nor the most unworthy that ever confided in his promise. He hath been with me, according to his faithful word, "Thro the Water & the Fire." He has upheld me (tho' at times almost sinking) upon the tumultous sea of life. And tho' in seasons of sore trial & temptation, The floods have lifted up their voice, & the waves seem'd ready to o'er whelm my frighted soul, yet, "The Lord has been mightier than the noise of many waters, Yea than the mighty waves of the Sea." I can indeed adopt the language of the Psalmist & say—"O how great is thy goodness which thou hast laid up for them that fear thee, which thou has wrought for them that trust in thee before the Sons of men, Thou didst hide me in thy secret presence from the pride of man: Thou didst keep me secretly in a pavilion from the strife of tongues." Blessed be his name, He is indeed my strength & my Son, & is become my Salvation; And by his power I will rest upon his faithfulness while I sojourn in this vale of tears, 'till my last change shall come, & then I trust thro' grace to join the innumerable multitude in ascribing, Blessing, & glory, & wisdom & thanksgiving and honor & power & might unto our God forever and ever Amen."

But to return to the Chronological account of events from which my full heart upon the recollection of past, & present mercies, had led me to digress. There was at this time a gracious work begun in the hearts of many especially in the Town of St Johns & among the free people of Colour. The ministry of the word by Doctor Coke may be compared to a net which he cast into the Sea, which took in a large draught of fishes, & this net drawn to shore by the faithful labors of Mr Warrener who he left behind & who labor'd among us for two years. The society began to be regulated more according to Mr Wesley's mode of discipline. The word was indeed like marrow & fat things, and all that could relish divine things were sure to feed richly on immortal food while sitting under the preached word. The society has continued to increase from that time to this. We have seen, more real converts added to our numbers under the ministry of some, than of others. Some of our preachers that have only paid us a visit of a week or two, have sown the precious seed in good ground & the fruit has appeared to the honor & glory of God; Among these Mr Graham, Mr Black, Mr Cook, Mr McCornock & Mr Ray stand foremost. Their labors were peculiarly bless'd in stirring up those that believe to press after the full image of God. That blessed servant of God Bartholomew McDonald arrived here 24th December 1797 and departed this life 4th Dec 1798. His labors on our favored Island were of short duration, but crowned with abundant success. He was but little seen or known, except in the pulpit, where of a truth he shone, with all the excellencies of a holy man & a very able minister & Steward of the mysteries of God. He carefully avoided seeking any honor & glory that cometh of man; And having in one peculiar instance in his life acted somewhat in opposition to the pride & prejudice of worldly-minded professors, some of them beheld him at a distance, & vainly attempted to pour contempt upon his labors: But the end of his coming to the West-indies was full answered; as is indisputably proved, by the testimony of many precious seals to his ministry; who by their holy & useful lives proclaim to all around, that "The Gospel (by his instrumentality) came not unto them in word only, but also with power, and with the Holy Ghost and with much assurance." *

He lived in our house & all our family felt the influence of his holy conversation. During the time he labor'd among us there was a deep and genuine revival of religion. Our vigilant enemy finding that his Kingdom was shaken, began to work by an instrument which he had prepared to prevent our further success. The immoral conduct of ———— who had been received among us as a preacher, stumbled many in the society in the country. He had been a missionary in a Sister Church & for proper reasons was excluded from their communion; unhappy for us he got into our connexion in the capacity of a preacher. His evil deeds being proved, he was also excluded from among us. After his expulsion the redoubled usefulness of Mr McDonald both in Town & Country soon repaired the breaches that had been made, & the word of God ran & was glorified. He had been indisposed, but was in some measure recovered & left us to go

---

*St. Paul, 1 Cor. 9:2; Eph. 1:13; 1 Thess. 1:5 [Ed.].

into the country, where he relapsed & was brought to Town on a very rainy day as soon as he step'd into the house I perceived he was in a high fever, a fever that seemed like a messenger sent to demand of us, one who we highly, & justly esteemed, & with whom were very reluctant to part. He instantly got to bed, but his disorder with all its dangerous symptoms rapidly encreased. The room he occupied in our house being too small, he was removed to the Chapel house. I spent as much of my time with him as the calls of my family would allow. I observed he grew worse & worse every hour: This he was sensible of himself, & sent for Mr Gilbert & told him how he would have his little effects disposed of. As the hour of his dissolution approached, The glorious scene of a dying Saint, giving his last testimony for God, & closing a useful life with the most powerful effusions of his ardent faith & love, grew brighter and brighter. He preached with his departing breath & heavenly countenance, the free unbounded love of Jesus. The Redeemer's name seem'd like music on his tongue. He called for the Doctors that he might tell them how perfectly the heavenly physician could cure the soul of the dreadful malady of sin. He begged some of the friends to carry him upon his bed into the pulpit & assemble the people, that he might tell them the awful realities he felt in his soul; & almost every thing he said was concluded with those words "Glory! Glory!" He asked us to sing & pray alternately with him; but such were our feelings upon this trying occasion that (tho' dying) he had often to take the lead himself & also to conclude the prayers begun by others. We attempted to sing. "My God the spring of all my joys" etc. And finding that we failed in the attempt, He struck in with the last verse "Fearless of Hell & ghostly Death," He sang with such strength & vigor as amazed us all. Seeing some in the room with him that had under the guise of zeal of the cause of God vented their pride by speaking evil of him & rejected him because of the proofs he had given of the dis-similarity of his sentiments with those so generally received by the world. He lovingly justified his conduct, He told them however the people of the world might be excused for indulging their prejudices it did not become the people of God to despise & traduce each other. He declared that in that awful moment he enjoyed the witness in himself that he had in no wise acted contrary to the will and word of God. He continued to pray & praise, to re-joice with Joy unspeakable & full of Glory 'till about 12 Oclock on the fifth night of his illness, his happy spirit freed from mortality took its joyful flight to the thrice blessed abode of Angels & God. The sorrow had filled our hearts at the loss of our dear Brother yet we had precious seasons of joy & love when those newly brought to God and the believers who were vigorously pressing after Holi-ness met together in our private prayer- & Class-meetings. Nothing remarkable occurred either one way or the other for sometime. A few months after Satan by some means or other sent us another enemy in the character of a preacher. I do not learn from any quar-ter that he came with recommendations from any of our European Brethren: How he came to commence preacher in the West-indies I cannot positively say having heard various accounts, but this I know he did not succeed well in playing the hypocrite; his mask was soon discovered by a faithful few. He did not stay long in Antigua after this, but was a few months in one of the other Islands, & happy for the West-indies has returned to Europe. Mr Murdock's labors were bless'd, & we may say with truth that he was a faithful preacher of the Gospel, & upright in all that was committed to his care as super-intendent. Many who at first felt it a cross to be subject to discipline under his uniform administration of it; now bless the Lord that ever he laboured in Antigua. He was opposed & vilified by two of the Leaders upon the Estates in the country who he found destitute of either gifts or grace & only zealous to have great numbers upon their papers & to possess great consequence among them: He took the classes from them and appointed proper persons to meet them; in consequence of it they left the society & took along with them some that were like-minded and such as we ought to rejoice to get rid of. Upon the arrival of Mr & Mrs Birkinhead, She opened a meeting for the religious instruction of children, & also a meeting for teaching the young people to sing, these meetings were the means of drawing many young people of colour, some of which are now steady mem-bers of our Society, others in the day of temptation withered away & are no more seen among the people of God. She also established a public prayer-meeting conducted by women and intended for the benefit of young women: The Lord has been pleased greatly to own these meetings, which are still continued: many that were halting between the paths of vice & virtue, have been confirmed to follow the more excellent way; in short they have in general had the effect of enlightening the ignorant & fixing the resolve of wav'ring minds in the side of truth & virtue.

Blessed be God, notwithstanding the many open & insidious efforts of earth & hell to prevail against the Work, many witnesses of the truth have continued to increase the cloud ever since it first appeared "little as a human hand." And tho' there are many who swell the numbers transmitted to Europe every year, who have scarcely the form of Godliness, others who make vain professions of religion, & yet hold fast their sins. Still I say blessed be the God of our Salvation, there are also many even among the abject & despised children of men, whose Garments are unspotted from the world, who deny themselves daily & take up the cross following the Savior of the world thro' evil and thro' good report; and I scruple not to say there would have been multitudes more, had the preachers as they succeeded each other from time to time been men of one heart & one soul with respect to their own conversation and the exercise of discipline among the people; and had the Leaders both in Town & Country co-operated heartily with those preachers, that adhered most strictly to Mr Wesley's rules: but sorry I am to say that some from a total neglect of discipline, others from irregularity, have at times pulled down, or passively suffered that to go [to] wrack which their predecessors had with many prayers much labour & indefatigable care built up. Allow me Dr Sir to observe that the work in the West-indies should not be entered upon by the sanguine & indeliberate: It should only be handled by humble, judicious men; who [are] well disciplin'd in the school of Christ, & have only one single aim in view; The glory of God & the good of souls: men who count not their lives dear; who for the glory that is set before them endure the cross despising the shame; whose principles are fixed by the revealed will of God, whose motives spring from unfeigned love to God & to ev'ry soul of man & fashion all their conversation by the life of Christ; who are not easily driven about by the corrupt & partial opinions of every vain and carnally-minded professor, that fawns & heaps favors upon him, for the express purpose of brib-

ing his self-denial & stability, to yield to their Luxury & conformity
to the world. Such thank God we have been and are now favoured
with in Antigua. From what I observe of the work at present, it is
not a time of in-gathering, but a deepening of the work of hearts
of the truly sincere. Many that were weak & easily cast down by the
apostasy of some, & the inconsistency of others, that made great
professions, appear to have learnt that wisdom that discerns the de-
vices of the Devil & runs for safety to him that is mighty to save.
I am truly thankful to find that you & your dear partner begin to
see some fruit of your labours to have a well regulated society of
people who embrace the salvation you preach: On Sunday last when
I visited you, I rejoiced to see the attention & seriousness of the
congregation under the word, & indeed the whole face of things,
speaks, that the people are no longer kept in ignorance & under the
influence of Blind leaders of the blind in the Circuit committed to
your care. Be not easily discouraged but labour on in patient humble
love; and if only one sinner, among many be saved from the guilt, &
power of sin, & escapes the wrath to come; be thankful, and rejoice
with Host above, participate in that joy which there is in Heaven
over one sinner that repents. I cannot but remark that it very frequently happens that when a preacher comes into a circuit who is
disinterestedly zealous for the good of souls, & not seeking to be in
high reputation among men, it may sometimes appear by the return
of numbers sent home that the work under his superintendence is
greatly at a stand, or when the decline; merely because he cannot
tolerate a corrupt society; & searches into the life & conversation of
every member, and a few who had lain by in silence, having been
dismayed & borne down by a majority of Latitudinarians, encouraged by his zeal & impartiality come forth and rejoice to hold up
his hands in excluding Drunkards, Swearers, Adulterers & Adul-
teresses, Sabbath breakers & Dancers, that have crept in unawares
from private partialities in the Leaders, & neglect of discipline in
the preachers. While those who rush into the labours of others full
of their own sufficiency, & suppose that all who weep under their
sermons, & profess to be much pleased with their disposition, are
beyond all doubt seals to their ministry; and without knowledge
of the characters of the person who they take into the Church of

Christ, except what they learn from the recommendation of one or
two Lukewarm Leaders who advise "take them as you find them"—
and "bear with them 'till they know better"—they receive persons
into full connexion, who ought only to be taken as Catechumens
& the strictest scrutiny made into ev'ry particular relating to their
lives and conversations. These often appear to be doing great things
& monstrously Swell the Numerical Splendor of the Church. It has
long been very clear to me that the work in Antigua would have been
in a more flourishing & advanced State, but from the choice of improper persons as Leaders; especially in the country; many, who if
they had been faithfully dealt with would have been happy partakers
of a Gospel hope themselves, & useful to their fellow-servants, have
been lull'd to sleep in their sins, or led on Hood-winked in the paths
of formality and Superstition with a vain hope, that as they were in
Society, they were of course in the way to heaven. You well know
my dear Sir how difficult you have found it, since you have laboured
in Antigua, to drag some of the poor Souls out of this pit; others I
know have rejoiced to be freed from this Yoke, tho' the Subordination of their situations made them afraid to complain. You know on
the 2 of January last we removed from St Johns to English-Harbor,
Mr Gilbert having had the offer of an employment that suited him
in his Majesty's Yard. To my great but pleasant surprise I found a
small society of black & coloured people, consisting of 28 Members
& all but a very few in earnest for Salvation. They have never had
one half the advantages of the people of St Johns, having no place
of worship to go to on Sundays, & very few of them able to read
the word of God. They were also thrown back at different times by
the scandal which was brought upon religion in consequence of the
Apostasy of a few white people who were members of our Society
in England & came out here in the Kings service, & some that removed from other parts of the Island to reside here. My complexion
exempted me from those prejudices & that disgust which the instability of their white Brethren had planted in their hearts & they
tremblingly ventured to receive us as friends. Mr Baxter desired the
women to meet with me; I soon found that they were all desirous
to have a little Chapel, & to have service on Sundays; & at the time
Mr Lumb laboured here had collected five joes among themselves

for that purpose but it was never brought into effect. I told them
how our Sisters in St Johns had heartily united together and even
labor'd with their hands to forward the building of the Chapel, &
they generally agree to do the same. Previous to our coming here
they had been in treaty for a house for the purpose of preaching, but
the situation is so hot, and so low, that both Preacher, & hearers,
run the risk of getting sick as soon as they come into the open air.
We have therefore petitioned the Commissioner to give us a Grant
of Land to build in a more convenient place & he has readily granted
the petition. It was written in the name of "the Negroes belonging to His Majesty & others inhabiting English-Harbor." & it was
presented by me of the King's negroes. We intend as our means are
very small to build our Chapel of Stone with a ground floor, for the
present 'till Providence shall send us help. I am afraid you will not
find this account as interesting as you expected; but probably if you
had known the wickedness & ignorance, that prevailed even in my
time & the thrice blessed effects of the Gospel, not only in civilizing
but christianizing, the people of this Island, you would rejoice that
ever you were called to perpetuate the glorious sound among us.
Some of the blessed influences of a preached Gospel are often over-
looked, or ascribed to other causes. But those who view all things
as directed, or over-ruled by his wonder-working power rejoice to
ascribe all good to the bounteous Author of all our blessings both
in time and to all Eternity. I see with heart-felt joy that prostitution
is now esteemed abominable & disgraceful by the greater part of the
Colour'd Women in St Johns where the great bulk of them reside;
and lawful alliances take place as frequently among them as among
the whites. This is one happy effect of seeing the Gospel seed sown
in the hearts of their Mothers; and many of them seeing themselves
examples corroborating, those truths that recommend, chastity tho'
accompanied with labour & self-denial. The great civilization of the
Slaves, their gradual emergence, from the depths of ignorance &
barbarism, has imperceptibly had an over-awing effect upon the System of tyranny & cruel oppression that was formerly exercised over
them with little or no restraint when they differed in so few respects from the Beasts that perish; And as a natural consequence,
those that are set over them feel more cautious in dealing with ratio-

nal creatures than they did with beings imbruted in ev'ry way both
body & mind. The Slaves in general that attend a Gospel ministry,
whether they are subject themselves to Church discipline or not,
become more creditable & decent in their families & manners than
those that do not. There is in all a thirst for a knowledge. The greater
part of those that can afford it get themselves taught to read &
some to write also. There are hundreds of black & colour'd children
sent to school every year in this little Island; and the great change
wrought in the manners & condition of all people of this description is beyond any thing that could have been expected and such as
nothing could effect but the wisdom & power of God. Its having
been effected by the Unbloody Sword of truth that has almost unperceivedly cut its way thro' mountainous obstacles; And not by
tumultous distracting revolution, massacre & bloodshed, is cause of
unspeakable thankfulness to God; and has been the means of opening a door free of access to all the preachers of the Gospel. After all
that I can say, I only give a faint idea of the blessing brought to our
favoured Island by the light of the Gospel. Could our dear friends in
Europe conceive only one half of the benefit derived by numbers of
our abject & despised fellow-creatures, they would rejoice to contribute all in their power, to carry on the blessed work; nor would
they think any self-denial too rigid to impose upon themselves, nor
any moments spent in fervent prayer too many to aid or advance the
Redeemer's Kingdom among the poor Slaves. I beg leave humbly to
observe, That if a preacher is a married man he is doubly useful as a
Missionary. provided his Wife is an humble pious Woman. But not
else. It is a matter too delicate for a man to tell a whole Society that
his Wife is worldly-minded, & not worthy their confidence, or imitation; And often while his soul is cast down, & disquieted within
him, because of the Offences & stumbling-blocks that are laid in the
way of God's people, by her that should be his help-mate, & hold
up his hands in the good cause, He appears quite neuter, or sides
with his wife to the destruction of his usefulness. The Wives of the
Moravian Missionaries have no intercourse with the vain Women of
the World. Their station in the Church as the Wives of Missionaries
furnish them with sufficient employment from morning 'till night,
so that they have no time for Tea-parties & feasts, nor can they find

leisure to frequent the tables of the Wicked which the scriptures tell us are snares even to themselves. I have at times been grieved to see some of the Wives of our preachers that have been like works for Flatterers and Sycophants to shoot at; Who deceived, by what is falsely called, (and bears a strong resemblance to) Kindness & hospitality; & under the idea of doing good, & winning souls to Christ by familiarity with the World, have lost their simplicity, & deadness, to the world, been shorn of their spiritual strength & had their affections estranged from the real people of God. I am truly sorry to say that some others have appeared in that character in the West-indies, whose conduct has evidently shewn that they were destitute of every principle of vital piety, whose pride & extravagance have rendered them as painful & irksome to those who endeavor to adorn the Gospel themselves & promote the interests of religion, as "Smoke to the eyes & vinegar to the teeth." Proverbs 10th Chapt 26th verse. Thank God Antigua does not labour under such burdens at present; But it is from the piety and usefulness of those that are with us now, that we are more than ever convinced of the great Utility of a Preacher's being a married man. I think from what we have seen within the last 16 Months I may safely add that a Missionary who is zealous and active himself & has a Wife like-minded, who will meet the Women & deal faithfully with them & visit the sick etc etc, makes his way quite easily with respect to temporals as a single man who is not equally devoted to God & the good of his fellow-mortals.

After all we may with great propriety ask with the Apostle "Who is sufficient for these things?" "The Harvest truly is plenteous but the labourers are few. Pray ye therefore the Lord of the Harvest that he would thrust forth more labourers into the Harvest." Let us in faith come boldly to the throne of Grace, and pray. "Thy Kingdom Come."

I am My Dear Sir
Your sister & servant in Christ, Anne Gilbert

Memoir of John Gilbert

At this point, Mr. Gilbert's part of the narrative breaks off, and Mrs. Gilbert takes it up. [Internal references suggest she wrote it not long before she died:]

My beloved husband, though born with very different expectations, gladly set about baking, as an occupation in which I could assist him, and which, with such assistance, would enable him to employ himself in the use of his pen. A strong temptation had been set before him; but he resisted it, in the power of the Holy Spirit, with his usual decision of character. While he was in partnership with his friends Playfair and Crichton, and, as he thought, growing rich, he had been very liberal to the French emigrants who fled from Guadaloupe and Martinique, during the revolution in France. Some of them, though men of high rank in their native country, were constrained to seek a subsistence for themselves and families by various employments opposed to their former habits and education; while their wives, who were women of fashion and refinement, aided the

The *Memoir of John Gilbert, Esq., Late Naval Storekeeper at Antigua, to Which Are Appended a Brief Sketch of His Relic, Mrs. Anne Gilbert, by the Rev. William Box, Wesleyan Missionary, and a Few Additional Remarks by a Christian Friend* (Liverpool: D. Marples, 1835) contains the *Memoir* itself, finished by Anne Gilbert; "A Brief Sketch," by the Reverend William Box (reproduced in appendix A); and "Additional Remarks on John and Ann Gilbert by a Friend" (see appendix B). A copy is in the British Library, shelf-mark 4903 df8. Permission to reprint courtesy of The British Library Board.

design by the use of their needles, in which they were remarkably well skilled, and produced most beautiful specimens of ornamental work. Nor was the benefit of the laudable efforts of these ladies confined to themselves; for, from their example, many of the young females of Antigua learnt the importance of exertion in the feebler sex. These interesting individuals were much attached to my dear husband: he could speak their own language, and they felt great sympathy towards us both, regarding us as oppressed strangers in our native land. One of them, a Monsieur M——, offered to go into partnership with him in the business of baker and tobacconist, provided he would sell on Sundays, which was then the universal practice, and usually attended with great emolument. He said he knew, and admired, my dear Mr. G.'s principles, and would release him from all interference in the business from Saturday night till Monday morning; but Mr. G. told him that would not satisfy him, and therefore declined entering into any engagement. The Frenchman was so convinced that his motives were purely conscientious, that he turned over the house in which he lived, and all the apparatus belonging to the tobacco business, to him, and returned to Guadaloupe. We both laboured hard that we might "owe no man any thing;" but it pleased God to try our faith closely. My dear husband fell sick, and was brought nigh to the grave: soon after his recovery, I had an illness, which confined me to my bed for six months. As he was at this time (after being up from three o'clock in the morning to bake) engaged through the day in settling some intricate accounts of an extensive firm, it may be easily conceived his labour, both of body and mind, was great. He settled one account in particular, for which the sum of eight hundred dollars was awarded him by arbitration, and which would not have been put into his hands if any other person in the Island could have been found equal to it. The greater part of this money was appropriated to purchasing the freedom of a young person who had some claims upon him, and who was saved from vice and wretchedness by being rescued from slavery. His being obliged to spend some hours every day at the merchant's counting-house where the books were deposited, and my inability to attend to business at home, rendered our circumstances very trying; we therefore determined upon giving up baking, and opening a school, in which we could have the assistance of my late dear sister, Mrs. Thwaites. We accordingly hired a house, and every arrangement was made for our removal, as soon as I should recover my strength sufficiently to attend to it. My heart sunk at the prospect of his engaging in a school: I knew that he would find it impossible to obtain regular payments for the children, some of whom were to board with us; and that his punctual and upright mind would be continually upon the rack to obtain the means of defraying the daily expenses of the establishment; while, after all, his income would be fluctuating and precarious. We both went many times to a throne of grace to implore divine aid and direction, and, by the gracious interposition of our Heavenly Father, we were released from this trying attempt to procure a subsistence. Before I was able to leave my sick-bed, as my dear Mr. G. was sitting by me one evening, a servant brought a message, purporting that Mr. Dow (under whom he had served in the Store-keeper's Office when a youth, and who had always cherished a kind regard for him, and endeavoured to serve him,) wished to speak to him. My mind being weakened by long bodily indisposition, I apprehended new trials awaited us, and, as soon as he returned, eagerly inquired if it was the case. I remember saying, rather impatiently, "Do tell me, is it for the better or the worse?" With his accustomed tenderness, he soothed my fears, and strove to dissipate my alarm, but did not know what opinion to give on the proposal which had been made to him. Mr. M——h, the then Naval Storekeeper, had written to Mr. D. to request him to ask Mr. Gilbert to take the situation of second clerk in the Storekeeper's Office, as the first clerk appeared to be dying. Mr. G. requested Mr. D. to give him his advice, as he had already obtained a licence as a schoolmaster, and was promised a good number of scholars. Mr. D. told him, though he should be very sorry to lose him as a neighbour, and should not be able to procure any body to fill his place in settling the accounts in Mr. K.'s office, he thought employment in the Naval yard more congenial to his habits, as it was the place in which he had already spent many years of his life; but that he must at the same time warn him he would find the business of the Storekeeper's Office oppressive, as the clerks were negligent, and he understood the writing department to be in a very backward state; that as, in consequence of a French fleet being in these seas, there were constantly from six to eight ships of war in the harbour, he would probably be under the necessity of writing almost all night, and, he was afraid, would sink under it. Mr. D. concluded by advising Mr. G. to go to English Harbour, and speak to Mr. M——h himself, and kindly offered him his gig for the purpose. My dear husband told me his heart shrunk from the idea of taking me to live in a place where vice of every kind held its undisturbed dominion, and where there was scarcely a single female with whom I could associate. I told him I was willing to go with him under any circumstances, provided we were convinced that divine Providence pointed the way. He accordingly went to English Harbour, and waited upon the Store-keeper, who told him the office was much in want of an efficient clerk; that the second would of course expect to succeed the first, in the event of his death; and that then there would be a vacancy for the second clerk's place, which he would be very glad to see filled by my dear Mr. G. He, however, declined accepting the situation, as the income would be insufficient for the support of his family, and he had the prospect of more ample maintenance as a schoolmaster. The Storekeeper replied that the second clerk was not willing to give up his promotion nominally; but that he would let Mr. G. receive the first clerk's salary, and be content with that of the second. My dear Mr. G. objected to this, and preferred entering upon the school. Accordingly he concluded the lease of the house, and we removed into it. The week before the school was to be opened, an order from Commissioner Lane was handed him, appointing him first clerk in the Store-keeper's Office. He, with his usual consideration for my comfort in all things, referred it to me, and I had no hesitation in preferring English Harbour, though attended with many privations and new trials, considering it an answer to prayers which I had put up, in great anguish of spirit, at the prospect of his wearing out his valuable life without even suitable remuneration for his toils. He had to pay a sum of money to be released from the contract about the house. As the business at English Harbour was pressing, he went there immediately, leaving me to pack up, and follow him, which I did in about ten days.

We had not long taken up our residence there, when the integrity

of my husband's principles began to give offence, and to occasion
gross misrepresentations of his character. What was chiefly disliked
in his conduct, was his endeavouring, with the permission of his
superior officers, to arrange the business of the Dock Yard so as to
prevent working on the Lord's day; the violation of which had been
encouraged by a professor of religion, for his own emolument, and
in order that he might become popular with the artificers. The force
of truth, however, proved irresistible, and the attacks of Mr. G.'s
enemies were so powerless, that he rose in the esteem of his superiors, and of all those officers in the navy who knew how to appre-
ciate intelligence, a conscientious attention to duty, and, in short,
all those qualities which distinguish the gentleman and the christian. In the mean time, the malice of his enemies spent itself in low
secret abuse. As soon as Sunday work had received a check, we attended the Parish Church, the pulpit of which was not then, as thank
God! we have known it since, occupied by a minister who preached
evangelical doctrines; besides which, we had not conveyance without borrowing, and the distance was much beyond a walking one,
in this climate. Among the poor there were a few who loved the
Gospel, and were under the necessity of walking six or eight miles
on the Sabbath to hear it, and to enjoy christian communion; others
also had been long wishing for Sunday service at English Harbour.
My beloved husband, then filling a situation which all around us
thought incompatible with such an employment, preached in a small
thatched house, in what was at that time a most wretched place,
called Spring Gardens. None other could be obtained for such a
sacred purpose, and, oh! for ever blessed be the name of that God
who made him instrumental to the conversion of many precious
souls, some of whom not only hold fast the beginning of their confidence to this day (though they had to endure bitter persecution,
and even corporal suffering, for the truth's sake), but have been
eminently useful to others.

I cannot, in my present state of mind, attempt to do more than
relate circumstances as they occur to my recollection, and that without regard to systematic arrangement. There is one which I must
not omit, because I think it somewhat remarkable. A captain in the
navy, who had been told (by a man to whom my dear husband had

rendered essential services, which involved himself in great pecuniary embarrassment,) that he was "one of the greatest villains in the
Island," but could not credit the slander, used to go occasionally,
but privately, to hear him preach. It appears that this gentleman felt
the truths delivered, and wished to call on Mr. G., but thought we
should not like such a visitor; knowing that we did not cultivate acquaintance with the officers of the navy, and approving our motives
for it. He afterwards died at English Harbour, and, to our very
great surprise, left my dear husband money to purchase a mourning
ring. His preaching began to diffuse a new and better feeling in the
neighbourhood. Some in the town of Falmouth, who had been cold
professors, attended. Mothers, who had promoted the degradation
and impurity of their daughters, began to bewail their wickedness,
and to wish to screen their yet undebased offspring from the destroyer. More respect was paid to the Sabbath, and the rapid stream
of ungodliness, in all its varied forms, received a check which it
had never experienced before. About this time, my late dear sister,
Mrs. Thwaites, was united to Mr. Thwaites, who was also employed
in the Naval Yard. The congregations became too large for the little
thatched house in Spring Gardens, and Mr. T. opened his house for
the purpose.

We became acquainted with a Mr. A——r, Ordnance Store-
keeper, who had been religiously brought up, by a pious father.
Mr. A. sought the acquaintance of my dear Mr. G., and was very
desirous of having him in the same department with himself. Seeing that he had greater application to business than was consistent
with his health, in consequence of having to make up the deficien-
cies and neglects of others, he advised his writing to any friends he
might have in England, who had interest in the Ordnance department, with a view for exchanging his situation. It happened that
Gen. M——, who was then high in rank in that department, had
been an intimate friend of his father; Mr. G. therefore wrote to him
on the subject, and through his interference procured admission to
the department, "if he should still be disposed to leave the Naval
service." In the mean time, we had laid the matter before the Lord,
and prayed him, if the removal was contrary to His will, to prevent it; and it pleased that Almighty being, to whose control all the

arcana of visible and invisible nature are subject, on this occasion to direct my dear husband, by *a dream*, to remain where he was. The Naval Store-keeper, whose health required change of climate, had written to England to recommend a person he wished to favour as his successor in the Store-keeper's office, and a gentleman in the law as Deputy Treasurer to Greenwich Hospital, appointments which had till then been always united in the same person, but, in consequence of this recommendation, were divided, and Mr. M——h's friend appointed to the latter. In conversation one day with Mr. G., the Store-keeper said, very disingenuously,—for he had no idea that Mr. G. had any interest which could avail him, and at the same time hoped his own application on behalf of the person he favoured would be successful,—"Gilbert, you had better apply for the situation of Store-keeper. Have you any friends in England who can assist you by their influence?" Mr. G. replied that Mr. M——n, who had always shewn him the affection of a parent, was in England, and he knew would be glad to serve him, but he did not know if he had any interest with the then ministry. After he came home, however, he recollected that the then earl, since Marquis of N——n, had married a niece of his father, and with prayer, but with little or no expectation of success, he wrote to the Earl, and to Mr. M——n. From the former, he received a prompt reply, telling him he had written to Lord Melville on the subject of his letter, and that his Lordship had promised attention to his wishes, if a vacancy should occur. Mr. M——n, who resided at Southampton, went up to London,— and if Mr. G. had been his own son, he could not have exerted himself more on his behalf,—and finally succeeded in obtaining for him the appointment, in the year 1807.

While the answers to the letters were pending, the enemies of religion ridiculed the idea of a man who accounted worldly honours as nothing, and whose life was devoted to the conscientious discharge of his public duties, and the religious instruction of the poor, obtaining a situation which *they* thought would be better filled by one who gave his time sparingly to business, and devoted his income to the popular pleasures of the world. I recollect one opposer of my dear husband's principles and conduct riding up to our door, and telling me that a ship had just arrived, and brought a new Store-keeper for the Naval-yard. I told him we had expected some such event. The next morning, it appeared that the person from England was sent to supersede the very man who came to triumph over what he considered our disappointment; the same ship also brought letters addressed to "Mr. Gilbert, Naval Store-keeper," and the following packet, official notice of his appointment.

It was now generally reported, that Mr. G. did not intend to preach any more; in short, that we were going to lay religion aside. Some of the poor were much grieved at this, and one woman actually returned to her house on Sunday morning, weeping bitterly. But, for ever blessed be that God, who kept us by his grace, my beloved husband waxed stronger and stronger in confessing Christ, and as Mr. Thwaites's house became too contracted for the increased congregations, our own was opened for the purpose, and Mr. G. preached or expounded the scriptures every Sabbath, the Wesleyan missionaries preaching once a fortnight, on a night in the week. We had soon all our rooms, the bed chambers excepted, quite full, when the weather was good.

I could here mention the names of some who heard and received the truth in the love of it; four in particular, who were attached to the army. In the Methodist Magazine for 1823, page 704, one is mentioned, under the head of "Obituary," who finished his course with joy. His brother officers in the naval department, and their families, loved and esteemed him; and though the former were not at that time men of decided piety, they admired his consistency of conduct, and in all times of public or domestic trial he was their confidential friend and counsellor. There were always a few in the department, however, who were dissatisfied with his scrupulous integrity, because his example overawed and restrained them; but even some of these he visited at their own request, when they were about to leave the world, pointed them to the Lamb of God, and besought mercy for their souls in earnest prayer.

In 1809, the first Sunday School known in the West Indies was commenced in Mr. G.'s house, and he became a teacher in it himself. Any attempt to detail the benefits which have resulted from this institution would swell this memoir, intended only as a sketch, beyond its proper limits; suffice it to say, "many arise and call it blessed."

After the arrival in this Island of his brother-in-law, Mr. D[awes], at his suggestion to Mr. G., they united in forming an Auxiliary Bible Society, which was organized in our house, and many of its committee meetings held there. The Female Refuge Society was formed in the same year, 1815, and all its meetings carried on in the same place, until, in consequence of Lady D'Urban's kind patronage, a general meeting was held at the Honourable Lady Grey's school room, and the children, who before that period had been placed out in different families for instruction, were collected together, and a regular establishment was formed. From their vicinity to us, and the circumscribed limits of the house they inhabited, several of the children were constant residents at Clarence house, except when, in seasons of ill health, or other peculiarities of circumstance, others by turns took their places; but on some occasions they were all collected there, and at such times assembled round Mr. G. as their common parent, and now bewail his loss as such. Of this institution it may be truly said, the blessed effects are evident to all who know anything of it.

The congregations usually assembling for preaching increased so much, that they could no longer be accommodated in our house; subscriptions were therefore set on foot for building a Methodist chapel. Mr. G. gave all the assistance in his power, and when Mr. Thwaites, upon whom the responsibility of erecting the building rested, found himself deficient in the means of making up one of the installments, my dear husband, having already given all that he could spare consistently with other demands of a similar nature, sent him his gold watch-chain, and ever after wore a bit of black ribbon. A communication was made to him, from a superior officer, though not in the form of a direct message, that he had better desist from preaching. "I will die first," was his laconic reply. It was sarcastically enquired of him, how the chapel was built, and whether the land was public or private property. He replied, the land had been purchased and was private property; and the chapel was built by subscription; adding, that he was trustee for it. Thus, on many occasions, did he silence malice and opposition, by a firm and calm acknowledgment of the truth.

Soon after we became resident at English Harbour, Mr. G.

formed a fund for relieving the poor, to which he liberally contributed. He was the treasurer, and, from the period of its formation until a few months before his death, though the number of
subscribers was few, had distributed nine hundred and sixty-one
pounds, three shillings, and three half-pence. At the time of his decease, he was twenty-five pounds in advance. But was it from this
fund alone that he relieved the poor? I ask my sorrowing heart. Ah!
no. There were many poor people to whom he made a weekly allow-
ance, independently of it: indeed, none applied in vain that it was
within the compass of his ability to relieve. On returning home, after
office hours, he has often said to me, "My dear, I have had such and
such applications from the distressed today; did they come to you?"
He dreaded the thought of laying up treasure on earth; and said the
words of our Lord were plain and forcible, "Where your treasure
is, there will your heart be also." Thank God! we were of one heart
and one mind, in this as in other respects, so that I have often felt
inexpressible satisfaction that he was so minded, and never had any
fears of want if I should be the survivor. He often felt anxious on my
account; but we could never persuade ourselves to refuse assistance
to those who had not common necessaries, from the fear of having
to endure privations in our own persons. At the time of his death,
Mr. G. was secretary and treasurer to four charitable institutions in
this neighbourhood, and the friend, director, and upholder of three
others.

At the conclusion of the peace, 1815, the naval establishment at
English Harbour was reduced, and the department left in charge
of the Master Shipwright. My dear husband settled his accounts
honourably with Government, and we removed to St. John's, never
expecting to reside again at English Harbour. He engaged in selling goods on commission, and soon obtained so much business,
that, though he was assisted by myself and an active clerk, both
his health and my own began to fail under incessant exertion. The
Master Shipwright being advanced in years, and wishing to retire,
recommended to my dear Mr. G. to apply to be re-entered as Store-
keeper. It seemed a hopeless attempt, as there were many applicants
on the spot; he yielded, however, without reluctance, to the solicitations of his friends, and wrote to the Board. He was in consequence

appointed, and, after an absence of twenty months, we returned to
English Harbour. Many were astonished at his reinstatement; but
most persons saw the divine hand in it, and were convinced that
God was with him. During my life, I have had frequent occasion
to notice, with gratitude to our Almighty Benefactor, not only His
goodness in delivering us *unexpectedly* from painful and embarrass-
ing circumstances, but in providing at the same time a comfortable
situation for us in future; and thus conferring a *double* benefit at
once. So it was in this instance.

It pleased God, after our return, to pour out His blessing on the
Sunday School particularly; its numbers greatly increased, and some
young persons, who were the first objects of its care, were brought to
a saving acquaintance with the truth as it is in Jesus; and, I am happy
to add, continue to this day, and are among its most valuable teachers. He re-commenced preaching in the chapel, and some of those
who appeared dissatisfied with his return became steady hearers of
the word, and doers of it also. He had occasionally to contend with
unreasonable men; but the result, blessed be God, was invariably
such as proved favourable to the cause of religion, and creditable
to his own character: insomuch that a certain individual, who had
shewn more enmity to him on account of his religious principles
than any one else, upon his retiring from office in April, 1832, wrote
of him to the Admiralty in strong terms of recommendation and approbation. But it is not to public testimonies that I need appeal, for
the most important fruits of that grace, which wrought effectually
by the Holy Spirit upon his heart to make him a Christian in word
and deed. If there was one *trait* more conspicuous than the rest,
amidst the lovely harmony of graces visible in his character, it was
his *total renunciation of self*, and *entire dependence on the atonement of
our blessed Saviour*: and that which made him so remarkable as a man,
and a man filling an important station in society, was his scrupulous
integrity, and an openness and candour in all his intercourse with
others, which even persons not devoid of piety and wisdom thought
sometimes carried too far, in a disingenuous and unfriendly world.
Upon his retirement from office he presented a memorial to the
Navy Board, the reply to which, through mistake, went so circuitous
a route, that he was kept in a state of suspense for some months. He

thought it necessary, therefore, to forward another to the Board of Admiralty, a copy of which may be seen at the end of this statement; and in consequence, a pension of 350 sterling was granted.

For the last three or four years of his residence in this vale of tears, he was a considerable sufferer from local complaints, of a nature seldom removed at an advanced period of life; but his active habits and astonishing patience kept him to the steady performance of all his duties till within a few months before his death. Then indeed the cup of bodily suffering was greatly augmented in bitterness. In January, 1833, a severe bowel complaint as succeeded by a degree of nervous excitement which occasioned incessant restlessness, exhausting to the animal frame; and a frequent rush of blood to the head and lungs produced sensations of suffocation, and other feelings, the effects of which it was distressing in no small degree even to witness. In the midst of his severest sufferings, no impatient expression escaped his lips; sometimes he would cast an imploring look upward, and exclaim, in the most affecting manner, "Pity me, my Saviour!" As far as related to spiritual concerns, his mind was calm and undisturbed, though his superior understanding was clouded and impaired by disease. He had often declared to me, when in his best health, that the subject of death was more familiar to him than any other, and he experienced no dismay at any time when it seemed to approach. He said to his kind medical friends, "I am not afraid to die. I love my Saviour, and my Saviour loves me too well to dispose of me in any way that will not be for my everlasting benefit; but I should be glad if any thing could be done to mitigate my bodily sufferings. This want of breath is very distressing." His heart glowed with the tenderest affection towards me, and with almost parental kindness to all around him, particularly to a dear, amiable niece of mine, and an interesting and affectionate young person in the family, who read to him daily; both of whom attended upon him with the most assiduous and reverential regard.

The day of his death, July 16, 1833, (ever memorable to me!) he took his usual drive out, and, when he returned, his accustomed refreshment, and did not appear worse than he had been latterly. He dined at table, carved a chicken, and ate a small bit; he then called my attention to the large drops of perspiration which fell from his eyelids and under his eyes. Alas! it was the dew of death, though I knew it not. I begged him to lie down a little. He rose, and I accompanied him into the chamber. Being much fatigued and indisposed myself, I was preparing to take a little rest, and one of the young friends already mentioned assisted him into the sitting-room. Almost immediately one of them came in, and, not wishing to alarm me, said he appeared poorly. I went instantly to him, and found him lying in a posture of ease on the sofa, but his complexion darker than usual. With a sensation of anguish not to be described, I took hold of his hand, and fancied I felt his pulse beat; but it was a delusion—the medical men came, and found the happy spirit had fled to the paradise of God! Oh! what tongue or pen can express the agonies of that moment.—I could only fall upon my knees, and afresh commend myself and the orphans around me into the hands of God. I afterwards learned that when his young guide was leading him into the sitting-room, he asked with a smile, "Where are we going to now?" to which she replied, "I will go wherever *you* please, sir;" "I am going to a *good* place," he said, (meaning heaven,) "where I hope you will meet me." His other young attendant asked, as he reclined upon the sofa, "Shall I fan you, Sir?" He smiled at her, and playfully repeating her words, "Shall I fan you, Sir?" added "Yes, very gently." She had scarcely begun to do so, when he threw his head back, shuddered, groaned, and died! The whole was almost instantaneous.

Many were the mourners made by this event. The poor, the widow, and the fatherless, as well as friends and relative, lament it; but what are all their losses compared with mine? The lapse of almost thirty-five years, with many scenes of sorrow and suffering endured together, had cemented our union, and increased the tenderness of our affection to each other; but he is gone; and to me

> "The disenchanted earth has lost its lustre,
>   The great magician's dead!
>   No, not dead!
>   He lives! he greatly lives! a life on earth
>   Unkindled, unconceived; and from an eye
>   Of tenderness lets heavenly pity fall
>   On me, more justly numbered with the dead."

Elizabeth Hart Thwaites
History of Methodism

St Johns, May 5th 1804

The Reverend Richard Pattisson
My Dear Sir,

I am induced by two considerations to a compliance with your re-quest, one is, that I would be obedient, and the other, that in so doing in this case, I afford myself a fresh opportunity of making mention of that goodness and mercy which have followed me, the most unworthy, all my days.

Knowing the interest you take in the concerns of Immortal Souls, I would give you a more circumstantial detail of my spiritual course, and for your satisfaction, add some account of others with whom I am acquainted, but time will not at present admit, I hope to write you again on the subject.

I am as you know, a native of Antigua. My deceased Grand-mother, who was converted to God by the ministry of the Rev. Francis Gilbert and who died in the Faith, with my Dear Mother (gone to Glory) were united to the Methodists and trained up the younger branches of the Family, myself among them, in the fear of God and the observance of religious duties. I was also blest with an affectionate Father who ever watched with the tenderest solicitude over the morals of his Children, as did others of our near Rela-tions, who by their kind attention prevented our feeling the want of Mother's care after her Death.

Like her sister's, Elizabeth Thwaite's *History of Methodism* was solicited by the Reverend Richard Pattison and took the form of a letter to him. The holograph copy is now in the Missionary Society Archives, School of Oriental and African Studies, University of London. Reprinted by permission.

Having soon imbibed a great regard to the Duty of Prayer, and believing in its efficacy, I never omitted the performance of it without feeling some compunction, and upon all occasions of danger or difficulty, I would either retire to prayer, or at the moment, lift up my heart to Heaven for assistance or direction, notwithstanding this, I was from my earliest days, subject to many painful temptations concerning the being of a God and of a future state, and would often be led into such labyrinths of inward reasonings on some parts of scripture and things that I could not comprehend as have made me wretched.

After my Mother's death, I principally attended the Preaching of the United Brethren at St Johns; the retirement of their situation, together with the simplicity of their manners and Preaching, greatly pleased me, and their Preachers used to dwell in such a pathetical manner on the sufferings and death of the Savior, as never failed to affect my heart. I thought they were happy, and in the midst of my Childish follies, often wish'd that I was of their communion. About this time, one night several severe Earthquakes were felt all over the Island. I was exceedingly terrified, and spent most of the night on my knees, imploring mercy and resolving that if the Earth did not open and swallow me up, but I was spared, that I would be very religious. Towards morning the shocks ceased, but not my tormenting fears, all the day following I was sad and could not take pleasure in anything. On being told in the Evening that Mrs. Mary Gilbert (now in England) was to have a public prayer-meeting at her house, I made haste to go, hoping there to find ease to my troubled mind, but I became worse, as I thought and wished myself home; I returned about bed-time, but was afraid to lay myself down, lest I should fall asleep and wake in a world unknown. I had many comforters around me crying, "Peace, Peace," but they understood not my distress. One would ask me whether I had been guilty of any Sins that I should be so much more concerned than the rest of the family, and that it was only for the wicked to be under such terrors. Another would tell me of my good life, virtuous Education, etc. Indeed I was consoled by Pharisees, Fatalists and Antinomians, though not professedly such, but rather accounted good Christians, nor did I know the Forms by which they were distinguished 'till I read the

Polemic writings of the Rev. John Fletcher. While in this state of alarm, I asked one who had really gone to much greater lengths of vanity and folly than I had at that time, and was several years Older, whether she had no dread, and if She had any certainty of going to Heaven should the Earth devour us before Morning? She told me confidently that She did not fear, and that relying upon the merits of the Savior who had done all for her, She had not a Doubt but that he would take her to himself, that admitting I was a great Sinner, He had made atonement for me, and I was safe. I was staggered at first, and thought that if I was unprepared for Death, She must be so too, and therefore was deceived; nevertheless, I laid me down after much persuasion. I slept and awoke in safety and began to take courage. At length my wound was slightly healed, and I was again lulled into Carnal security.

Some time after this, Mr. Lambert, a Methodist Preacher came here from America; curiosity led me to go and hear him, his preaching was alarming and impressive, and always had the same effect upon my mind as Earthquakes, Thunder and lightning, rousing me to greater seriousness, to pray and read my Bible more, and it operated on like manner on some of my relations, yet did we not submit to the truth, but contrived after all, to hold fast our own Righteousness. Mr. Lambert returned to America, and I remained destitute of the power of Godliness, and for the most part, content with the form, Yea, a Lover of pleasure more than a lover of God. I continued my attendance at the Methodist Chapel, the Established Church of that of the Brethren, experiencing more or less of the strivings of the Spirit and the restraints of conscience, but none of all the preaching which I had heard produced any lasting or saving effects upon me, 'till the arrival of the Rev. Doctor Coke and the Missionaries which accompanied him. I heard the Doctor's first sermon with a sort of delight, yet, because it was Christmas, I went into the country for the purpose of amusement, and spent the evening in dancing. The next day, I was restless and very desirous to get back to Town, to attend the Preaching. I did so, and was made really ashamed of my conduct by the sermon which the Doctor Preached on my return, and in which he mentioned the evil consequences of Dancing in particular. I heard him eagerly and all his Brethren in turn, and my heart was now powerfully attracted to the truth. The Doctor and all the Preachers after having been some days in the Island, went to spend a day at my Father's home in the Country, and there, One introduced my Elder sister (now Anne Gilbert) and myself to him as persons much farther advanced in religion than We really were, and desiring to join the Society. He presented us with a Ticket each, we received them, but I was fully resolved not to meet in Class, nor even to attend constantly at the Chapel after the Doctor was gone. He soon left Mr. Warrener here, and with the rest of the Preachers went to visit the other Islands. Contrary to my intention, I became a constant hearer. There were no young persons, that I knew of, who were in Society at this time, that were not Slaves; on this, and some other accounts, I proudly held out as long as I could, from wholly joining them, tho' I gain'd admittance to many of the private meetings. Every Sermon which Mr. Warrener preached, that I heard, entered my heart, enlighten'd my darkness, and showed me the path of Life. I was at last stript of my fancied goodness, beat out of every false refuge, made willing to be saved on the terms of the Gospel and brought humbly to seek for Pardon and Salvation. In this state, I joined the Society, and some months after, one night, in private Prayer my Soul was set at liberty, my prayer was suddenly turned into Praise, and with the eye of Faith I viewed a smiling Savior. It is not possible for me to describe the transports of my Soul on that glad hour, and so much the more did I rejoice in this clear manifestation of his favour, because I had so often been told that I was not to expect it, nor any who had lived morally.

My beloved sister Anne Gilbert, joined the Methodists at the same time that I did. She was brought to God in the same way, and first found peace. This was a Providential circumstance for me. She was the only Person to whom I could communicate my Joys and Griefs. We walked hand in hand, and mutually helped each other on. Blessed be God, we are at this Day of one heart and soul. Upon our becoming Methodists all the Self Righteous in the circle of our acquaintance opposed us. They thought the steps we took were a reproof to them, and laboured to persuade us, that we were doing works of supererogation of which we would soon be tired and return to our former way, which was good enough. We knew for our-

selves that the Service of our God was perfect freedom, and would
not be influenced by the opinions of the Day. Indeed Mr Warrener's
preaching was unspeakably blest to our Souls; it seemed remarkable
that whenever we went to the Chapel labouring under any temptations, trials, doubts or fears, he would speak as appositely to our
case as if we had asked direction or advice of him. I well remember
one Wednesday morning after a long and painful debate with some
who said we had taken up with a new religion, which had done us
no good, I was much grieved and tempted to think that I was not
right. They were Persons whom I loved though they would scarcely
believe it, because we differed in sentiment. We had been on very
affectionate terms 'till this time and I found it hard to bear the dif-
ferings which now took place. On the afternoon of the Wednesday
alluded to, we went to the Chapel, Mr. Warrener's text was from
Matthew 10th Chap. 34th Verse: "Think not that I am come to send
Peace" a most encouraging Sermon it was to me. I was satisfied that
such disagreeables were unavoidable, when all did not sweetly think
and speak the same. Mr. W. in the course of that Sermon mentioned
an instance which happened in a family, almost exactly similar to our
Case, so that One who was present, thought we had been complaining to him, it was far otherwise, we were young and diffident and
seldom spoke a Word to him. I now began to discover the Sinfulness
of my nature and deeply to feel the plague of my own heart; though
I think I had power over Sin for more than three years. The doctrine
of Sanctification was not preached and enforced as I have since heard
it, but happy would it have been for me had I gone on to perfection
and obtain'd a compleat victory, but alas! I loitered, and almost imperceptibly lost ground. Company, conversation and Books which
did not tend to the Glory of God, together with Music's charms and
Worldly attachments, bewitched, and in a measure stole my heart
from God. Long suffering, and of tender Compassion, he never gave
me up! I constantly felt for every deviation from the self-denying
path, but had not power to overcome. I often wept, and prayed
and strove, revived and was slain; alternately hoped and despaired. I
used all the means of Grace, and never came under Church censure,
during this time I met a Class of young women who were Slaves and
to whom I said nothing of my then experience, which, when at the

worst, did not prevent my enforcing upon them the necessity of a
present Salvation. I abated in nothing my severity against Sin, and
continually enjoined upon them to avoid the very appearance of evil.
Most of these are still in the good way. At this season, I frequently
laboured under grievous temptations, and sometimes brought them
upon myself, one night in particular, at my Aunt's, when after supper a relation of mine who had been beguiled from the simplicity
of the Gospel, entered into a controversy with two of our Preachers
on the subject of the Trinity, and the Divinity of Christ, some that
were much stronger than I, left the table and went out of hearing.
One of the Parties being able and interesting, I was induced to stay
and hear them out, though many things that were advanced, made
me shudder; by the time the Company were dismissed, I was filled
with perplexing thoughts. I attempted to pray, but could not; tor-
tured with horrid injections from the Enemy, I threw myself upon
my Bed and fell asleep. In the morning I was more composed and
prayed as I could. My deliverance came while calling on the name of
Jesus, which Dear name, has often rescued me from Satan's power.

While in a comfortless and discouraging situation, that chosen
messenger of the Lord Mr. McDonald arrived here, his first Sermon
came with indescribable power to my heart. I was, as it were broken
to pieces and all my bones were out of Joint. My ingratitude stared
me in the face and every instance of my unfaithfulness; the anguish
of my spirit was very great, and I could have wept my Life away for
having grieved his Love. A few nights after Mr. M^cD's arrival we
had our Covenant meeting, and while all around me were repeating
the solemn words after the Minister, the language of my desponding
heart was:

My solemn engagements are vain,
My promises empty as air,
My vows I shall break them again
And plunge in eternal despair.

Mr. McDonald preached soon after. I really thought that someone
had told him my case, or that he could discern spirits and this made
me ashamed to look toward the Pulpit. The word Preached by this
servant of God, to my diseased and helpless soul brought life and
liberty. It seized on all my powers. I was again enabled to venture

on the Sinners friend, my bands were burst; the Captive was Delivered, and I could once more say, "O Lord, I will praise Thee! tho' thou wast angry with me, thine anger is turned away and thou comfortedst me." Not only the Ministry, but the life of conversation, and happy death of this good Man, I shall never forget. He was not a man of Learning, but he possessed the great requisites for a West India Missionary, a strong sense and steady Piety. *The various scenes which the Preachers have to pass through, after they leave Europe makes it indeed necessary that they should be men of wise and understanding hearts in order to preserve an equal, an untainted mind, this was his case, and thus he died.* My full heart could say much concerning him. Let it suffice that I believe, I shall find it matter of praise through all Eternity, that ever he visited this Land. I am thankful, I can say at this time, I know in whom I have Trusted, and having obtained help of God, I continue to this day, determined to devote my little all to him, to whom my more than all is due. I do not find anything at present in my Soul opposing the operations of the Spirit, but I see heights, and depths, lengths and breadths of Love Divine to which my Soul aspires. I trust, through that Grace by which I am saved, all that is lacking will be accomplished; that I shall be preserved faithfull unto Death, and be found of him in peace, without spot and blameless. The Blessings which I have experienced by the Ministry of the word, from the coming of Doctor Coke to Antigua, to the present day, and its salutary effects upon others, makes me bold to declare that the Gospel has not visited these Parts in vain; and I know of a truth, that the labours of every Minister who himself adorns the Gospel, and propounds the Truth in the plainest terms, is more or less attended with success. This was evidently the case during Mr. Murdoch's labours here. The Congregations are princi-. pally composed of illiterate People, who are neither interested nor affected by what they cannot understand, and those who are better informed, well know that the Preacher is doing his duty when he seeks rather to Edify the many than please the few.

Having to meet upwards of 160 in Class, affords me an opportunity of knowing several who have a hearing ear, and understanding heart, two of them are Whites who have a saving knowledge of the truth, the others are Black and Coloured from 13 to 60 years of Age.

Some of the poor Africans can particularize such parts of a Sermon as they felt most, and one of them told me a few Sundays ago, after Preaching, "Massa open me poor sinner heart. He tell me every thing me do," with many of such expressions. I rejoice in the certainty that there are many real converts in St Johns, both of young and Old. I am inclined to think, that one reason why so many of the poor Slaves upon the Estates, cause you trouble and discouragement is, that they are in general received into the Society, as Catechumens, and not convinced Sinners, and if a genuine work of Grace does not take place, they soon relapse into those Sins, which habit and custom have rendered as their meat and drink, particularly Quarreling and Unchastity.

You know, Sir, that very, very few are brought up with any sense of decency or regard to reputation, with respect to the forming of their connections they are obliged to be governed more by convenience than affection and being bound by no Laws human or divine, their engagements are easily broken. It is mostly the case that when Female Slaves are raised to wealth, and consequence (may I not say respectability) it is by entering into that way of Life, that cause women in another sphere to fall into disgrace and contempt, I mean concubinage. Of this you have many Instances. Truly labour and want are not the evils of Slavery (horrid system!) though these, as well as the Oppressor's Yoke, cause many still to groan.

In my late visits to Parham, I have been very glad to see the prospect brightens there, and that it wears a very different face to what it did a year ago.

May the good hand of Our god, who brought you and your Dear Partner among us, enable you with patience and perseverance to continue your Labours of Love, among the Outcast of Men, and crown the same with abundant success, prays.

My Dear Sir; your affection^{te} and respectful,
Sister and Servant Elizabeth Hart

Hymns and Verse by Elizabeth Hart Thwaites

[Untitled]

What would I have on earth below?
Thine utmost mercy would I know,
    And quit this vale of tears.
I long on mercy's wings to fly,
To leave my sins and griefs and fears,
    To love my God and die,

Jesu, I cry for help to Thee!
Thou hast, O Lord, the double key:
    Open the gracious door,
And let me live with pardon bless'd,
And then obtain one blessing more,
    And lay me down to rest.

In love, forbid my longer stay;
O beckon me from earth away!

The hymns and verse by Elizabeth Hart
Thwaites appear in John Horsford, *A Voice
from the West Indies: Being a Review of the
Character and Results of Missionary Efforts in
the British and Other Colonies in the Charib-
bean Sea, with Some Remarks on the Usages,
Prejudices, etc., of the Inhabitants* (London:
Alexander Heylin, 1856), chap. 7.

Fulfil my heart's desire,
And sign my pardon'd soul's release,
And then my pardon'd soul require,
    And let me die in peace.

[Untitled]

Weary world, when will it end,
    Destined to be purging fire?
Fain I would to heaven ascend;
    Thitherward I still aspire.
Saviour, this is not my place:
Let me die, to see Thy face.

O cut short Thy work in me;
    Make a speedy end of sin;
Set my heart at liberty;
    Bring the heavenly nature in:
Seal me to redemption's day,
Bear my new-born soul away.

For this only thing I wait,
    This for which I here was born:
Raise me to my first estate,
    Bid me to Thine arms return.
Let me to Thine image rise:
Give me back my Paradise.

For Thine only love I pant:
    God of love, Thyself reveal.
Love, Thou know'st, is all I want:
    Now my only want fulfil.
Answer now Thy Spirit's cry:
Let me love my God and die!

[Untitled]

Thy nature I long to put on,
    Thine image on earth to regain.
And then in the grave to lay down
    My burden of body and pain.
O Jesus! in pity draw near,
    And lull me asleep on Thy breast;
Appear to my rescue, appear
    And gather me into Thy rest.

O take a poor fugitive in;
    The arms of Thy mercy display,
And give me to rest from all sin
    And bear me triumphant away,—
Away from a world of distress,
    Away to the mansions above,
The heaven of seeing Thy face,
    The heaven of feeling Thy love!

VERSE

On the Death of the Rev. Mr. Cook

What mournful tidings these salute our ear,
Alarm our hearts, nor can our grief forbear?
Another Prophet from our church has fled,
And Cook is number'd with the happy dead!
Another dead! how doleful is the sound!
How sad the stroke! Our Sion feels the wound,
Awakens all her sons with awful call,
And makes us tremble, as her pillars fall.
How soon, alas! he gains the immortal shore,
And we shall hear his warning voice no more!

In tender years, ere sin, with treacherous arts,
Had spread its baneful influence o'er his heart,
The Saviour drew him with the cords of love,

Wean'd him from earth, and raised his heart above;
Commission'd him to spread the Gospel grace,
And offer mercy to the fallen race;
Nor in his native land alone proclaim
The saving power of Jesu's precious name:
But distant climes the adventurous youth invite,
His labour with the faithful few to' unite,
Who, in obedience to the heavenly call,
And for our sakes, had left their early all.
The cost he counted; this his aim and end,
His health and strength in the blest cause to spend.
Nor now with flesh confers; the time was come,
When he should bid adieu to friends and home,
Himself, his friends, his all to Heaven resign,
Sail with new life and fortitude Divine.
With lively faith that Israel's God would keep,
He now encounters the tremendous deep;
Preserved o'er rocks unknown to him before,
At length is landed on the wish'd for shore;
With joy is welcomed to our favour'd Isle,
When soon he enters on his happy toil,
With strength Divine to sinners cries aloud,
And mercy offers to the listening crowd;
While we with pleasure heard the stripling bold,
With wondrous voice, the sacred truths unfold;
In all the warmth that language could express,
He urged repentance, faith, and holiness,
Was ever for this duty well prepared,
And the whole counsel of his God declared.

The season soon arrived when we should join,
As long accustom'd, in our feast Divine.
He by the simple board with pleasure stood,
A happy guest, partaking heavenly food;
With rapture heard the diff'rent tribes converse,
In Canaan's tongue redeeming love rehearse,
And Afric's sable sons in stammering accents tell

of Jesu's love, immense, unspeakable.
The grace that reach'd his heart, to all it came;
Their language, as their spirit, was the same.
Thankful he to our feast of love had come,
With heart elate, he left the sacred dome.

Like faithful Abram, call'd, he must obey,
Cross the great deep again, pursue his way,
Till reach'd a neighbouring Isle, and there proclaim
His welcome embassy in Jesus' name.
They now conclude, and, as by God's command,
Once more embark'd, he seeks the destined land:
The haven gain'd,—but ah! some fell disease
Resistless on his youth and bloom did seize,
Nor could their prayers nor human art detain;
The struggling spirit press'd its home to gain;
Arrested by the ruthless hand of death,
No more does Cook here draw his labouring breath.

Mourn him, Tortoia, and your loss deplore,
Who brought you light; but, ah! it shines no more.
Your Pastor and his flock united mourn;
Your gratulations into sorrow turn.
He living, would have taught you how to live:
An equal lesson from his death receive;
To the blest task your every heart apply;
His steps pursue, and learn of him to die.
His title clear to mansions in the skies,
He breaks from earth, and gains the glorious prize.
Repine not at this awful providence,
Nor ask, what urged his swift departure hence.
'Tis Heaven has call'd its youthful favourite home
In mercy taken from the ills to come.
Let every murmur cease, no more complain;
Our loss is his unutterable gain.
No more shall gloomy clouds o'ercast his sky,
Nor the destroyer's piercing arrow fly:

His happy soul exempt, secure from harms,
It now encircled in the Saviour's arms.
'Tis there he rests, his griefs are all laid down:
He waves the palm, has won the glorious crown.
Let us ascend with him above the skies;
Let our rapt minds to that bless'd state arise.

[Untitled]

O Thou whose ear attends the softest prayer!
Redress our wants, our cries for Zion hear.
Resign'd we to Thy dispensations bow.
Nor tempt Thee more, nor ask Thee, "What dost Thou?"
But on Thy Church a blessing we implore:
Thy servants save, nor thus afflict us more.
Regard our sorrows, for the Saviour's sake,
Nor all Thy watchmen from our Israel take;
But grant the blessed few who yet survive
May for Thy cause and to Thy glory live;
That every sacred precept they enjoin
With brightest lustre in their conduct shine.
O may they ever speak in Thy great name,
Thy glory and our good their single aim,
While they advance the kingdom of Thy grace,
United spread Thine everlasting praise!
And give, O give us eyes to see our day.
And hearts that may the glorious truths obey.
May all who hear (through Thee) by them be taught,
Nor spend their precious time and strength for nought!
Borne on our minds, to Thee their wants we bear,
While Thou for us regard'st their faithful prayer.
Protect by day, be Thou their guard by night,
Nor scorching sun nor sickly moon shall smite;
Rest them secure beneath the Almighty shade,
Nor troubles nor untimely death invade.
And then, when each the appointed race has run,
Ready that "glory end what grace begun,"

In years and labours rich, their farewell give
To earth, and "cease at once to work and live;"
With rapturous joy receive the signal given
To 'scape from earth, and hail their friends in heaven,
There to remain in glory with the just,
Till life Divine re-animate their dust.

Letter from Elizabeth Hart
to a Friend

Popeshead, October 24th, 1794

Dear Sir,—

Had I not promised in my last to say something concerning slavery, I should certainly have dropped the business; for I have since thought myself a very unsuitable person to write on controverted points; and were I equal to the task, I do not know it will answer any end that I should take the subject in hand: however, I am (and I believe you are likewise) on the side of truth. I have never declared my sentiments so freely to any person (except my sister) as to you on this head. I find none disposed to receive such hard sayings; and why? Because they are not disinterested, self is concerned; and as I cannot, to please the best and wisest, lower the standard of right, or bend a straight rule to favour a crooked practice, I am, for the most part, silent.

I thank you for your kind intention to guard our minds against unnecessary solicitude at evils which we cannot remedy. In doing this, you first ask, "Is not the being so very anxious concerning it, in some measure, letting go our own work, and meddling with God's?" Undoubtedly it is, if I am very anxious. I acknowledge I am not easy about it; nor is it possible, as the matter stands, that I should feel that Christian indifference so necessary upon some other occasions. It is not the stoical, but submissive, spirit that should pervade our minds. Believe me, Sir, I do not leave my own work to meddle with

---

This letter to an unidentified male friend was published in John Horsford, *A Voice from the West Indies: Being a Review of the Character and Results of Missionary Efforts in the British and Other Colonies in the Charibbean Sea, with Some Remarks on the Usages, Prejudices, etc., of the Inhabitants* (London: Alexander Heylin, 1856).

God's. I do not pretend to scan His all-wise dealings with the children of men; nor am I bold to tempt the Lord, or ask Him, "What doest Thou?" Far be it from me.

I do not recollect that I ever made any objections to the merely being in a state of servitude, including much labour. This has been almost from the beginning, and perhaps subsists, more or less, in all parts of the world. Nay, were I obliged to provide for myself, I should desire no higher station than that of being servant: but Heaven forbid that I should be a slave! Nor have I said much about the shocking practice of taking the Africans from their native land, where—

> "The sable warrior, frantic with regret
> Of her he loves, and never can forget,
> Loses in tears the far receding shore,
> But not the thought that they must meet no more.
> Deprived of her and freedom at a blow,
> What has he left, that he can yet forego?
> To deepest sadness suddenly resign'd,
> He feels his body's bondage in his mind."

It is not, I say, the being merely placed in a state of subordination; for this is by choice the condition of many; but it is the black train of ills which I know to be inseparably connected with *this* species of slavery: such as may you never know, if it will give you needless pain,—such as my eyes see, and my ears hear daily, and makes my heart shrink when I write. When any thing is said like compassionating persons in this situation, it is urged by some, who seem wilfully blind, that they are much better off than the poor Europeans. Now, when things are clear to a demonstration, I know not what to say of such assertions, unless, as a good man observes, "it is sometimes in morals as in optics: the eye and the object come too near to answer the end of vision." I know that persons in a state of indigence, free as well as slaves, are exposed to many troubles; and are subject, especially if dependent, to every insult from those above them, who have little minds. These take every advantage of, and oppress, the poor. They have, however, laws made to redress their personal injuries. Slaves either have not, or they are never put in force; so that many of them suffer all these distresses, besides those peculiar to *their* situation. All who have their liberty, though servitude and penury may be their portion through life, have yet some of the greatest earthly joys within their reach; comforts such as give vitality to existence, and are really necessary to the being of man. They need not be deprived of those dear relatives,—

"Whose friendly aid in every grief
Partakes a willing share;
In sickness yields a kind relief,
And comfort in despair."

But, alas, how is it reversed with the others! It appears to me that pains are taken to prevent, or break, the nearest alliances, often in times of sickness and distress, and sometimes from the basest views. On the neighbouring estates the sick are removed from their comfortable abodes to large, hot rooms, made for the purpose, where frequently husbands and wives, parents and children, have no intercourse but through the grates. This is to prevent their lying by longer than necessity obliges; many make their escape from these dark abodes to those blessed regions "where tyrants vex not, and the weary rest." I know several who have been mothers of ten children, who never had the satisfaction to call *one* their own; and this, not from the hand of death, or separation by mutual consent; but sold, given away, or otherwise disposed of, according to the will of man. Others have an only darling child, whom they wish to see do well, taken from them and sent to some other Island, where they would sell for the best price, no more regard being paid to the feelings of the parents than if they were cattle. I very lately saw an old lady take an only son of one of her Negroes, and with seeming pleasure declare, he would serve her to buy bread with by and by; and in a house not far from hers is a young woman who was bartered for a horse. In such cases who can tell what those feel that have not—

"Put off their generous feelings, and, to suit
Their tempers to their fate, assumed the brute."

Christians who are not slaves, need only to be subject to the will of Heaven and of those they love; while most of those who

LETTER TO A FRIEND

are in bondage must either continually submit their wills to that of some irreligious, unreasonable being, or undergo a sort of martyrdom. There are likewise others, who, being endued with good natural understanding, aspire after refinement, useful knowledge, and sweets of social life, &c., &c.: were there a possibility of changing the colour of their skin, and emancipating them, with culture they would become ornaments to society. These are not permitted to emerge; they are bound down by some unenlightened, mercenary mortal, who perhaps has not a thought or wish above scraping money together. You may suppose such slaves find it a galling yoke,—

> "And oft endure, e'en while they draw their breath,
> A stroke as fatal as the scythe of death."

Again, free men may enjoy the fruit of their labours; but slaves are allowed a very small portion of their earnings. Many who undoubtedly earn their masters fifteen shillings *per* week by field-work, are allowed one shilling *per* week to provide meat, drink, clothes, &c.; and those who are not very industrious, are but half-clothed and half-fed; and, if not religious, are consequently thieves. But that which pains me most is, that every contrivance is made, by the generality of those who have rule over them, to baffle their efforts for decency and virtue; sometimes punishing them for that which is highly commended in persons in the opposite situation. A fair reputation, which, a pious author observes, is one of the most laudable objects of human ambition, is out of the question with them; for, in the earliest stages of their lives, every thing like modesty or rationality is crushed as it appears. I will give you one instance out of a thousand, by which you will see they are not allowed many privileges above the beasts that perish. During the Conference (District-Meeting) before the last, a black woman in the Society went with her husband one evening to hear Dr. Coke preach. When the meeting was over, seeing some of the noble crowding the gates with their implements of mischief, with fear and trembling she stole her husband's arm, which was not sooner observed by the gentlemen and ladies (so called,) than she was as much ridiculed and abused for doing that which would have appeared strange in them not to do, as though she had committed a crime: the poor affrighted creature withdrew from her husband, to stop the clamour of this narrow-hearted *gentry*, and made haste out of the way. Considering all things that respect this people, I stood amazed that so much conjugal, paternal, and filial affection remains among even the irreligious part of them. Another cause of wonder to me (knowing something of the natural heart) is, that such as do not possess Christianity should display such Christian graces as subjection of the will, long-suffering, &c.; and that towards persons to whom they are bound by no other tie than that against which you would suppose the heart would continually rise; in short, adhering to St. Peter's blessed precepts to converted servants, "Being subject, with all fear, not only to the good, but to the froward, enduring grief, suffering wrongfully, being buffeted and taking it patiently." &c. It is not uncommon to see old persons, who have spent their health and strength in this unreasonable service, and whose conduct merits every respect, receiving the utmost indignities at the hand of some untaught capricious little Master or Miss, who thinks nothing of lifting the hand or heel against them. Now, Sir, I have only given you a specimen of the situation of the slaves in this part of the world. It does not suit me to say the worst I know concerning it: only I assure you it comprises a mystery of iniquity, an endless list of complicated ills, which it is not likely you will ever know. You will not, perhaps, find the sufferers disposed to complain of their case. Not many are capable of *explaining*, however keenly they may *feel*, their disadvantages. As to the opposite party, while blinded by self-interest, (and who among them are not more or less so?) they will not allow that they act unjustly. As I do not think it possible that those whose property consists in slaves can be persons of *clean hands*, must I not think you feel something on this account? And particularly for those who are dear to me, that have been so unfortunate as to gain this wretched pre-eminence. Those of them that are any way enlightened are themselves uncomfortable, and would be extricated. They are unhappy at their deviation from the golden rule, "Whatsoever ye would that men should do unto you, even so do ye unto them."

But you farther ask: "Is it not, at least, *permitted* by the all-wise Governor of the universe, and will He not do all things well? Might there not be some clue to it quite unknown to us, such as the sins of the Africans, as it was the case of the Israelites before their bondage in Babylon?" I readily allow their being in a state of servitude is permitted by the Almighty, and do not question but He *may* intend bondage for this race of men; but I account the abominations that follow to be purely the will and work of corrupt, fallen men, and displeasing to God. "He doeth all things well." But we cannot take upon us to say, "This is the Lord's doing." I agree with you, that there might be some clue to it quite unknown to us; but this does not strike me as being the sins of the Africans; for, from all I can learn of them, according to their light, though barbarous and uncivilized, they are not so depraved as the generality of the Europeans, but more especially the West Indians; neither are they acquainted with so many methods of drawing down the vengeance of Heaven. England, however, has the advantage of the West Indies; not only as being a land of liberty, &c., but because there are some corners in it less corrupt than others. You will not, perhaps, find in every county the same degree of vice and extravagance; but slavery has rendered every part of the West Indies equally iniquitous. There are no asylums from the tainted throng. What I conceive to be partly the reason of this is, that the Europeans who have not independent fortunes, for the most part labour with their hands; (and I always look upon employment as being next to religion for the prevention of crime;) while most of the free people in this part of the world, of all complexions, are supported, by the toils of the slaves, in every degree of idleness and excess. Slavery affords them a wide field for the indulgence of every diabolical disposition, in which they "riot unscared." We do not read that the Israelites, in any of their captivities, were exposed to these miseries, though we have no doubt but *theirs* was the desert of sin.

Another thing to be observed is, that many of the slaves are not Africans; some white people sold themselves for a term of years, and shared the same fate with the blacks, being debarred their civil and religious rights; and many who now suffer as slaves, are much more nearly allied to the whites than to the others: so that I do not give full assent to your proposition at the conclusion of your queries, that the perpetrators of guilt, whether fair, black, or brown, are doing God's work. He has, and does still make use of the wicked (being most fit) as His sword to punish wickedness; but if these are in *this* case doing God's work they have mixed so much of their own with it, as at length to be bringing the same sort of punishment upon themselves. I have thought, that when the Almighty afflicts a people, *for sin*, they repent and are humbled before deliverance is brought near. But I believe the Africans remained in their original darkness when He raised up men in Europe to espouse their cause. Nor have we reason to suppose the Negroes in St. Domingo, Martinique, &c., are one whit better than ever they were. Concerning these we have strange accounts, many of them having taken their masters' places; and the oppressors are now the oppressed. I believe, with a good man, that "present impunity is the deepest revenge."

But, lastly, you inquire, "Will all our solicitude make the least change in the matter? Have we not reason to believe that a brighter scene is approaching, and that this dark night will be the precursor of a brighter morning? Should we not by all means rejoice in hope, and be thankful that we are not in bondage, either in a literal or spiritual sense?" It is certainly wrong to be solicitous about these things, it ever makes bad worse; nor do I suppose that any thing I may feel, say, or do, will make the least change in the matter, however the disposition of soul is inculcated by Him whose heart was tender; and pity is not apathy, but sensibility resigned; it is to this that I aspire, that while I feel my own and others' woes, I may recline on Heaven, and meekly and patiently say, "Thy will be done." I think with you, we have reason to believe that a brighter scene is approaching; and agree with the sentiments of a pious writer, (who has nothing in his book respecting slavery but what follows,) when he says, "I indulge myself in moments of the most enthusiastic and delightful vision, taking encouragement from that glorious prophecy, that 'of the increase of His government there shall be no end;' a prediction which seems to be gradually accomplishing, and in no instance more, perhaps, than in the noble attempt about to be made for the abolition of the African Slave-Trade." For what event can human wisdom foresee, more likely to "give His Son the heathen for His inheritance, and the uttermost parts of the earth for His possession," than the success of such an enterprise? What will

restore the lustre of the Christian name, too long sullied with oppression, cruelty, and injustice? We should indeed rejoice in hope of
this bright morning, be abundantly thankful that we are not in the
chains of sin or *slavery*, and pray that God would hasten the time
when "violence shall no more be heard in our land, neither wasting
nor destruction within our borders, but our walls be salvation and
our gates praise." Then shall we—

> "Love as He loved,—a love so unconfined
> With arms extended will embrace mankind;
> Self-love will cease, or be delated, when
> We each behold as many *selfs* as men,
> All of one family in blood allied,
> His precious blood, who for our ransom died."

I assure you, Sir, it is not any thing which I have read that has furnished thoughts upon the subject; I do not recollect to have seen any
writing respecting it but Mr. Boucher's pamphlet, (which I think
you have,) and a piece on "Charity" by Cowper, from which I have
quoted a few lines in the first sheet of this letter. My mind was perfectly made up before these came into my hands. I was no sooner
capable of thinking, than my heart shuddered at the cruelties that
were presented to my sight; but more have I felt since I began to
think seriously. I am, however, most concerned to have the evils
within rectified, or rather cured; this will perhaps render some of
those that are without less poignant, though I do not expect that
religion will deliver me from fellow-feeling, nor do I desire it should;
only I wish that I (and all who are in those things like-minded) may
be enabled to live—

"Unspotted in so foul a place, And innocently grieve."
I am, dear Sir, Your Sister in Christ, E. H.

Extracts from Elizabeth Hart Thwaites's Correspondence with Her Friend, Miss Lynch

[An unknown editor comments: "(The following) extracts convey an interesting view of the character of Mrs. Thwaites and of her multifarious and unwearied labours. In this pleasing task of teaching and training the young she continued till the year 1816, when a Society was established, denominated "The Female Refuge Society," designed to gather these orphans and others into an asylum, from the contaminating example of their fallen and depraved relatives. In this same year there was published in the Missionary Register a letter from Mr. Dawes, (then of Antigua, but formerly Governor of Sierra Leone,) agent of the Church Missionary Society in Antigua, showing the destitute condition of the young women growing up in the Island, virtuously and religiously, by means, under God, of Sunday-schools; at the same time pointing out the state of those children who lived with their guilty mothers, and earnestly requesting aid for the schools. This letter excited considerable interest in England, and the call thus made was promptly responded to by many benevolent Societies and ladies, who liberally sent aid in money and clothes from time to time; and afterwards the schools were patronized and supported by the Ladies' Negro Education Society."]

Elizabeth Hart Thwaites's correspondence with her cousin, Elizabeth Lynch, regarding the establishment of Sunday schools in Antigua (1809) was published in John Horsford, *A Voice from the West Indies: Being a Review of the Character and Results of Missionary Efforts in the British and Other Colonies in the Charibbean Sea, with Some Remarks on the Usages, Prejudices, etc., of the Inhabitants* (London: Alexander Heylin, 1856).

One of the bonnets sent has been bestowed on M. P. She attends our meetings whenever she can. Her poor mother called last week. On my asking how Marie behaved, she answered, "O Ma'am, God bless the child! I don't know what I should do without her, now I am so poorly; she is a little mother to the young ones; she is quite content with her poverty."—Many of the children are truly benefitted by religious instruction. I will give you an instance in P. O., the white orphan, who has to beg at the grog-shops, &c. I asked her, a few days ago, how her "mother," as she calls her, was: she answered with tears in her eyes, "She is very poorly, Ma'am, getting worse; but she don't pray; and when I beg her to pray to God, she swears at me."—M. M. is about eleven or twelve years old; you would hardly think, from the modesty and rectitude of her behaviour, that she lived in a house of ill-fame, the resort of the basest characters. Her mother, at present having no rest to the soles of her feet, and being miserably poor withal, sends every day to get her meal from a wealthy woman, of the most vulgar manners, who lives with Commissary D.

I hasten to inform you that our prospects brighten. Mr. Thwaites last Sunday invited the old country Leader, "Daddy Harry," to bring the poor little blacks he is teaching to read to our chapel, where we would furnish him with some of Lancaster's newly invented lessons, and put him in the way of teaching on that plan. The old man accordingly came in time to preaching with upwards of one hundred boys and girls. The chapel was very well filled when they came in, so that we could hardly stow them away. After preaching I sent them all away to our house, under the conduct of a careful person; for the old Leader went into the chapel cellar with Mr. Thwaites, and assisted him in meeting a large Class of men, while three female Leaders met above.

There are several children who cannot yet attend the school for want of clothes, and yet I have laid out upwards of twenty dollars cash from my own pocket since Christmas, exclusive of the seven dollars which you sent, and which have been well applied. I shall send the list to Mr. Brookes, &c. I think, if he and some others could once be roused to consider the wants of the children, they would interest themselves. The articles given by Misses Looby have enabled three clever little girls to attend for the first time last Thursday afternoon. We have ten girls learning to write. I ought in course to have observed to you that Mr. Thwaites has for some time past been so concerned about the poor children, that he has begged me, if possible, to get myself taught to make lace or any thing that I could teach the girls; and he has been trying to manufacture the long straw into hats for him to teach them; but he made no hand of it.

We have the happiness to see many bidding fair to be valuable and good women, who would probably by this time have been tending their steps to infamy and woe. But what would have been the use of schools, books, teachers, lectures, &c., had not a few benevolent hands been stretched out to enable the poor little creatures, as well as those who are growing up to womanhood, to come at these good things? Yours, Miss Looby's, and Miss Tait's subscriptions, with the many kind presents, have been very helpful. Our number has so greatly increased this year, I have been obliged to take active steps to obtain more ample assistance for the needy ones. I sent Mr. Brookes a subscription list, with Mr. Gilbert's name and mine. I hear he has twenty subscribers, exclusive of you, Miss Tait, and Miss Looby. I flatter myself that we are at length awakening the feelings of some from whom we might reasonably expect aid. The prospect brightens in every respect, and I hope I shall be able to convey the most pleasing intelligence to you in time to come.

The Rev. Mr. Whitehouse opened the meeting yesterday at Mrs. Gilbert's: he addressed the children with so much feeling and affection, that there was not a dry eye among them, nor have the good impressions of those I have seen to-day in any measure worn off; even Mrs. Gilbert's wild Sarah is deeply affected. Upon the whole, we had a good Sabbath. Mr. Whitehouse preached two such sermons, so plain, sound, and energetic, that many of all descriptions were touched. He was a Barnabas in the morning, and a Boanerges in the evening. Some of our family have felt the truths delivered. We had great and attentive congregations. This is indeed our Gospel day. God grant that the little flock may be kept simple and humble, loving and sincere, and that the blessed work may abundantly spread! Sunday after next, when there is to be no Preacher at Lyon's, Mr. Thwaites and I have promised to be there before ten o'clock, on purpose to meet the children, and commence a Sunday-school.

Appendixes

A Brief Sketch of Mrs. Anne Gilbert by the Reverend William Box, Wesleyan Missionary

Our lately departed friend was born of parents who were the subjects of regenerating grace, and who industriously strove to bring up their children in the nurture and admonition of the Lord. Anne, their first child, was, with her sister Elizabeth, early in life favoured with the friendship and ministry of the celebrated Dr. Coke, when he first, with several other missionaries, landed on this island; but this favourable circumstance was not fully improved by the two sisters, who, in the self-righteousness of their hearts, continued outer court worshippers, notwithstanding the affectionate and earnest overtures of those holy men to bring them into "the communion of saints." However, it was not long after the Doctor's departure, and of the Rev. Mr. Warrener's appointment to St. John's, that Anne, whose religious experience and history we are now especially considering, was brought to feel that in her, that is, in her flesh, dwelt no good thing; that she was very far gone from original righteousness, and needed some one to answer the enquiry, "Who will shew me any good?"—The ministry of Mr. Warrener served to exhibit the way of salvation, and to encourage her in the pursuit of it. She joined the Methodist Society, in company with her sister, and soon became an

---

This sketch of Anne Gilbert by the Reverend William Box appeared as section 2b of the *Memoir of John Gilbert, Esq., Late Naval Storekeeper at Antigua, to Which Are Appended a Brief Sketch of His Relic, Mrs. Anne Gilbert, by the Rev. William Box, Wesleyan Missionary, and a Few Additional Remarks by a Christian Friend* (Liverpool: D. Marples, 1835). A copy is in the British Library, shelf-mark 4903 df8. Reprinted with permission.

ardent seeker of salvation through a crucified Redeemer. There was nothing peculiar either in her repentance unto life, or in the manner of her obtaining the pearl of great price; it was while secluded in her place of prayer and study, and while pouring out her heart to God for the manifestation of his mercy, that divine light filled her mind, and she was enabled to believe in Jesus Christ, as having loved her, and given himself for her; then it was that she found "redemption through his blood, even the forgiveness of her sins," and received the Holy Spirit of adoption, witnessing with her spirit that she was a child of God. From that time to the period of her exchanging mortality for immortality, a period of about fifty years, it is not known that she ever lost her assurance of being personally interested in the salvation of the gospel.

It is to be lamented that, some time ago, our dear sister (no doubt from the best motives) destroyed all the documents which had reference to her religious progress; so that we are left ignorant, to a great extent of her early career in the way to heaven; but in the absence of information written with ink, her whole life was "an epistle of Christ, written with the Spirit of the living God;" so that those who knew her longest and knew her most, "are witnesses, and God also, how holily, and justly, and unblameably she behaved herself among them that believe, (as also in the world;) and how she exhorted, and comforted, and charged every one, as a mother doth her children, that they should walk worthy of God, who had called them unto his kingdom and glory."

Perhaps no departed saint could be more appropriately denominated "a mother in Israel," than her whose remains we so lately committed to the silent grave. Deprived at a very early age of her mother, the management and care of a numerous family principally devolved on her, whose temporal and spiritual interests alike lay near her heart. Her advice, her prayers, her example were continued on their behalf, until "the weary wheels of life stood still," and they saw her no more.

Of her union with the late excellent Mr. Gilbert, it is unnecessary to say more, than that it was founded upon a mutual affection, which sprang from a perception of that moral excellence in each other which alone constitutes true greatness—which alone yields true happiness. It was an affection which could not be eradicated from their kindred spirits, either by the sneers of the scornful, the contempt of the proud, the animadversions of fools, or the combined influence of power, prejudice, and poverty. It was an affection resulting from that love, "which many waters cannot quench," and which is "stronger than death." The union which cemented and consummated this reciprocal regard was a long and blissful one; the Lord lengthened out their domestic tranquility for upwards of thirty-four years; until, in his wise providence, about twelve months since, he cut their earthly bond asunder, and said to his most infirm servant, "Come up higher, and behold my glory." But this union produced no change either in the principles or practice of our lamented friend, excepting that, while the former continued to improve, the latter was correspondent thereto. The commanding situation in life enjoyed by Mrs. G. gave her constant opportunities of exhibiting the nature, sincerity, and strength of her Christian principles, in that steady and undeviating course of practical piety, which, while it illustrated the excellency of our holy religion, enriched her with a degree of moral influence which rarely falls to the share of a single individual. It was this great and general influence, which she had the power of exerting, that rendered her so suitable and efficient an instrument in the hands of God for the furtherance of his righteous cause in this part of the world. Scarcely one servant of Christ, who has laboured in this island, but has enjoyed her friendship, and benefited by her judicious intimations; "many of them are now, as she is, sleeping in the dust of the earth," but many remain who can testify how she has laboured with them in the gospel, by obtaining doors for its promulgation, by personally declaring to others its hallowing truths, and by assiduously leading that part of the flock of God committed to her care in all the paths of righteousness and holiness.

In the establishment and support of Refuge Societies, for such of the female sex as were either comparatively or entirely destitute,— in the formation of Benevolent Institutions, for feeding the hungry, clothing the naked, and relieving the afflicted—in the extension of Sabbath and other Schools, for the instruction of the young—and in the promotion of every cause having for its object the general welfare of her undying fellow creatures, and especially of such as were too long accounted the filth and offscouring of all things, she was "instant in season and out of season;" nor is it too much to hope that scores, if not hundreds, of those whom she has nurtured in her domestic and religious life, will be the crown of her rejoicing in the day of the Lord Jesus.

There is, however, another, and an additional reason to be assigned for that extraordinary and successful influence which our deceased friend exerted upon the various objects of her solicitude; and that is, her intellectual superiority, her magnanimity, the which no one ever denied, whatever views might be entertained as to its proper application. Possessed of a vigorous and clear conception, of a discriminating and correct judgment, and furnished with no common measure of valuable knowledge, she was not only enabled to give her best advice to those who sought it, but her decisions were ordinarily regarded as wise and right—they carried conviction to the mind of the inquirer, and that, not only in instances where education had not formed it for private judgment, but also where the mind has been cultivated and matured. She had a piercing wit, which was sometimes admirably employed in the exposure and censure of vanity and sin. She displayed, on almost all occasions, a self-possession, a kind of moral majesty, indicative of conscious rectitude and mental strength; nothing perhaps was too great for her grasp, had not her numerous and pressing avocations prevented her from becoming, in the strict sense of the term, "a literary character." With the best literature—the records of eternal truth, she was intimately acquainted; they had been the subjects of her meditation day and night for half a century; her knowledge of these unchangeable verities conduced to her personal comfort and support throughout life, and especially when her heart and flesh failed her; and it gave her the means and ability of doing good to thousands in her day and generation. In her domestic concerns, she was conscientious, systematic, careful, economical, strict, and uniform. In her person, there were combined (especially before the infirmities of age made inroads upon it,) a kind, yet firm countenance, with noble, yet graceful mien; this, together with her many other amiabilities, have ever gained her the esteem and commendation of those who estimate their fellows, not by their exaltedness of station, not by any local circumstances, not by their caste or colour, but by that moral and mental excellence which alone is pleasing to God, and which alone is deserving the praise and imitation of mortals.

Having thus imperfectly shown the blessed effects of religion upon the renewed heart and enlightened mind of our dear sister, while in the dawn and meridian of life, let us briefly mark its operation when the time drew near that she should die. It is not necessary to state the nature of her last sickness; suffice it to say that, in spite of the greatest skill and solicitude of her medical practitioner, it was a sickness ordained to be unto death. From its commencement to its termination, it appears she had a presentiment that it would end in her dissolution; and so, after several weeks of severe, excruciating suffering, her anticipations were realized. "Who knows," said she, "but that this (pointing to her excoriated finger), is intended to take me home;" and it proved that this apparently insignificant accident issued in her separation from us.

The time would fail to mention all her dying sayings; they were heard by many, and can be forgotten by few; but it must suffice to observe, that during her final sickness she was fully resigned to the will of God, although she more than once feared that her faith would fail, so that her constant prayer was that the Lord would give her patience to the end. She ever spoke of herself as a sinner, saved by grace; and as having no other foundation for her eternal salvation than faith in the atonement of our Lord Jesus Christ. She regarded herself as a weak, unfaithful, and unprofitable servant, and as "less than the least of all saints." She exhorted all who came to see her, giving every one a word in season, and blessing them in the name of the Lord. She retained her faculties to the last moment, and enjoyed, throughout her affliction, the peace of God which passeth understanding. She could confidently say, in the immediate prospect of dissolution, "I know that my Redeemer liveth, and that he shall stand at the latter day upon the earth: and though, after my skin, worms destroy this body, yet in my flesh shall I see God: whom I shall see for myself, and mine eyes shall behold, and not another; though my reins be consumed within me." Job xix. 25–27. Being turned, for the last time, upon her weary and painful side, she said,

"Now let the pilgrim's journey end;
Now, O my Saviour, Brother, Friend,
Receive me to thy breast!"

The last words she was heard to utter were, "That is sin, sin,
sin!" pointing to the black matter which she had been vomiting;
and soon afterwards, without a struggle or a groan, her happy spirit
"was carried by angels into Abraham's bosom."

" 'Twas then the gates of paradise flew wide,
To embrace another spirit washed in blood;
And, fully tried in tribulation's fire,
Another trophy of the attractive cross,
Uplifted for the ransom of mankind.
Attendant convoys waft it to the throne
Of God's Messiah, loudly shouting there,
'Behold the travail of thy human soul,
O mighty Saviour, and be satisfied.' "

In the death of the late Mrs. Gilbert, the house of her father
has lost its chiefest ornament—its best adviser—its greatest inter-
cessor. The orphan and dependent family under her care have lost
their protector, their guide, and their friend. The Methodist Society
has lost a member, a leader, a shepherdess, a pattern, a pillar of the
first magnitude. The village of English Harbour has lost a burning
and shining light—a city set on a hill, which could not be hid—
a righteous woman. The young have lost a mother; the aged have
lost a companion; the poor have lost a benefactor; the rich have lost
a jewel; the Island of Antigua has lost one who for sixty years was
perhaps never excelled; and the world has lost a saint of the Most
High God! But our loss is her gain—she has gained a complete victory over weakness, want, pain, and sin for ever; a victory over death
and the grave, by the blood of the Lamb. She has gained the height
of knowledge, holiness, and love; in a word, she has gained eternal
life, through Jesus Christ the Lord! O may we die the death of the
righteous, and may our last end be like hers.—Amen, and Amen.

Mrs. Gilbert's funeral sermon was preached at English Harbour, by the Rev. William Box, Wesleyan missionary, on Sunday, August 3d, 1833, from Prov. xiv. 37—"The righteous hath hope in his death," to a large and attentive congregation, the greater part of whom were deeply affected while the above sketch of her life, written for the purpose, was read to them.

"Blessed are the dead which die in the Lord; yea, saith the Spirit, that they may rest from their labours; and their works do follow them." Rev. xiv. 13.

The following desultory observations [Appendix B] are merely intended to supply such information as is not included in Mr. Box's able sketch.

APPENDIX B

Additional Remarks
on John and Anne Gilbert
by a Friend

In the short space of twelve months and three days, Death has made
another breach in the circle of family love and friendship. Ere we had
ceased to mourn for one, another is taken. Varied as the trials and
afflictions of the Christian are, in his journey heavenward, there are
none which make this world appear such a dreary wilderness to him,
as the loss of those companions who shared his anxieties, fatigues,
and sorrows, and equally participated in his enjoyments and refresh-
ments by the way. He no longer beholds the smiling countenances
which cheered his heart under perplexities and discouragements; no
longer hears the loved voices which animated him to the performance of painful duties; nor sees the active limb in motion which
enabled them, like their Divine Master, to "go about doing good."
Sad and silent is the vacuum made by their removal. They have
reached the haven of eternal rest and peace; but he is still toiling to

---

These "few additional remarks by a Christian friend" appeared as section 2c of
the *Memoir of John Gilbert, Esq., Late Naval Storekeeper at Antigua, to Which Are
Appended a Brief Sketch of His Relic Mrs. Anne Gilbert, by the Rev. William Box, Wesleyan Missionary, and a Few Additional Remarks by a Christian Friend* (Liverpool:
D. Marples, 1845). A copy is in the British Library, shelf-mark 4903 df8. Reprinted by permission.

Editor's note: Since the "Additional Remarks" state that Anne Gilbert died one
year and three days after John Gilbert, and since Anne Gilbert refers to Elizabeth Thwaites as her "late dear sister" (Anne Gilbert, *Memoir of John Gilbert*), it
seems that Rev. Box's date recorded in appendix A as August 3, 1833, should read
August 3, 1834.

gain it. He had indeed the consolation of knowing that, if he perseveres to the end, travelling the same road that they did, he shall "go
to them, though they cannot return to him," and, in that city of his
and their God, "the New Jerusalem," join the song of the redeemed
through endless ages.

The solemn event which has induced these reflections, is the departure of the beloved Wife of the subject of the preceding Memoir.
She wrote a part of it, and was then sorrowing over his grave; now
her "light afflictions, which were but for a moment, have wrought
out for her a far more exceeding and eternal weight of glory." Then
she felt bereaved and solitary; now she has rejoined the kindred spirit
with whom she enjoyed such sweet communion on earth, and soars
with him through the regions of unlimited space, admiring, adoring, and rejoicing in the wonders of creating and redeeming love.
One who knew her well says, "Mrs. Gilbert was the eldest daughter
of the late Mr. Barry Conyers Hart, by his first marriage. Religiously
and usefully educated, she, at an early age, performed the duties of
a parent to a young and numerous family, having lost her excellent
mother while yet a girl of twelve years old. Her cares were not confined to her brothers and sisters, but embraced the negroes upon
her father's estate at Popeshead, and such of the neighbouring slaves
as chose to benefit by her instructions." He adds, "It may justly be
said that she was almost the founder, in that part of the country, of
those religious and moral principles which distinguish the Antigua
negroes, and have brought us through such a momentous change
without commotion or bloodshed." She was joined in these pursuits
and avocations by her sister Eliza, the late Mrs. Thwaites; and such
was the order and regularity of their arrangements, that when the
Rev. Nathaniel Gilbert, afterwards Vicar of Bledlow, Bucks, was on a
visit in this Island, being intimately acquainted and highly esteemed
in the family, he took his cousin, Mr. John Gilbert, then a married
man, to make an introductory call at Popeshead, and unceremoniously conducted him into the school room. His view in doing so was
to surprise his companion; and he was indeed surprised, at a sight
so unusual in the West Indies, and particularly at that time. Two
youthful sisters, surrounded by a number of little ones, endeared to
them by the near ties of kindred, to whom they were imparting the

elements of useful and religious knowledge, and who looked up to them, particularly to the elder, with the reverence of filial love, and ready obeisance, was an interesting subject even for a painter.

Perhaps there are few females, in any class of society, whose lives have been more successfully devoted to the benefit of others, than theirs were. A memoir of Mrs. Thwaites, which Mrs. Gilbert would have prepared to the press from the stores of her own knowledge, and documents in Mr. Thwaites' possession, if she had been spared, would have shewn this to be no hasty assertion with respect to one of them; and feeble and unskilful as is the pen which attempts to exhibit the truth of the position concerning the other, it is confidently hoped it will not totally fail of its purpose.

That Mrs. Gilbert was indeed a help meet to her husband, will in some measure appear from the preceding Memoir. In nothing was she more helpful to him than in encouraging and cheering him, when his anxieties were oppressive, and his animal spirits failed under the pressure of bodily infirmity, which they were apt to do, in the latter part of his life particularly. She was his principal clerk and assistant, when he carried on business in St. John's; and though her abilities could not with propriety be exercised in this way while they lived in English Harbour, she still found out methods of being useful to him, and of lightening his burdens. But the duties of a wife and mistress of a family (in which latter character, also, she was uncommonly excellent) did not engross her active and capacious mind. With the assistance of Mrs. Thwaites, she commenced a Sunday School in the year 1809. To this, poor children, whether slave or free, were admitted, and many of the former came from neighbouring estates; it was the first institution of the kind formed in the West Indies, and was formed at a time, too, when teaching slaves to read was so unpopular and suspicious a measure, that the missionaries were instructed to avoid it, lest it should prevent their admission into places where they might otherwise be allowed to preach the Gospel.

When it is considered that, even in *England*, instructing the children of the lower classes of society was so much disapproved of, at its commencement, that Mrs. H. More, the benefactress and ornament of her sex, incurred obloquy and slander for being engaged in it; it cannot reasonably excite surprise that a similar design should be unfavourably regarded in a *Slave Colony*.

The school, however, went on and prospered. The writer of this never can forget the impression made upon her mind by the first sight of it in 1813. It consisted of every shade of colour, from pure white to unmixed black; nor can she fail to remember her emotions while she heard them sweetly warble—

> "Lord, may a few poor children raise
> A hymn of gratitude and praise;
> 'Tis by thy great compassion we
> Are taught to love and worship thee."

The establishment of the English Harbour Sunday School having brought into more particular notice the unhappy condition of some of the free young females in that neighbourhood, and as it was found that, in many instances, little good could be effected in their behalf unless they were taken out of situations where they were exposed to great moral evils, Mrs. Gilbert planned a Society, which was afterwards designated the Female Refuge.

For reasons which existed then, but have less weight now, she delegated the office of ostensible manager to one who was greatly her inferior in natural and religious qualifications, but who ever deemed it a privilege to act in conjunction with her. Sneer and sarcasm were not spared upon the occasion, notwithstanding this precautionary measure; several persons said it would prove an encouragement to vice; and one lady tore the prospectus in a rage, before the messenger, and threw it out of the window. Happily, we have now many ladies in the community of a very different description; and even then there were a few—and the fewer their number, the more conspicuous did *their* liberality appear,—who contributed to the undertaking, and kindly wished it prosperity. The appointment of Sir Benjamin D'Urban to the Government was an auspicious event to all the charitable institutions in the Island. Lady D'Urban afforded her countenance and sanction to each, but particularly patronized the female ones. She esteemed Mrs. Gilbert highly, often consulted her on subjects of benevolence, and bestowed her bounty through her hand to many. She corresponded with Mrs. Gilbert for some years after her departure from the Island; but this intercourse gradually ceased. Lady Ross, while Sir Patrick was Governor, encouraged, and was the kind patroness of, the Female Societies in particular, and knew and appreciated Mrs. Gilbert's character and exertions in favour of morality and religion.

At the time of her death, the English Harbour Sunday School had been in operation about twenty-five, and the Female Refuge Society nearly nineteen years. Of the good effected by these Societies numbers can testify; while it is not asserted that *all* the subjects of their care have profited by the advantages they enjoyed.—Alas! of what seminary of public education can this be said with truth.—Nay, of a few of those who were born under such unfavourable circumstances, it must with pain be acknowledged, that their benefactress reaped only disappointment and sorrow. Others of them, there is good reason to believe, after outriding the storm, wind, and tempest, have found safe anchorage in the haven of eternal rest and peace; and not a few are respectable heads of families, bringing up their children in the nurture and admonition of the Lord, and sending them to the same school where they themselves were first taught to know and love the God of their salvation. Another, and not the least interesting class, are those young women whose virtuous and pious conduct "adorns the doctrine of God their Saviour" in various situations of life; those also who now act as teachers in the School; and others, at present scholars, who, it is hoped, are treading in their footsteps.

These were not the only charitable institutions which Mrs. Gilbert was engaged in—there were several others. She kept a weekly school, to teach writing and arithmetic. She superintended, and had the direction of, a large Infant School, supported by the Ladies' Society in London. She was the dispenser of blessings through the poor's fund for many years; visiting the sick, comforting the afflicted, clothing the naked, and feeding the hungry. She devised and organized a Juvenile Association, which has been more useful than could have been imagined in prospect. She presided also over other modes of charity, and lent her influence and support to very good work. And when it is considered that she was the leader of several classes in the Methodist Society, out of which branched duties that occupied a considerable portion of her time; and that Mr. Gilbert's situation and character, though he avoided entertaining company in his public capacity, subjected them to numerous and often unexpected visitors, it is wonderful how she could accomplish one half of what she did; yet no department was neglected; "whatever her hand found to do, she did it with her might, remembering that there is no wisdom, nor knowledge, nor device in the grave, whether she was going."*

Many affecting anecdotes might be introduced, illustrative of the benefits which she was the channel of conveying to others; but it would swell this sketch beyond the limits assigned to it, and might be painful to the feelings of the parties concerned.

While she lived at English Harbour the first time, excuses were often made by poor slaves for not attending public worship, because they had not clean clothes to appear in; she therefore established a weekly meeting for women of this description. It was held in the dusk of the evening, and only one light was admitted on the table, to enable her to read a chapter in the Bible, which she expounded, beginning and ending the service with prayer and singing. There, many stole in, who would have been ashamed to appear in a place of worship by day, or even in a well lighted one by night. It was surprising to themselves, and to occasional hearers of a different sort, how she could so minutely trace the workings of their ignorant and untutored minds, and contrive to express the instruction she meant to convey by elucidations and language so suitable to their comprehension. That her knowledge of the human heart was not confined to this class of her fellow creatures evidently appeared, when, after Mr. Gilbert's removal to town, upon the reduction of the naval establishment, a meeting was appointed, one evening in the week, at the house of a near relation of hers in town, where, by particular desire, she expounded a chapter, and adapted her remarks to her own sex, of very different grades of society from her English Harbour auditors. Here they were many, and a large room often was filled to overflowing. None but females were admitted, among whom were many ladies; and those heard, with delight and surprise, her apposite modes of exhibiting truth, which were as well

---

*She had been in the habit, for many years of her life, of rising at four o'clock.

suited to them, and brought as closely home to their consciences, as her expositions at English Harbour had been to the dark and ignorant minds of her hearers there. In this, her variety of talent was strikingly evidenced and, there is reason to believe, productive of much good.

Mrs. Gilbert's health declined from the period of her husband's death; though, like him, she was upheld by the energy of her mind, and casual observers saw no difference in her. It was with apprehension and anxiety, however, that her friends recollected his often declared conviction, that she would soon follow him. The reason he assigned for this persuasion was, that they had "a prayer registered in heaven" that one might not long survive the other; and when the extraordinary answers they had frequently received to their petitions were remembered, it could scarcely be hoped that he, who "as a prince had power with God, and prevailed" remarkably at other times, should be unsuccessful in this instance. Another circumstance, tending to increase their apprehensions of losing her, was the impossibility of obtaining any permanent provision for her, notwithstanding the exertions of kind and influential friends in England. This was considered as an indication that her Heavenly Father would call her home to her inheritance above; and she often spoke of the event herself as probable.

Her illness commenced with an apparently trifling accident to one of her fingers, which produced violent erysipelas in the hand, that eventually became nearly universal. Her sufferings were extreme. She was confined to her bed for five weeks, without any cessation of pain. It was most affecting to see her uplifted hands and eyes, and to hear her plaintive voice, beseeching her "compassionate Saviour to grant her a few minutes' ease, if it were his gracious will." Much, and fervently too, did she entreat for faith and patience to endure unto the end, and that she might not be suffered to grieve the Holy Spirit by impatience. No murmuring or repining word escaped her lips, though she endured such agonies of pain as it was impossible to witness without most distressing sensations. She greatly affected those bout her by talking much of her death, and giving a frequent word of admonition to them. She spoke strongly of her own sinful and corrupt state, and her entire dependence on atoning blood. More than once she repeated those lines of Mr. Toplady—

"Nothing in my hand I bring,
Simply to Thy cross I cling," &c.

and "Not by works of righteousness which I have done, but according to His mercy he saveth me, by the washing of regeneration,
and renewing of the Holy Ghost." Sometimes she had a hymn sung
in her chamber; and one night it was peculiarly affecting to hear
her once powerful and melodious voice, now tremulous through
weakness, set the tune to those words—

"Thee, Jesus, full of truth and grace,
Thee, Saviour, we adore;
Thee in affliction's furnace praise,
And magnify thy power."

It consists of four verses, remarkably appropriate, and may be
found in Mr. Wesley's Collection of Hymns, page 313.

To the Rev. Mr. Walton, Wesleyan missionary, who observed to
her that as her afflictions abounded, no doubt her consolations
abounded also; she replied, "I will tell you how I feel. I have an
unshaken confidence in the love and faithfulness of my Heavenly
Father, which diffuses a delightful sensation through my mind; but
I have no rapturous joy." She added—"Jesus had done more for her
than she could find words to express—He had purchased pardon,
purity, and heaven; and when she thought of those as the portion
of such a wretch as herself,—so corrupt, so vile as she was—." The
last expression was not heard by the writer, but Mr. W. said, "that
doubt arose from the tempter." She answered "No—her Heavenly
Father kept him at a distance, and what she felt was not *doubt*, but
amazement."

She admonished and exhorted all who came to see her; and her
visitors were numerous. Among them, the Rev. Mr. Jones, rector of
St. Philip's, paid her a kind Christian visit. They conversed suitably,
and he concluded with prayer. She expressed herself pleased after he
was gone. She blessed, and prayed for, her medical friend and his
whole family; and often did the same for those who assisted her in
her helpless condition. She required many attendants; and having
shewn much love and compassion to others, in their time of need,
it was returned to her in hers, by affectionate relatives and fellow

Christians. Once she said, "I could almost long for my release." At another time, being raised up on her pillows, from which she had slipt, it was observed by the writer, "You look more comfortable." "Comfortable! my dear," she replied. "Ah!" it was rejoined, "I fear you know little of comfort in any posture." Casting her eyes upward, she answered, "I know none, but what streams from above." She sent her love to all her relatives and friends, and said, if she saw them no more on earth, she hoped to meet them in heaven.

She gave Mr. Walton directions about having her grave prepared as near as possible to her beloved husband's; and minute ones to a female friend, as soon as she should hear she had changed for death, respecting what she wished her to do. Once she said, "I do not think my Heavenly Father has forgotten me, but my faith is weak this morning." She occasionally apprehended the failure of it altogether, but generally she was "strong in the Lord, and in the power of his might."

In the night of the 18th of July, she suddenly sank; and on being asked, on account of her laborious breathing, if she had pain in her stomach, she replied, "No pain any where, but weakness inexpressible." She retained her senses perfectly to the last—complained of being prevented meditating on the glories of Heaven—and said to her sister, [probably her cousin Miss Lynch, since Elizabeth Hart Thwaites was now dead]* who offered her nourishment, which at her intreaty she took—"You want to keep me from heaven." Soon after, she was turned upon her side, and quietly entered into the rest which remains for the people of God.

> "O think that, while we're weeping here,
>   Her hand a golden harp is stringing;
> And, with a voice serene and clear,
> Her ransomed soul, without a tear,
>   Her Saviour's praise is singing!"

---

*Note that "sister" was used as a term of deep familiarity. Miss Lynch, for example, refers to her cousins Anne and Elizabeth as sisters. See appendix D [Ed.]

Extracts from Charles
Thwaites's Journal, 1829

Willoughby Bay, 5th May 1829

Rev. & Dear Sir,

I take the opportunity of our valuable friend Mr. Garling's going to England to forward by him an extract of my journal for the months of January, February & March. I also send you short accounts of the happy deaths of a few Sunday Scholars if you think them worthy to be printed in the form of a reward book. We believe it will be acceptable and useful among the slaves, who delight to read anything of this kind concerning their own class. With respect to the articles the schools require, I beg to refer you to my former letter, particularly to the reward books.

To the Reverend Geo. Morley
I am Rev. & Dear Sir
Your most Obedient Servant
Charles Thwaites

EXTRACT OF CHARLES THWAITES'S JOURNAL NO. 1

Thursday, January 1st 1829. Mrs. Thwaites and I attended at the School room in English Harbour. A large company of children assembled as is usual on this day to receive awards. It is evident that the

---

This letter was sent "To the Reverend George Morley, One of the Secretaries of the Wesleyan Missionary Society, No. 77 Hatton Garden, London." The holograph copy is in the Methodist Missionary Archives, School of Oriental and African Studies, London, West Indian File. Reprinted by permission.

blessing of God still rests upon this Sunday school. In the evening we went to Gilla[m]s, taught and catechised the children.

Friday 2nd. Assembled and taught the children at Archbolds' at noon and at Lynch's at night.

Saturday 3rd. Went to teach at Watson's at noon and at the Hope at night.

Sunday 4th. Mrs. T. and I at Willoughby Bay School, a large company attended, in the afternoon at Sion Hill.

Monday 5th. Mrs. Thwaites and I having received a summon from a Committee of the House of Assembly, to appear before them for examination, respecting a supposed correspondence with a Society in England, for the relief of the destitute slaves in Antigua. We attended there today.

Friday 9th. Taught at Upper Walrond's and at night at Lynch's.

Saturday 10th. Went to Lynch's at noon and at Lower Walrond's at night.

Sunday 11th. Mrs. T. and I at Willoughby Bay. I went to Sion Hill in the afternoon, from thence to Lyon's at night, to hold the young people's prayer meeting. Many earnest and humble supplications were offered up by them.

Monday 12th. Held a meeting of the same kind at Lynch's at night. The young people prayed in an affecting manner, bewailed the sinfulness of their hearts and begged to be renewed by grace. I was summoned to attend the Court House the next day concerning the business before mentioned, and although we denied having any correspondence with any person or persons in England, relative to the treatment of slaves, it appears from the angry feelings which are excited, we are not believed, and therefore we expect the worse. One of the girls in her prayer mentioned the subject, and began to pray for us, on which the whole company spontaneously burst forth in strong cries to God to avert the evil to us and to them, some adding, but should our teachers be taken away from us, yet keep us Lord, and let us never turn our backs upon the good way. A pious man, who had married a Sunday Scholar, prayed in a very emphatic manner, "Lord! Thou reignest in the Heavens above, thou reignest also in the Earth below, all hearts are in thy hands. Hear the cries of these little ones who cry to thee &c &c." An Inspector afterwards prayed with many tears, with faith and submission. At the conclusion none would go away as usual on my bidding them good night, but came forward weeping to shake hands and say good bye.

Tuesday 13th. I went to town and appeared before the Committee, who told me they did not want me, but Mrs. Thwaites. This seemed strange as they had sent me a written summons to attend. I returned home persuaded that the Lord had so far heard prayer in our behalf.

Sunday 18th. Mrs. Thwaites and I at Willoughby Bay in the afternoon at Sion Hill, the children attended well.

Tuesday 20th. Took my wife to town and attended her to the Court House. She did not approve of the questions [about her anti-slavery activities], nor with the design apparently with which they were asked, and therefore declined replying.

Wed. 21st. Went to Lynch's and regulated the noon school and in the afternoon to Colebrook's.

Sunday 25th. Mrs. Thwaites and I at Willoughby Bay. In the afternoon she and Patrick Skerrett went to Sion Hill, where they held the monthly prayer meeting with the young people, who were not backward in humble simple language to make their complaint to their heavenly Father, and to implore his grace that they might be enabled to persevere in running the heavenly race.

Tuesday 27th. My wife having received a summon to attend *the Bar* of the House of Assembly, to answer for having objected to the interrogations of their Committee, I attended her there. The Speaker addressed her from the Chair, desired to know if she would return to the Committee and answer all *proper* questions proposed to her. It had been determined, that if she refused, she should be sent to jail: which we hear, was cleared out for her reception. She had been previously advised to consent to reply to the questions, as they had withdrawn all that were improper. There was no law to punish persons for giving charity to slaves, and she had done no injury to their proprietors. She therefore consented to answer their interrogations; she was after a short time dismissed.

Tuesday 3rd. Mrs. Thwaites made her appearance before the five gentlemen who formed the Committee. She mentioned such of the cases which she relieved, as she could recollect, and on being closely examined on the nature of her correspondence, they found nothing censurable; she was therefore acquitted.

Saturday 7th. Attended the noon school at Lynch's, was informed by one of the inspectors, a pious woman who belongs to the estate, that one of our teachers, who is in the habit of reading his Bible every night, a few nights ago, was reading those chapters in Deuteronomy where the blessings of God are particularly mentioned as consequent upon obedience, with the threatenings denounced against disobedience. He went to bed deeply affected and when he awoke next morning told his wife he had not been doing the work of God aright. The Inspector said he appears deeply convinced of sin, and cannot conceal his distress from his fellow servants, but vents it in tears. He tells them what he feels and speaks to them in a way of warning. This young man grew up in the school, was to the best of our knowledge strictly moral, though much exposed to temptation, and had married a Sunday school teacher of the same description.

Sunday 15th. Mrs. Thwaites and I at Willoughby Bay, at Sion Hill in the afternoon, and at Lyon's at night to hold the young peoples' prayer meeting. It was attended with life and power as at other times.

Monday 16th. At noon went to Morris's, was much pleased to find the child doing well. At night held the young peoples' prayer meeting at Lynch's. It was truly interesting, and we felt that the Lord was in our midst. In the confusion I felt a desire to know the individuals who had been particularly blessed, and requested that such should come forward and declare it, to the glory of God. On this a young man, who had backslidden, stood up and acknowledged his fall, the wickedness of his heart & his former self-confidence which had almost proved his ruin, he said. He could not sufficiently praise God for recalling him before it was too late, and not leaving him to go any farther in sin. He never before felt it to be such an evil and bitter thing, and he was determined not to rest till he should find pardon. When he sat down an elderly man said that his had been a life of sin. That the blessed Spirit of God often spoke to his heart (especially when he heard the experience of the people of God), telling him, he never felt the like, therefore he had no religion. He confessed that shame and the love of the evils made him drive away these impressions but that the last two weeks, he felt himself such a hell-deserving Sinner, he could take no rest, but gave himself up to God and earnestly prayed for pardon. And he praised the Lord, he now felt his grace in his heart. When I saw this aged man making a good confession before a company of children, my heart rejoiced. Another young man stood up and declared his experience and also some of the young people came forward. This kept the meeting till late.

Wednesday 18th. Mrs. Thwaites and I went to Delap's. A large company of children attended who we are glad to find are improving.

Tuesday 24th. Went to William Harman's at noon, had most of the children whom I taught and catechised. In the evening to Lynch's were with other leaders. We met a large class of adults.

Wednesday 25th. Went to Dr. Dues's, a good company attended, and in the evening to Lyon's, only the small children could attend.

Friday 27th. Went to Upper Walrond's, Mr. Bladen the manager having interested himself in the instruction of the children, they are taught every noon.

Saturday 28th. At night at Lower Walrond's assembled the children and had a good company.

Wednesday 4th. Went to Dr. Dues's at noon, the children are improving, at night at Lyon's only the small children attended.

Friday 6th. Mrs. Thwaites and I visited Sir George Thomas in the Parham circuit. After calling upon Mr. Cranistoun the Attorney, who favours the instruction of slaves, we went down to the prayer house and had a good company. Appointed five teachers and three inspectors to carry on the night teaching, the whole to be under the superintendence of Richard Jackson, a leader and local preacher, who has lately obtained his freedom as a reward for his good conduct.

EXTRACT OF CHARLES THWAITES'S JOURNAL NO. 2

Tuesday 10th March 1829. At night went to Redhead's. Some evil disposed persons had introduced dancing on this estate on Sunday nights. I had to reprove some of the young people for being spectators.

Wednesday 11th. Mrs. Thwaites and I went to Vernon's, an estate in the Parham quarter. The proprietor Major Vernon, on application immediately sent the young negroes to the prayer house. 92 in number. I appointed teachers and inspectors who have engaged to assemble the children three nights in the week. At night taught the children at Lyon's.

Thursday 12th. Assembled the young people and children at Harman's taught and catechised them.

Friday 13th. Attended at Upper Wolrond's at noon. Lynch's at night.

Sunday 15th. Mrs. Thwaites and I at Willoughby Bay School in the morning. In the afternoon my sister accompanied me to Sion Hill. I held the young people's prayer meeting afterwards went to Lyon's and held a meeting of the same kind, at both these places we had a good time.

Monday 16th. At Morris' taught the children at noon, many attended, and they are going on well. At night held the monthly prayer meeting at Lynch's, we are thankful that these meetings are still attended with the divine blessing.

Tuesday 17th. Met a large class of adults at Lynch's with the assistance of other leaders.

Wednesday 18th. Went to Delap's and was gratified at having a large company of children who are improving, at night at Lyon's where I taught and catechised.

Thursday 19th. Mrs. Thwaites and I went to Blackman's, an estate in the Parham quarter. I waited on the manager who gave permission for the children to assemble, but not expecting us, all did not come, neither was the principal person who looks after the children on the estate present, so that I could not establish noon and night teaching or do anything effective.

Friday 20th. At Skerrett's at noon, had very few children in consignment, of the group. At night went to Lynch's and was gratified at the improvement of the little ones. At night went to Garland's as they were not grinding we had the children and young people. After teaching I met them in class, and had reason to believe they were making progress. As they did not seem inclined to go home, I called upon the teacher to pray, which he did with much earnestness, particularly for the young people, himself and his fellow servants, some of whom are very wicked. I then called on three of the girls to pray, one after another and they offered up their petitions with much feeling and simplicity after this the teacher gave out a verse of hymn, while we remained upon our knees. He then called upon a lad about fourteen or fifteen years of age to pray. My heart rejoiced to hear the humble and earnest pleadings with God, of this youth. He prayed much for his mother and his aged uncle (both Africans) that the Lord would open their eyes and save them. Most of these young people are in the Society, and received tickets this night for the first time. I left the place feeling my own soul blest.

Sunday 22nd. Mrs. Thwaites and I at Willoughby Bay in the morning and in the morning and in the afternoon at Sion Hill, about 100 children present.

Monday 23rd. At noon taught the children at Lavington Gordon's. In the afternoon buried a child at Dr. Dues's and endeavored to improve the occasion, remained till night, and taught the children.

Tuesday 24th. Taught at Lynch's at noon, in the evening went to Redhead's. Set the evil of dancing before the young people and I hope not without effect.

Wednesday 25th. Mrs. Thwaites and I went to Vernon's, we were gratified to find that our former visit had not been in vain; they had attended to the night teaching and discovered a desire for instruction, seldom exceeded. The young negroes who teach seem to be steady characters. Mrs. Thwaites and I took the big girls apart, as is her custom, to point out and warn them against the dangers and snares which beset them. On enquiring into their attendance at the Parham School, we found that a girl about 14, who can read in the testament, seldom went, she was very ragged and on being asked, who was her mother? The tears started in her eyes, and she replied, "She is dead, Ma'am." A sympathetic feeling caused all the others to weep with her. After teaching and catechising we left them much pleased. In the evening went to Lyon's and taught the children.

Thursday 26th. Went to Dr. Dues's. Their teacher being dead, I intended to have appointed another, but *business* prevented his attendance.

Sunday 29th. Mrs. Thwaites and I at Willoughby Bay in the morning. In the afternoon at Sion Hill, the small children came in first. I asked them several questions individually according to their ages. To a girl about 10 years of age I said, Are you a sinner? She answered with seriousness, "Yes Sir" and paid attention to me while I endeavoured to improve that conviction. To another little girl, I asked, Do you know you must die? With some hesitation, she answered in the affirmative. I made the same enquiry of a little boy some days past; he seemed quite startled and answered quickly, "No Sir." The elder scholars came in and we commenced the prayer meeting. The young people prayed with their accustomed humility, simplicity and fervour, and the dew of heavenly grace seemed to descend upon us. The little ones looked very serious, especially the girl above mentioned and another much of the same age whose eyes were fixed upon me, and who seemed to drink in all I said. I told them Jesus invites such as you to come to him, and no one can hinder you, and repeated to them the passage. Those of you who want to love and serve him must kneel down to pray to him, upon which a little girl about 6 years old began to pray; after her, the girl who looked at me so earnestly, cried to God in a very affecting manner, some of her expressions were Lord I sin every day, have mercy upon me, and pardon me, I want to go to heaven," etc. After ceasing to pray she wept and sobbed a great deal. I then called upon the first mentioned to pray, which she did in a very humble manner, begging earnestly that her sins might be forgiven. There was a blessed feeling, and it was to us a house of God and the gate of heaven.

Biography of Elizabeth Lynch

Miss Elizabeth Lynch, daughter of Nicholas Lynch, Esq., and Lucy his wife, was born in St. John's, Antigua, on February 1st, 1783; and had completed her sixty-sixth year, when it pleased God to remove her by death, on Sunday, August 26th, 1849.

The parents of Miss Lynch had been attendants on the ministry of the first Wesleyan Missionaries,—Messrs. Gilbert, Baxter, Dr. Coke, and others; and, having profited by the ministrations of those eminent servants of Christ, they resolved to train their numerous family in the paths of virtue and righteousness. Their house was the constant resort of those men of God, to whom Antigua is so deeply indebted for their labours of love in promulgating the truth amidst great obloquy and opposition.

Miss Lynch's maternal grandmother had embraced the Gospel, and felt its saving power, under the ministry of the Hon. Nathaniel Gilbert, Speaker of the House of Assembly, who first introduced Methodism into Antigua; and the journeys on horseback of this admirable woman, every Sunday, to Gilbert's Estate, to hear the word of God, indicated her indefatigable zeal and ardent love for the truth, at a time when the means of grace were not so easy of access as in subsequent more highly favoured periods.

This brief biography of the Hart sisters' cousin Elizabeth Lynch appeared as an appendix to chapter 4 of John Horsford, *A Voice from the West Indies: Being a Review of the Character and Results of Missionary Efforts in the British and Other Colonies in the Charibbean Sea, with Some Remarks on the Usages, Prejudices, etc., of the Inhabitants* (London: Alexander Heylin, 1856).

Miss Lynch at her birth was ushered into an atmosphere of virtue and religion in the domestic circle, which was by no means common at that time; and though her father did not until a more recent period become a partaker of converting grace, yet were his convictions of parental obligation so deep, such enlightened views did he cherish on the subject, and such was the tone of morals which he assiduously cultivated, that his family were most virtuously and religiously trained. Her mother had at an early age become a member of the Wesleyan body.

Miss Lynch was naturally of a most gentle and amiable temper, of a kind and affectionate disposition, free from envy, jealousy, and suspicion; and consequently was much beloved by her parents and every member of the family. Her docility and obedience, and her love for books, made her the friend and companion of her father, by whom she was often employed to read to him out of his favourite authors, and by whose intellectual conversation she greatly profited. But though she was not entangled in the sinful pleasures of the world, and was strictly attentive to the duties of religion, and its public ordinances, yet she was a stranger to the converting grace of God. She had the form of godliness without the power, though she was often much impressed by the ministry of the Gospel. At length, in her seventeenth year, (A.D. 1806) under the preaching of the Rev. Mr. Murdock, her heart was deeply convinced of the importance of a personal attainment of vital religion. "The law was" her "schoolmaster to bring" her "to Christ." Groaning under the burden of sin, and feeling her lost and guilty state before a heart-searching God, she poured out her soul in supplication for pardoning mercy through our Lord Jesus Christ, and at length attained the blessing of justification, and the witness of the Spirit to her adoption into the family of God. She thus became a partaker of that new birth, or change of heart, which is absolutely necessary for all the children of men, whether they are moral or immoral, virtuous or profligate, and which constitutes the turning-point in their religious history. She could now exclaim, "Being justified by faith, we have peace with God, through our Lord Jesus Christ," and, feeling the pardoning love of God shed abroad in her heart, her exulting soul uttered its emotions in the language of St. John, "We love Him because He first loved us."

The exact time when her sorrow was turned into joy, I cannot ascertain. Like too many other excellent people, Miss Lynch, we lament to say, destroyed those journals and papers which doubtless contained a description of the commencement and completion of this work of saving mercy; and we are deprived of the pleasure and edification which would have resulted from the perusal of the details of that important revolution in her feelings, as well as her religious experience in after years. From this memorable period, when she became a child of God, and a member of Christ's body, and consecrated herself to the Lord in an everlasting covenant never to be forgotten, her course was decided and unwavering to the end of her pilgrimage; and I think I cannot more profitably delineate the life of our departed friend, than by bringing before you the various prominent features in her history and character, properly classified. This is the more necessary because, in the absence of a journal, it is impracticable to give the experience and proceedings of every year consecutively.

1. The first feature, then, which demands our attention is her decided and consistent piety. This is the foundation of all those moral excellencies for which we glorify God in her. Her conversion to God I have described; it was clear and undoubted. The fruits of the Spirit were now exhibited in her daily walk, to the praise of the glory of His grace. She was stable and persevering: she was not "a reed shaken with the wind." The seed had taken deep root in her heart. There was no vacillation in her character: having embraced the truth, she retained it firmly: having found the "pearl of great price," no earthly consideration would induce her to part with it. Those lovely virtues which existed in her previously to her conversion, were now hallowed as the results of Divine Grace. They became Christian graces, acceptable to God through Jesus Christ; being purified by the operation of the Spirit, and proceeding from the impulses of those new motives which now filled her heart.

Nor was Miss Lynch's character disfigured by those inconsistencies which we sometimes witness. She resolved to adhere to the rules of that religious body to which she had voluntarily united herself. She was "not conformed to this world, but transformed by the renewing of her mind;" and her external appearance indicated the feelings of her heart. She was remarkably plain and neat in her dress, and adhered to the apostolic injunction, that women should not indulge in the outward adorning of wearing of gold, pearls, and costly array. She deplored—as did her beloved cousins, Mrs. Gilbert and Mrs. Thwaites—a growing tendency to indulge in gaudy and extravagant dress, unbecoming the spirituality of true religion, and so manifestly inconsistent with the word of God and the rules of Methodism. She therefore eschewed the needless ornaments of rings, jewels, artificial flowers, and other vanities to which the young are commonly addicted. O that her example in this respect may impress the minds of the young persons in this city and elsewhere, and lead them to imitate such laudable consistency, and to secure the inward beauteous adorning of the heart and mind!

In this, and in every thing else which was "lovely and of good report," she became "an example of the believers, in word, in conversation, in charity, in spirit, in faith, in purity." She lived in subjection to the authority of that Saviour to whom she had consecrated her ransomed powers. Never did she depart from God's people. Never was a charge justly brought against her moral or religious character; but, "walking in the fear of God and the comfort of the Holy Ghost," her path was that of the just, "shining more and more unto the perfect day."

2. The second characteristic to which I call your attention, is her regular attendance on the ordinances of religion. Daily secret prayer she constantly offered to her heavenly Father. The word of God was her never-failing companion; its promises were the solace of her chequered life. She was most conscientious in the performance of family devotion. Even when her state of health made her almost incapable of attending the usual exercises, still was she found at the post of duty; and in some cases, from her extreme feebleness, she had almost fainted after its performance. Her sisters call to mind her frequent admonitions, that the family might be regularly summoned to this privilege when she could no longer conduct it.

Her devout and constant attendance on public worship must not be forgotten. Often has she come to the beloved house of prayer, when suffering acutely from sickness and infirmity, which would have detained at home the great bulk of religious professors, and might have been justly considered as a reason for absence. But she loved the habitation of His house, and longed for the courts of the living God. Her soul panted for the water-brooks; and her language concerning herself and her household was, "Our feet shall stand within thy gates, O Jerusalem." (Psalm cxxii. 2.) Often, when absolutely unable to go, she would insist on all her servants observing the sanctity of the Sabbath, and repairing to the means of grace. One only would be permitted, *by her consent*, to stay to minister to her convenience. And her attendance was punctual. The fashionable and culpable habit of coming to God's house late, always met her decided reprobation; and great delight did she feel, on the return of the family, in receiving an account of the service, and especially of the sermon. For a year or more, when she was the prisoner of the Lord, shut out entirely from the house of prayer, she was frequently found by her sisters weeping at the sore privation. She greatly prized the week-night services of the house of God, and regularly enjoyed them, until her state of health precluded the possibility of her attendance at them. She was incessant in urging others to go also, and to endeavour to secure sittings in the chapel. Rarely did a Saturday pass in which she did not dispatch notes or messages to some individuals, reminding them that to-morrow was a "holy convocation."

She always remembered the thanksgiving days, and quarterly days of humiliation and prayer, urging others to attend the public services on those occasions, and to encourage their friends to do likewise. When one of her sisters was recently leaving the house, in order to solicit contributions to the bazaar, she requested her to consider it as a part of her errand to invite persons to attend at God's house on the next day,—the day of intercession with reference to the hurricane months.

I cannot omit another matter, to which I attach considerable importance. She never allowed invitations to social parties, or the visits of others, to interfere with her own attendance, or that of her boarders, on the regular services of the sanctuary. If the family were visited by friends resident in Antigua, or any other place, on the evening of public worship, they were kindly invited to accompany them to the Prayer-Meeting or week-night sermon. These precious means of grace were not neglected under the plea of miscalled "civility." This is a sacred duty, and I hope our people will remember it, and never permit the hour that ought to be devoted to the worship of God, to be employed in visits to friends, or in receiving calls from others.

3. I must now notice her extensive and unwearied benevolence. This was a prominent trait in the character of our deceased sister. She was possessed of a largeness of heart, and a tenderness of sympathy, which not only called forth the tear of pity over the various forms of human woe, but prompted her to great efforts for the relief of suffering and degraded humanity. She was always employed in endeavouring to do good, and in devising schemes of usefulness. There seemed to be in her soul a ceaseless spring of activity. And it is easily understood: "The love of Christ constrained" her; for she thus judged, as did the Apostle, (and none can dispute his judgment,) "that if One died for all, then were all dead: and that He died for all, that they which live should not henceforth live unto themselves, but unto Him which died for them, and rose again." (2 Cor. v. 14, 15.) This was the source of her persevering exertions for the benefit of others. It was a gushing fountain that never ceased to flow, until "the weary wheels of life stood still," and "the pitcher was broken at the fountain."

Selfishness was well-nigh annihilated in Miss Lynch; she appeared to live mainly for the welfare of others. In various ways was this exhibited. Hence arose her visits to the sick, and aged, and afflicted, so full of sympathy and tenderness, and her prayers for them, so rich in pathos and earnest desire. For she remembered the words of Christ: "I was sick, and ye visited Me." Hence her frequent resort to the most dark and degraded streets and avenues of the city, in order to find out children for the Sunday-school; and this at a period when gross darkness pervaded those regions and dens of iniquity: hence her earnest reproofs of the ungodly, and her pressing invitations to them to attend the house of God, and to forsake their sins. Frequently would they fly from her approach; or so conceal themselves as to escape her vigilant eye. Hence her importunate solicitations, that they would allow their children to attend the Sabbath-school either at the Point chapel or Ebenezer, actually entreating that as a favour, which the parents ought to have regarded as a precious boon and privilege.

Miss Lynch was appointed the first Female Superintendent of the Sunday-school instituted in the old chapel, in 1815; she was most faithful and indefatigable in the performance of the duties of this office until the year 1837, when increasing years and infirmities obliged her to resign it to her sister. She was a great lover of order, and rigidly attended to the regulations of the institution; was a strict disciplinarian, and insisted on the observance of rules with reference to time and attendance, suitable apparel, and becoming behaviour in the classes.

Her efforts in this interesting department of Christian philanthropy were abounding; and the extent of her usefulness eternity only can unfold. In conjunction with others, Miss Lynch hired a room at the Point, in which to conduct the school in that quarter, before the warehouse of our respected friend, Mr. Garling, was set apart for the purpose; and she deeply regretted its unavoidable dissolution.

The Juvenile Society was formed under her auspices, and its annual meeting was held under her roof. Greatly did it minister to the physical wants of some poor afflicted pensioners, and help the education of others, as well as send its annual guinea to the Chapel Fund. The necessity for the formation of the Distressed Females' Friend Society arose out of the benevolent efforts of Miss Lynch to secure the attendance of children on the Sunday-school. The parents pleaded want of clothes and other necessaries; and often was she employed in soliciting old clothes, and shoes, and bonnets, to supply this lack. Many of these fathers and mothers were so abandoned to iniquity, that it was deemed an act of real charity to take the unhappy offspring, and lodge them in a place of refuge. In the commencement of this work of mercy Miss Lynch induced some like-minded with herself to take the children, and feed them on the Sabbath-day, that they might be enabled to attend the Sunday-school, and then to lodge and board them during the week. At length a house was hired as a shelter for these lambs, in danger of the devouring wolf; and ultimately a building was purchased, and constituted the Asylum of the Distressed Females' Friend Society. This work is mainly to be traced to the indefatigable toil and unconquerable energy of this excellent woman. Many of its inmates have arisen to call her blessed; and many of those who have been trained and led to Christ there, have already welcomed her into the heavenly habitations.

But in a countless variety of other ways was this compassion for

souls exhibited. In the distribution of suitable tracts,—in the loan
of useful books,—in individual exhortation to those who came to
her house, or into whose company she was accidentally thrown,—
in invitations to the house of God,—in urgent addresses to parents
and guardians concerning their youthful charges,—in stimulating
others to do good where opportunity appeared to offer,—in short
in almost every imaginable method did the ingenuity of Miss Lynch
devise and execute schemes of mercy. So absorbed was she often in
these labours of love that she forgot to take her daily food; and it
is easily conceivable that on such occasions her inmost soul could
say, with undissembled sincerity, and in the spirit of her benevolent Master,—in reply to pressing solicitations of her affectionate
friends, "Sister, eat!"—"I have meat to eat that ye know not of.
Wist ye not that I must be about my Father's business?" One of her
former pupils, who tenderly loved her, assures me that she often sat
up at night, in order to induce her, on returning home from errands
of mercy, to take needful bodily refreshment. It was truly her delight to do good; and her charity extended to the bodily wants of
the poor also. Often has she fed the hungry, and clothed the naked,
and with her own hands been a succourer of many.

In the consideration of these facts, it need not excite our surprise
that Miss Lynch should have been so generally beloved, and that so
much solicitude should have been manifested during her illness, and
so many tears shed at her lamented removal, and so many tokens
of respect exhibited for her memory. I was struck on two or three
occasions, when she accompanied me in visits, to some of my flock
in the most distant parts of the Point, to hear the affectionate recog-
nitions and greetings of some aged persons, who were once more
permitted to see their old friend, whose presence was well known in
those scenes of sorrow and sin, when youthful vigour enabled her to
go about doing good. I was reminded of the words of Job: "When
the ear heard me, then it blessed me; and when the eye saw me, it
gave witness to me: because I delivered the poor that cried, and the
fatherless, and him that had none to help him. The blessing of him
that was ready to perish came upon me: and I caused the widow's
heart to sing for joy;" (Job xxix. 11–13;)—and earnestly did I pray
that a greater number might arise and emulate her example. In this

connexion, I may also mention that the missionary cause was dear to her; and great pleasure did she feel in perusing the periodicals containing intelligence of its triumphs. She was a missionary collector until decaying health forbade such an occupation.

4. Closely connected with this subject is another,—her calm endurance of sufferings in the prosecution of these philanthropic purposes. It is a lamentable proof of human depravity, that those who have signally and disinterestedly laboured to promote the moral regeneration of the heart have been most awfully vituperated and persecuted by the very objects of their benevolence. But there were subsidiary and special causes, which secured for Miss Lynch the honour of a large measure of reproach and calumny at this period of her history. Most courageously opposing prevalent and unblushing enormity this heroic lady encountered opposition and violence for such a length of time, that even some of her most judicious friends urged her to give over the conflict, as utterly hopeless and personally dangerous. But she was firm and immoveable. She had nailed her colours to the mast; and, trusting in the strength of the Lord Jehovah, her motto was, "No surrender!" Before a court of justice she was ready to go, had it been necessary, to plead the cause of the oppressed victims of unhallowed passion, but the triumph was secured without it; and great was her thankfulness to the Lord of heaven and earth, who, in that memorable case, broke the arm of the oppressor, and secured the object of her trembling solicitude.

In some cases the opposition and reproach to which Miss Lynch and her coadjutors were subjected, arose from the parents of the children whom they were anxious to pluck from the grasp of infamy and ruin. O "tell it not in Gath! Publish it not in the streets of Askelon!" But knowing the excellence of her plans, supported by conscious rectitude, and the smile and approbation of the virtuous and godly, and by the strength of the great Lord of all, the subject of our memoir was "steadfast, unmoveable, always abounding in the work of the Lord." Her heart was filled with compassion and forgiveness for her bitterest opponents; and she earnestly prayed for them.

5. I should be inexcusable if I did not mention another striking feature in our friend's character; and that was her love for the doctrines, disciplines, and institutions of Methodism. Most catholic in

her principles, and enabled heartily to say, "Grace be with all them," of every name, "that love our Lord Jesus Christ in sincerity," yet she was warmly attached to that system of church government which she had, from thorough conviction, voluntarily espoused. Knowing the awful moral condition of Antigua previously to the introduction of Methodism in 1763; being well acquainted with its history, and the beneficial results which it had effected in this and neighbouring Islands; perceiving its advantages in the large families of her father and her uncle,—Mr. Barry Conyers Hart, of Popeshead,— and in the households of the Clearkleys, and Cables, and Gilberts, and others, in her earlier days, as well as the rich and numerous blessings which it had conferred on the black and coloured population especially, to whose spiritual wants it most generally ministered, while they were neglected by more influential bodies; and rejoicing in its adaptation to human wants and the purposes of church government, by its Prayer-Meetings, Class-Meetings, and other peculiar institutions, and the warmth and vigour of its operation;—it is not marvellous that she should have highly prized it herself, and earnestly commended it to others. To those who were beginning to exhibit serious emotions she would, without any morbid fastidiousness, recommend a Class-Leader and a union with the church of Christ, that the gracious work commenced might be fostered and brought to maturity. Her personal obligations to it she always acknowledged; and she was ever anxious to maintain it in efficiency, because she conscientiously believed it to be the best church organization extant.

As a Class-Leader,—an office which she profitably filled for many years,—she was most acceptable and useful, entering, as she did, into the various circumstances of her people, exhorting, admonishing, and comforting, as occasion required. Nor did she neglect her absent members. The sick and aged she sought after with most tender assiduity. Her anxiety was awakened by any appearance of negligence or back-sliding; and most diligently did she personally seek after them, or, when too feeble to do so, send to them, and stir up their minds by "putting them in remembrance."

She was concerned for the temporal support of the work of God also, and sought to deepen the conviction in the minds of her members, that the servants of Christ who ministered of their spiritual things were unquestionably entitled to a due proportion of "carnal things" from those who profited by their ministry.

6. I proceed to notice, in the next place, her gratitude to God for the "Temperance movement." When the subject of total abandonment of alcoholic fluids was first broached, she, like many other good people, was sceptical as to the practicability and usefulness of it. It is true, that the children of her father's family had been trained in the most moderate use of such drinks;—were, indeed, rarely allowed to taste them on any occasion. But the doctrine of the pernicious influence of alcohol was so contrary to maxims which had been received and cherished by all around them, that it was difficult to accept it. But reading, reflection, and observation of the utility of the Temperance movement, soon produced most decided conviction in its favour, and she embraced the cause with the utmost cordiality. Every year confirmed her attachment to it, and earnestly did she advocate it in every quarter. She had long groaned over the ravages of strong drink; and, perceiving in Teetotalism the most probable cure for them, it is not surprising that one of her sanguine and benevolent temperament should throw her whole soul into the movement. While she was not insensible to its advantages, socially and economically, in cutting off a most useless and culpable expenditure, she especially prized it, as taking out of the way of the ungodly, and godly too, a prolific source of sin and misery. She knew that intoxicating liquors had been the bane and utter destruction of some valuable young men and women, as well as others; that they were a most formidable foe to the interests of true religion; and that no classes were free from peril in the use of them, while the solemn cautions of Holy Writ were frequent and decided against it, especially in the wondrous embodiment of Solomon's wisdom. She well knew also that the only safe course was to abstain altogether; and that it was the imperative obligation of Christians to take such a stumbling-block and occasion of falling out of their brother's way, and so not incur the woe denounced by God Himself against those who give their neighbour drink, and put the bottle to his mouth. (Habakkuk

ii. 15.) Most earnestly did she warn and exhort all classes to espouse this principle. A steady and consistent example of thorough temperance was observed in all her household.

7. But we must now contemplate Miss Lynch in a most distinguished sphere of usefulness, that is, as a teacher of the young. Her seminary for the education of females was commenced in the year 1809; and since its formation, some hundreds have been trained in it from Antigua and the neighbouring Islands; and there have been boarded and lodged in it one hundred and thirty-two. So highly prized have been her labours in this department, that children from all the adjacent Isles were sent to enjoy the advantages of her faithful and effective training. Miss Lynch was peculiarly qualified for this important work. She possessed great energy and activity and buoyancy of spirit, superabounding cheerfulness and vivacity, a most affectionate manner, combined with a commanding tone and a resolute enforcement of order, and a superior tact for communicating instruction, and eliciting the dormant energies of her pupils. The delight she felt in the work, and the hope of profiting the minds and hearts of her youthful charges, made her task pleasant; which would have otherwise become wearisome drudgery.

She had a peculiar facility in communicating religious instruction; and her sisters have remarked that it was profitable to *them* to hear her apt and striking illustrations of the word of God as read in her classes, and the pointed and faithful application of it made to the consciences by this skilful teacher. Some have traced their first religious impressions to her godly admonitions in this way; and doubtless many will be her crown of rejoicing. She would often take her pupils into her closet, lead them to self-examination, teach them to pray, and commend them in prayer to God. She was not merely a schoolteacher, but cherished a maternal care for the children under her charge; as if she heard the voice of Jehovah saying, "Take this child, and nurse it for Me; and I will give thee thy wages."

Miss Lynch endeavoured also to awaken and foster a literary taste in the minds of her scholars, by drawing their attention to the beauty or grandeur of style in a hymn, or in some of the magnificent portions of the word of God, or in any other remarkable volume; as well as by recommending useful works suitable to their circumstances, and by urging them to commit to memory choice pieces of prose or verse.

Her fascinating and attractive manner greatly contributed to success; and most affectionate epistles from pupils here and elsewhere have often cheered her heart with the assurance that her labour was not fruitless. She principally gave that impetus to youthful mental culture which now exists, feeble as it still is, compared with what it ought to be. Schools were by no means common when she began her work of elementary education, and to act as a pioneer in literary improvement. We earnestly hope that those who have been under her roof, and have not yet exhibited proofs of real benefit from her godly admonitions and maternal counsels, may hear her voice from the tomb, or rather from the skies, calling on them to walk in the real "ways of pleasantness" and the true "paths of peace."

But I cannot on this occasion pretend to dwell at length on many other features of the character of our venerated friend. The subject grows under my hand. I can only glance at her tender compassion for souls,—a flame that seemed ever to burn;—her anxiety for relations, both young and old, asking if they were at the house of God, administering godly counsels, advising, warning, beseeching them to fly from the wrath to come;—her buoyancy and exuberance of spirits, which were a mighty help in sustaining the manifold burdens and afflictions which she had frequently to endure;—her unfeigned humility and lowliness before God, increasing with years, and producing feelings of self-abasement and repugnance when her useful labours were adverted to;—her evident preference of others before herself;—the Christian courtesy, suavity, and urbanity of temper, for which she was remarkable;—the absence of all affectation;— the constant desire to please and to make all around her happy;— the holding frequent religious conversation with her servants, and giving wholesome advice to young females on their peculiar dangers and duties;—her anxiety to procure for them useful situations, in service or otherwise, by which they might secure an honest and respectable livelihood;—her unabated interest in the care of the Asylum, and perseverance in maintaining it amidst difficulties which appalled many stout hearts, and produced frequent despondency;— her tender affection for numerous brothers and sisters, and other relatives, evinced by earnest prayer and by epistolary correspondence;—her constant efforts to promote their comfort, and to mitigate their sufferings in affliction;—her habits of early rising, most diligently redeeming the time, as well as her punctuality and fidelity in business;—her industry and Christian economy, that she might have to give to those that needed. On these topics we cannot enlarge; but they all constrain us to say, that a "mother in Israel" has fallen; and they lead her sisters to feel that not only a sister, but a mother,—one whom from early age they have regarded as a second mother,—has been taken from their head.

But we must hasten to the closing scene. You know how long she had suffered from painful and harassing sickness. You know also, that her indomitable activity would induce her to come forth to the house of God, to visit the afflicted, and to attend to the duties of her school, whenever an interval of ease allowed her, and often without any such intermission. But at length disease progressed with such rapidity and power, that it became evident to all that the time had arrived when she must die. It was most difficult for her affectionate sisters and friends to realize the dread certainty. So often had she been brought to the margin, and wonderfully raised up again, that hopes were fondly entertained to a late period; but they were gradually annihilated, although not followed by the "black grief of despair." The light of the Sun of Righteousness illuminated that sick chamber; the Rose of Sharon shed its fragrance there; and the promise was fulfilled, "I will not leave you comfortless: I will come unto you." Some of us will not soon forget the enlargement of heart experienced while pleading with God on her behalf, and singing hymns of thanksgiving, nor the surpassing delight enjoyed in beholding the steadfastness of her faith in Christ. She was a "wise virgin," who had oil in her vessel with her lamp: and therefore when the cry was made, "Behold the Bridegroom cometh!" there was no confusion, or unseemly trepidation. Calmly did our beloved sister address herself to the task of gathering up her feet to die. The Lord was her Shepherd: her cup was full; she was led into the green pastures of spiritual comfort, and Christ fulfilled His promise: "I will come again, and receive you to Myself; that where I am, there ye may be also," (John xiv. 3.) The nature of her complaint and the medicine administered produced much nervous agitation, but there was a deep tranquility within the soul. The surface was occasionally ruffled, but in the depths within there was undisturbed quietude. Every inquiry was answered satisfactorily; directions were given, with patriarchal dignity and perfect self-possession, for the disposal of various mundane affairs. The numerous young friends and others who crowded around her dying bed, were welcomed most cordially, and addressed according to their respective conditions, as long as strength permitted: and then the weary saint, bending herself upon the bed's head, said, "I have waited for Thy salvation, O Lord!"

She continually breathed the spirit of prayer. When apprised, on one occasion, that it was probable she would be detained on earth some days longer, she was evidently disappointed, though submissive. And when, at another time, upon her inquiring, "When does the doctor think I shall be released?" the answer was, "To-day;" "Amen," exclaimed the dying child of God. During her illness the graces of the Spirit shone out in their full maturity, and appeared in all their heavenly loveliness. She was most grateful for any attention, and often uttered a fear that she should impose on the strength of numerous kind and voluntary nurses. To her sisters she expressed a hope that her death would be rendered profitable to them all, as a means of grace, leading them nearer to Christ. To one she said, with perfect composure, "You will write to Mrs. Fraser and Mrs. Whitworth." Her sisterly affection was burning brightly while life yet flickered in the socket, and she added with tremendous emotion, "Be kind to my sisters." The dying request shall be fulfilled.

She said to Miss M'Kinnen, her companion in the kingdom and patience of Jesus for nearly fifty years, "I feel that my sickness will be unto death, and pray that my will may be lost in God's." She felt it a severe struggle to part with her affectionate sisters, to whom she was most tenderly attached; but at length she said that by the grace of God she had obtained the victory over nature, and was enabled to resign them in submission to His will; and then exclaimed, "O the precious blood of Christ! Upon this only I build my hope!" On the Sunday morning, (the day of her death,) in holy rapture she said to Miss M'Kinnen, "Great joy! I have had such a glimpse of glory! Great joy! The sufferings of this present time are not worthy to be compared with the glory which shall be revealed in us." Miss M'Kinnen replied, "Presently you will join the blood-washed throng who sing, Unto Him that loved us, and washed us from our sins in His own blood, and hath made us Kings and Priests unto God and His Father; to Him be glory and dominion for ever and ever. Amen." She replied, "Yes; but not yet the fulness, not yet!" Miss M'Kinnen proposed prayer; and immediately after the dying saint exclaimed, "Oh, the joy! 'Tis worth living for this, and worth suffering for this!" Her earthly vessel was full to overflowing; her cup ran over; she often prayed that the Lord would finish His work, and take her home.

In this tranquil frame of mind she continued to the end of her pilgrimage. That dying chamber was truly a Bethel, a "house of God." Jacob's ladder was there; it reached from heaven to earth, and the angels of God ascended and descended upon it. This is not poetical imagination or hyperbole. For "it came to pass that the beggar died, and was carried by the angels into Abraham's bosom:" and is this restricted to Lazarus? "Are they not all ministering spirits, sent forth to minister for them who shall be heirs of salvation?" The atmosphere of heaven was breathed in that upper chamber; gentle gales from the spirit-land reached us there. Holy tranquility marked the dying hour of this devoted woman; and in her we had a witness to the truth of the lines:—

> "Jesus can make a dying bed
>   Feel soft as downy pillows are,
> While on His breast I lay my head,
>   And sweetly breathe my soul out there."

A dying Christian of the eighteenth century called one of his volatile and thoughtless relatives to his bedside, and gently said, "See how calmly a believer can die." And, my beloved friends, I call you to behold this attractive spectacle. Learn here the value of vital religion. What can infidelity do before a magnificent scene like this,—a feeble child of God exclaiming, "O Death! where is thy sting? O Grave! where is thy victory?" while renouncing all confidence in her own merit, and putting her only trust in Jesu's blood and righteousness.

At length "the weary wheels of life stood still;" and while her watchful attendants supposed she was still sleeping, her spirit had escaped to the inheritance above. The welcome summons,—

"Sister spirit, come away!"

was not heard by human ear. How quietly was the angelic mission performed! How easily did she glide from earth to heaven! "Thanks be to God, who giveth us the victory through our Lord Jesus Christ!" The pearly gates have received her. Her exulting spirit has seized its harp of gold, and united with her beloved sisters Gilbert and Thwaites, and others, in everlasting hallelujah. And the burden of their songs is, "Blessing, and honour, and glory, and power, be unto Him that sitteth upon the throne, and unto the Lamb for ever and ever!" "Our Jesus hath done all things well." Who will not unite with us in saying,—

"O may I triumph so,
When all my warfare's past;
And, dying, find my latest foe
Under my feet at last!"

But on whom shall her mantle fall? Concerning whom shall it be said, "The spirit of Elijah doth rest on Elisha?" Young people of Antigua! arise, and imitate her example. The same grace which she obtained at seventeen years of age, you may also secure. God is willing to bestow it: with unremitting earnestness implore it. Let your hearts become the hallowed temples of the living God. Consecrate your energies to the Lord of Hosts, and live for the benefit of your generation.

How will it gladden the soul of our beatified friend, if she can be assured that through her death, or the services of this night, spiritual life has been brought to any of you! Will you not allow the ministering angels, who are about to wing their flight in returning to the skies, to proclaim there, that "the dead is alive, the lost is found?" How joyfully will all the enraptured host attune their golden lyres to the praises of the Eternal! and none will sound more sweet and loud than hers.

Letter from John Baxter to a
Fellow Methodist in London

Antigua 12 June 1804

Very Dear Brother

I received your letter dated February 14th about two months ago. The packet that brought it having sailed before I arrived in town I had not an opportunity of answering it, and the three last packets being taken I have had no opportunity of writing to you or the Committee till the sailing of the fleet. I fear you will not receive this. I shall give the Committee and yourself all the information I can respecting the spiritual state of the mission in this island. The number in Society has been large, but when the state of our people [becomes] a state of ignorance and gross darkness the effect of which is the gratification of every lustful passion and unchaste affection, with greediness both in male and female without restraint, the edge of conviction becomes dull, and it is hard to imprint purity of manners and chaste affections on the mind of those who have been lit by their appetites and passions; so that they are parted by death, or in case of sickness we have been obliged to exclude many who run well for years for forming improper connections. And with regard to the rising generation, although we have a pleasing prospect concerning many that bid fair for leading virtuous lives; yet I fear not a few will fall a prey to a vice, so prevalent in this country. And many that have been baptised in an infant state with us, when they grow-

---

John Baxter's letter was sent to Mr. Joseph Benson, City Road, London, "by the packet." The holograph copy is in the Methodist Missionary Archives, School of Oriental and African Studies, London, West Indian File. Angle brackets indicate material that had been crossed out but was still legible. Reprinted by permission.

up, will not take husbands & wives properly. As for living a single life properly and chastely there is no such thing known among the Blacks after they are eighteen years old I believe. I believe few of the females at sixteen, and their coming together improperly without affection, young women taking old men and young men old women is the cause of constant jealousy and separating from each other in which case we exclude the guilty person and never receive. But notwithstanding many evils which remain, and are not done away, I can say with truth there is a wonderful change for the better within the twenty-six years. These general evils exist among so large a body of illiterate people who I am sorry to say have the example of their superiors to countenance them. We have, at present, many young women in the society who are an ornament to their profession, and in their behavior manifest both chastity and purity of manners. And many of the aged prove that they have held fast [from] the beginning of their confidence firm unto the end. I believe we shall now have a fitting time, as we are determined to pay a strict regard to discipline.

As we have not the opportunity of visiting our people just because they are at a distance from us, except when we visit the estates in town; and as we have no intelligent persons to give us just information concerning them, we cannot present you with accounts of the experience of many of them. I shall endeavor however to write everything that I think worthy of notice. On Tuesday, April 16, our sister Euphemia Chapman was buried, a young white woman who had been a member of our society for years. She was much enlightened and affected under the preaching, and gave up the vanities of the world in the prime of life. She had many trials but bore them with patience. Six months before her death she caught a violent cold and lost the use of her limbs. She bore her affliction with christian patience and resignation in hope of a resurrection to eternal life.

The next day I rode to Doctor Athel's estate, to bury the remains of John Quash[?] Gilbert. He had been a member of the first Methodist society in Antigua and was a seal of Mr. Gilbert's ministry. He had been in society three and thirty years and walked as became the gospel soberly and uprightly. He was a faithful trusty servant, a good husband and a loving father. Being deaf for some years, he could not converse much. He always attended the means of grace; and though he was ninety years old, he labored for his master till a fortnight before his death. He observed to his wife in his sickness "I have not much to say: but my great master is preparing a place for me and going to take me to himself. He left issue six children, forty four grandchildren, four great grandchildren and he buried one son and thirteen grandchildren. He requested to [be] buried among his children, which was willingly agreed although they had seven miles to carry his corpse. His body was followed by his family and many friends. I preached a funeral sermon on the occasion which I hope was of use to the living.

You desire we would give you an account of our local preachers. In order that you may form a proper judgment of them you must observe we have but a few white men, not more than six in the society. One of these is a local preacher. And we have but one free coloured man that is willing to be so reproached for Christ's sake. We have very few coloured men that are free in society, although we have many women. Some of the coloured women have good gifts in prayer and hold prayer meetings: but the free women in general have no relish for religion. We have a few men who are slaves that exhort and are leaders but they have not gifts neither will the law of the country allow[?] of their being publicly useful, that is. Mr. Richardson, books, clothes and what money he left are with[?] Mr. Shipley at Dominica. He wrote me word he would sell his books and clothes and send the money home to his father; with respect to state and experience I must refer you to the letter he wrote before his death if you inquire of his Yorkshire friends as I have forgot the person's name ⟨the letter was directed to⟩. I bless God and my fellow labourers who labour together in love. And I am as well at present as when I left England: but I have had two severe attacks of the fever last year, and feel the infirmity of old age advancing upon me. I beg leave to come home next year, and be a supernumerary if I am not able to take a circuit.

Our numbers are Whites 22

black and coloured 3516

Many have died this year. I believe more than three hundred.

⟨Give my kind love to the London preacher's sister B——[?] and families.⟩

That God may bless you is the prayer of your affectionate brother John Baxter.

Since I wrote this letter the packet which we supposed was taken and I write by it rather than by the fleet that you may have the accounts by conference. I have received a letter from Brother Shipley, Dominica; he is much in want of help and Brother Hawkshaw wants me to[?] go so that there is a preacher more than is wanting in St. Kitts: and one wanted at Dominica. I shall enclose the account of money received and disbursed in my letter to the committee. I received your letter dated April 18 by the packet.

Chronology of John Gilbert

1767 Born in St. Johns on the island of Antigua, July 31
1776 Death of his mother
1779 Death of his father; moves to the estate of Nathaniel Gilbert
1781 Moves to English Harbour and is introduced into Store-
    keeper's Office of Antigua Yard without pay, May 27
1784 Moves to the home of John Baxter when he is ill
1784 Begins receiving pay in Storekeeper's Office, June 1
1787 Admitted to Freemasons
1789 Marries Miss Lorin, May 30
1793 Quits His Majesty's service, March 31; moves to St. Johns to
    open liquor store; arrival of his cousin, Reverend Nathaniel
    Gilbert, in Antigua
1794 Joins Methodist Society
    Enters copartnership in firm of Playfair, Gilbert, and Crich-
    ton, but leaves shortly thereafter
1797 Begins to act as a local preacher; appointed a steward of the
    Methodist Society
    Death of his wife
1798 Marries Miss Anne Hart, October 7

The chronology of John Gilbert was compiled from the material in the *Memoir of John Gilbert, Esq., Late Naval Storekeeper at Antigua, to Which Are Appended a Brief Sketch of His Relic, Mrs. Anne Gilbert, by the Rev. William Box, Wesleyan Missionary, and a Few Additional Remarks by a Christian Friend* (Liverpool: (D. Marples, 1835). A copy is in the British Library, shelf-mark 4903 df8.

1803 Appointed storekeeper's first clerk, December 23
1807 Appointed storekeeper and naval officer, April 20
1809 Becomes a teacher in the first Sunday school in the Caribbean
1817 Leaves Storekeeper's Office, February 16
1818 Reappointed storekeeper and naval officer, June 26
1832 Retires from post in naval stockyard, April 10
1833 Death, July 16

Charles Thwaites's Report

The state of the Wesleyan schools will appear from the following remarks, kindly drawn up by Charles Thwaites for our use. Most of his observations are applicable to the schools of the island generally.

The schools in connexion with the Wesleyan stations are as follow:—

Sunday Schools, 7 in numbers, attended by 1800 children.
Day   ditto   18 "   "   "   "   1365   "
Night   ditto   24 "   "   "   "   500   "

The total number under instruction is about two thousand five hundred; of whom about two thousand two hundred are children of slaves, liberated on the 1st of August, 1834.

No regular system of instruction is pursued in the Sunday and night schools. The infant school system is *imperfectly* taught in the day schools.

The children's capacities to learn are equal to those of any other class of people. They excel in reading, and the girls in needlework. They are deficient in writing and arithmetic.

Charles Thwaites prepared this report for Joseph Sturge and Thomas Harvey during their visit to the West Indies in 1837. It appeared in Joseph Sturge and Thomas Harvey, *The West Indies in 1837: Being the Journal of a Visit to Antigua, Montserrat, Dominica, St. Lucia, Barbadoes, and Jamaica, Undertaken for the Purpose of Ascertaining the Actual Condition of the Negro Population of Those Islands*, 2d ed (London: Hamilton, Adams, 1838).

Adult schools have repeatedly been established; but, for want of regularity in the attendance of the scholars, have been given up. There are notwithstanding many adults learning to read in their spare time; some of whom are taught by their own children.

The funds have never been sufficient to hire teachers of competent ability. Of those we have, (twenty-three in number), three are very capable; the rest are liberated slaves. Some of them receive four dollars per month, others three and a half, and some three dollars. This pay is much too small; and some of them suffer from pecuniary difficulties. They are pious and indefatigable in their duty, and love their work, which makes them engage in it at so reduced a sum. Many of them have also greatly improved themselves since they have been employed.

In most of the schools, each child is required to pay three farthings sterling per week; and those taught writing and needlework three halfpence per week.

The schools have been supported chiefly by the "Negro Education Society;" who have given an annual grant of 50, and sometimes 60, besides paying the rent of the Church Mission Society's premises in Willoughby Bay, for the use of the superintendent and Willoughby Bay school. The Ladies' Antislavery Societies at Chelmsford, Birmingham, Westbromwich, Clapham and Liverpool, have also given considerable assistance in money and articles of reward. The regular funds are, notwithstanding, very inadequate; and a continual reliance on God is necessary, not only for the regular supply that it may be kept up, but also for the deficiences; and it is a matter of gratitude that we can say, "Hitherto He has helped us."

Besides the schools under the superintendence of the three religious bodies, there are several on particular estates, supported by the proprietors or managers.

The want of a normal or model school, is felt by all in the island who take an interest in the subject of education. The rector of St. Johns's, previously to his recent visit to England, raised an amount by subscription sufficient to bring out a master and mistress to establish such a school for the training of teachers. On his arrival in London, he learned that the trustees of the Mico Institution were about to appoint an agent to carry that object into effect. Their agent subsequently sailed; but his destination was suddenly changed from Antigua to Barbadoes, to the great disappointment of the friends of education in the former island.

The Case of the Neglected and Deserted Negroes in the Island of Antigua

The voice of humanity on behalf of the deeply injured African race has so far aroused the feelings of the Legislature of this country, as to induce it to free this nation from the blood-guiltiness consequent on the infamous traffic in the persons of men on the coasts of Africa; nevertheless, slavery, with its unavoidable accompaniment, a traffic in human flesh and blood, still exists in our West India Islands. To arrest the attention of the humane and benevolent to this fact, and to the scene of human woe that is necessarily connected with this fact, is the object of the present address; for though the iron hand of oppression may not lie with quite the same weight as formerly on this part of suffering humanity, yet the groans of the oppressed continue to call for our sympathy and relief.

What has been heretofore said, may be again urged by the interested partizans of Slavery, "that the Legislatures of the Islands have provided various salutary regulations for the protection of Slaves, which place them in a situation even of enviable security and comfort." But this attempt to stifle the cries of the oppressed, will be as vain now as when it was first made. That some such regulations may exist will not be denied, but we fear that it will also appear equally

The Case of the Neglected and Deserted Negroes in the Island of Antigua was issued as a pamphlet shortly after 27 March 1814, presumably in London. A copy is found in the John Rylands Memorial Library, Manchester, England, shelf-mark 21.5 (pt. 8). Reprinted by courtesy of the Director and University Librarian, the John Rylands University Library of Manchester.

clear that the same obstacle prevents their efficacy as when Governor Prevost, the Governor of Dominica, in a letter to Earl Camden, dated the 17th of January, 1805, said, "The Act of the Legislature, intitled, 'An Act for the Encouragement, Protection, and better Government of Slaves,' appears to have been considered, from the day it was passed until this hour, as a political measure, to avert the interference of the mother country in the management of Slaves. Having said this, your Lordship will not be surprized to learn the seventh clause of that Bill has been wholly neglected."

This was the report of the Governor of an Island that was distinguished from the others for the Laws it had passed for the encouragement, protection, and government of Slaves. That such Laws, made perhaps by persons who were the first to break them, should produce any permanent salutary effects, is not to be expected:—of their efficacy, we may judge by the following accounts received from another of the Islands.

A Letter from a humane person on the Island of Antigua, written in the year 1807, thus states the condition of the Slaves in that Island.

"In this country it is a frequent case for the Owners of Negroes to desert them in times of sickness, and especially if the complaint seems likely to be of long continuance. A species of scurvy, or contamination of the system, frequently breaks out upon these unhappy creatures, many of whom suffer from it under all the horrid forms of disease that can be imagined, and so truly dreadful as to make them fearful objects to look upon; they may thus linger many years a burden to themselves, and very obnoxious to society: frequently they are turned out by their Owners in this case, to shift for themselves, under the idea of giving them freedom; and although we have a law to prevent this cruel desertion of Negroes, yet it is still too frequent. A case I have recently visited was truly distressing, where the poor wretch was perishing, and only dependant on the assistance of a poor relative, who was himself a picture of wretchedness and poverty; the state in which I found him will not bear description: he departed a few hours after, in, what I may justly call, the extreme of human woe. My attentions came too late, and we were obliged to apply to the Coroner to remove his remains, lest they should be an offence to the neighbourhood."

A Letter written in the year 1808, contains among others the following Case:—"Being out on business at a remote part of the town, I heard in an adjoining yard some cries, which I conceived proceeded from some poor creature who was being tied up to be flogged; I rode up, and was struck with horror at the sight of the object before me;—almost naked, exposed to the burning sun, lay a poor wretch, who appeared half consumed with the horrible disease I have before spoken of; she held up with most piercing entreaty her mutilated hands, enlarged by the putrid and distorting operation of the malady, they exhibited rather the irregular appearance of fungus than a human hand; the fingers were eaten off near the hand, and what was left, as well as the hand and arm, was full of holes, and at any motion of the wretched stumps, crowds of flies hovered round her, impatient to settle and renew their work of misery. Her legs and feet were as bad as her hands; the whole body appeared to be literally full of sores: I asked her who she belonged to, and found it was to a lady living in the town, who had long since discarded her on account of her complaint: she said she had been four days without food, the woman who had attended her having left her; this I found was one almost as bad as herself, but still able to crawl about; they had lived some time together, till the increasing sickness of this poor thing, added to an almost frantic impatience from the extreme agonies of her situation, had worn out the patience of the other, herself almost sinking under her distresses. I sought out the latter, and persuaded her to attend her companion. I sent immediate relief: they lodge on some logs of wood, without bed or scarce any thing to cover their nakedness." In three days after she was discovered, the first of these wretched objects was released from her miseries by death; and in a month, the second obtained a like release.

Another instance is mentioned in the same year of a young girl named *Betsey*, who was discarded by her Mistress, and forbid to come on her premises, because she was much afflicted with the scurvy.

We will give one more instance, from an account received in 1912, of the effects of this dreadful disease, and of the cruel neglect of the

Owner of the diseased Negro, who is described as "a most miserable object that can be conceived; no hands, no feet, no eyes; has scarcely the power of articulation left; is an aged man, and has no relation or friend to assist him: a small piece of land was given him by his owner as a support for his wretched life, but being incapacitated by his calamitous situation from cultivating it, it has been of no service to him." Indeed such an offer from his owner, was only insulting his distress.—Such are the facts in an Island where a fine of £300 is incurred upon conviction of such neglect and desertion: but prosecution must precede conviction, and no one could commence such a prosecution without raising to himself a host of enemies. To a Briton, conduct that manifests a disposition so insensible to the common feelings of humanity, may appear strange, but from the following extracts he may discover to what extent these feelings operate in the breast of a West Indian.

"Before you can persuade people *here* of the injustice, cruelty, and depravity of their conduct to their wretched dependents, you must remove deep-rooted prejudices of education; must convince them that a Negro is any thing better than an horse, or has a stronger claim on their humanity than the beasts that perish." Again: "None are more to be pitied than the deluded inflictors of misery, many of whom are Europeans who are educated with [in] principles opposed to tyranny and oppression, but they are now West Indians. The way to promotion is, to work your fellow creatures almost to death; to contrive how to make them do with as little of the real necessaries of life as possible, to brow-beat and stifle every sentiment of refinement and virtue that dares to shew itself in them." These descriptions of the low scale of moral feeling in the West Indies, are not given from common report, but are the testimonials of persons resident on the Islands, who have formed their judgment by their own experience and actual observation, having been themselves, at one time, under the influence of West Indian prejudices.

The accounts received from Antigua of the sufferings of those Slaves, who, either through injuries arising from ill treatment, sickness, or old age, were deserted by their owners, induced a few benevolent persons to contribute something towards alleviating their condition. The good done by the casual relief afforded them by this means, much exceeds what could have been expected from the comparative smallness of the contributions; and the pleasure of thus mitigating the sufferings of our fellow men, and children of the same Father, was increased by the grateful expressions of their thankfulness for the smallest relief.

Encouraged by the benefit that had been produced by the sums thus contributed, the friends of these distressed objects were induced to endeavour to establish a regular Fund, by annual subscriptions, for their more permanent relief. These endeavours have not been altogether in vain; the Subscriptions for the year 1813, amount of £88 18 6: and Donations to £116.

A Committee is formed on the Island of Antigua, to whom are entrusted the application of the Funds raised for the relief of the Negroes. This Committee has, from time to time, sent to the Association formed for their relief in England, accounts of the distribution of its funds, and of the cases towards the relief of which they have been appropriated. From which accounts are extracted the following cases, as they prove, if Laws have been passed in the Islands to improve the condition of the slaves, their inefficacy to eradicate the evils which are entwined, as it were, into the very system of slavery.

"*Catharine Redhead*, with several other old women, were some time back exposed to sale: the stronger were bought, but she with two others were turned away to pick for themselves, and to this day, live on charity. One of them had suckled several of her late mistress's children, and had known comparative prosperity."—"*Frances*, an aged woman, permitted to pick for herself (or in other words, turned away as unfit for labour) was found hiding herself behind a door, with only what may be called a few shreds to cover her, and in great distress, having scarcely any thing to eat, and nothing to wear but what she had on. She received a suit, viz. a coat, wrapper, and handkerchief for the head, which she wore with great thankfulness." This last person died about the 10th month, 1813.

"A Lady, possessing property in the island, by untoward circumstances being much reduced, instead of feeding her Negroes, allows them half their time to procure what they can for their own support; but they are so situated, that they are very little bettered by it, and nearly the whole of them are half starved, especially the children, of whom there are several, whose practice it has been to wander about the country in search of wild fruits, &c. to satisfy the cravings of nature. Lately we heard that the housekeeper had sent a message to her mistress, to say, that the poultry and children had nothing to eat; when money was sent to procure food for the fowls, but the children were ordered to be sent to their mothers. Knowing the condition in which the children were, we advanced a dollar to buy them corn-meal, to satisfy their hunger for a few days."—The foregoing cases are extracted from a letter dated Nov. 23, 1813.

Such are the miseries attendant on, and inseparable from, slavery; and though it is a melancholy reflection, that whilst the cause exists, there are little hopes of their entire removal, they are calls on the humane and benevolent to contribute their mite towards mitigating the distresses of these their fellow men, and some of them their fellow professors of the Christian name. The gratitude expressed by these poor people for the smallest relief, forms so pleasing a trait in their character, that we cannot close this statement without giving a few instances of it.

Our correspondent gives an account of an elderly woman named *Grace*, who, with her husband, only received from this fund 1s. 2d. per week between them, and after mentioning her decease, adds, "She several times assured me, that she often prayed the Lord to bless, in a rich manner, those unknown friends, who so kindly assisted in supporting her by their weekly donation." And, speaking of them collectively, the same correspondent says, "They request us to return their heart-felt thankfulness to their benefactors, praying that the Lord may reward them with heavenly blessings." In a Letter just received, dated March 27, 1814, is the following case, "*Henrietta Daw*, an aged woman, who of late, has found it very difficult to support nature, came under the notice of the Committee. About three years back, when the property she belonged to was *appraised*, she was *valued at Six-pence*, and dismissed. For many years she worked out, that is, maintained herself and paid hire, as she could afford, to her master; but being now unable to advance any money, is left to care for herself. The first time relief was handed to her, she was quite overcome with gratitude, and wept for joy. It was agreed to allow a trifle towards her support."

Subscriptions are received by William Allen, Plough-Court, Lombard-Street; Thomas Christy, No. 35, Gracechurch-Street, London; and Matthew Wright, Bristol.

N.B. An account of the Cases, and the manner in which the monies have been appropriated, lies at Thomas Christy's Gracechurch-Street, for the inspection of the Subscribers.

Antigua: An Act to Provide for the More Effectual Support and Education of the Poor Children of Several Parishes of This Island, and for the Establishment and Maintenance of a Central School Therein

Whereas the present system of Education of the poor Children of the several Parishes throughout this Island is very inefficient, from their being so widely separated in small numbers in the respective Parishes, whereby not only is an uniform system of Education precluded, but obstacles are opposed to the due and sufficient remuneration of Teachers, in such a manner as would insure respectable and proper persons to fill those offices.

And whereas it would obviously be of great benefit not only to such Children themselves, but to the Community at large, were a more condensed system adopted, better calculated to advance the important objects of forming the youthful mind to industrious and useful habits, and of training the young in those paths of religious and moral duties, by which alone their own happiness, and that of all connected with them, may be promoted.—

We therefore your Majesty's dutiful and loyal subjects, the Governor and Commander-in-Chief of your Majesty's Islands of Antigua, Montserrat, and Barbuda, and the Council and Assembly of this your Majesty's Island Antigua, DO HUMBLY PRAY YOUR MOST EXCELLENT MAJESTY THAT IT MAY BE ENACTED, AND BE IT, AND IT IS HEREBY ENACTED AND ORDAINED, by the authority of your Majesty's said Governor and Commander-in-Chief, and the Coun-

---

This act was passed by the Antigua legislature in 1831 and published in Antigua by Loving and Hill.

cil and Assembly of this your Majesty's Island of Antigua aforesaid, that there shall be established a School within the Town of Saint John, which shall be termed the "ANTIGUA CENTRAL SCHOOL," the objects of which establishment shall be, first, the Support, Maintenance, Clothing and Education of the Parish Children generally throughout this Island;—secondly, the useful and plain Education and Instruction of other Children in Reading, Writing, Arithmetic, English Grammar, History and Geography; and thirdly, a good Classical Education embracing Greek and Latin; as well as Instruction in the modern Languages, provided competent Teachers can be engaged.

II. *And be it further enacted*, that from and after the publication of this Act, it shall and may be lawful for the Vestries or Churchwardens of the respective Parishes, whenever application shall have been made to them for parochial relief on behalf of any Child or Children, to make immediate application to the Guardians hereinafter specified, for admission of such Child or Children into the said Central School, to which such persons are required to pay immediate attention, and to signify their assent in writing accordingly, or otherwise, if peculiar considerations should render it improper, specifying the grounds of such their objection; and on receiving their assent as aforesaid, the said Churchwardens shall forthwith forward the said Child or Children to the Master of the said School, having previously given in to the Treasurer or his lawful Deputy the name or names of such Child or Children, taking from him a Certificate of the same; and the said Master, who shall have been duly instructed to receive the said Child or Children, is, on production of such Certificate, to enter him, her and them upon the list of Parochial Scholars, to be maintained, clothed, and instructed at the Public expense.

III. *And be it also enacted, by the Authority aforesaid*, that for the payment of such expense it shall and may be lawful for the Vestires of the respective Parishes to raise, by assessment in the usual manner, and they are hereby authorized and required so to do, at and after the rate of Thirty-two Pounds per annum for each and every Child or Children sent to the said Central School by such Parish, to be applied to their maintenance, clothing, and education; which said sum shall be paid quarterly by the Church-wardens of the said Parishes into the Public Treasury of this Island. Any Act of this Island to the contrary hereof notwithstanding.

IV. *And be it further enacted*, that admission, for education only, into the said School may be obtained for other children, on similar application as hereinbefore provided, and on production of the certificate of the Treasurer, or his lawful deputy, that the quarterly payment has been made in advance into the Treasury, at and after the following rates; viz:

Twelve Pounds per annum for every Boy admitted:

Four Pounds per annum, in addition, for instruction in French and Spanish, or either of those Languages:

Four Pounds per annum, in addition, for instruction in Greek and Latin, or either:

Six Pounds per annum for every pupil learning to spell and read only, in the Female School:

Ten Pounds per annum for every Female instructed in reading, writing and arithmetic:

Four Pounds per annum, in addition, for instruction in the French language.

V. *And be it further enacted*, That in order to ensure effectual support to this useful Institution, the same shall be conducted under the direction and management of seven members of the Legislature, (of whom two shall be appointed from the Council and five from the House of Assembly, to be nominated, respectively, by the President and Speaker, whose names shall be by them transmitted to the Governor,) of the Right Reverend The Lord Bishop of the Diocese, of the President of His Majesty's Council, and the Speaker of the House of Assembly, of the Venerable the Archdeacon who is or may be resident in this Island, and of the Rector for the time being of the Parish of Saint John, and of one member from each Vestry, to be chosen from among themselves; the whole to be under the superintending care and patronage of His Excellency the Governor, or the

Commander-in-Chief for the time being; who may at all times be deemed members of the same; and the said personals before named shall be called "Guardians of the Antigua Central School."

VI. *And be it further enacted*, That in the event of any dissolution of the Legislative Body, or of any other event by which their functions may be suspended, the duties and powers of the Guardians, members of those Bodies respectively, shall not be thereby concluded, but the said members shall continue to act in the management of the affairs of the said school, conjointly with the other before named Guardians, until the next calling together of the Legislative Body, and, further, until a fresh nomination from the respective Bodies shall have been made, which nomination shall on their meeting be immediately made, and whenever from time to time any vacancy may arise, either from absence or death, it shall and may be lawful for the said Council and Assembly to fill up such vacancy, by a fresh nomination, signifying the same, as provided in the preceding clause.

VII. *And be it further enacted*, That on the said Guardians shall devolve the power of making such rules and regulations for the general government of the Schools, and for the interior economy of the same, as they may deem most advisable; which rules and regulations shall be forthwith submitted for approval to the Three Branches of the Legislature respectively, and if the same be not objected to within sixty days, they shall be considered as adopted, and be deemed the standing Rules and Regulations for the government of the said School.—And the said Guardians shall also have power from time to time, an occasion may require, to draw out further rules, if necessary: provided always that the same be not in direct contravention of those which may have been already submitted and approved, and that the same be in like manner submitted for approbation.

VIII. *And be it further enacted*, That all applications for admission into the said School as directed herein, shall be addressed to the Guardians of the Antigua Central School, who are hereby required thereupon to decide agreeably to the provisions contained in the said clauses, and to carry the same into due and proper effect, and the said Guardians are hereby also required to make a report to the

Legislature of the state of the said School at least once in each year. And of the said Guardians five members shall constitute a Board for the transaction of all business relating to the said Schools: Provided nevertheless, that of that number one shall have been nominated by the Board of Council and two by the House of Assembly.

IX. *And be it further enacted*, That in order to afford instruction to the respective Scholars, there shall be appointed a Head Master, an Usher, and a Mistress; that the former shall receive from the Treasury a yearly Sum or Salary of Three Hundred Pounds, the Usher the sum of One Hundred and fifty Pounds, and the Mistress the sum of one Hundred and fifty pounds, respectively, payable quarterly out of the Treasury of this Island.

X. *And be it further enacted*, That out of the rates hereinbefore mentioned and provided for the education of Children, not parochial, the Head Master shall receive for every pupil the additional sum of Nine Pounds each per annum, and be entitled also to receive the further rate laid down herein, of Four Pounds for instruction in Greek and Latin, and the remainder of the said rate of twelve pounds per annum, viz.—three pounds, shall be paid to the said Usher in like manner.

XI. *And be it also enacted*, That the rates for pupils in the Female School, not parochial, and hereinbefore fixed and allowed, shall be and wholly enure to the use of the Mistress of the said School: provided always, that whenever the Guardians may consider additional assistance requisite, the same shall be furnished at her proper cost;— it being hereby reserved to the Guardians to point out what additional assistants may be requisite, and to appoint or approve the same, as well as of the remuneration to be allowed.

XII. *And be it further enacted*, That from and after the publication of this act, it shall and may be lawful for the said Guardians to enquire out and recommend for the approbation of the three Branches of the Legislature, fit and proper persons to undertake the duties which will be required of them in the immediate care of the Schools; and on approval by the House of Legislature, signified to His Excellency the Governor, through their respective organs, and by him confirmed, the said persons shall be allowed to enter on their respective offices;—in like manner it shall be competent to them the said

Guardians to recommend, from time to time, should death or other causes make it necessary so to do; or on good and sufficient reason to recommend dismissal and re-appointment.

XIII. *And be it further enacted*, That in every year examinations shall take place in the several Schools on the second Tuesday in January, before the said Guardians, who are required to report the same, as hereinbefore made necessary in other cases, within thirty days after such examination, or as soon after as the Legislature may hold its first meeting next ensuing such examination; and as far as respects the Parochial children, the said Guardians are authorised and empowered to put out to apprentice such of the said children, as to them shall appear to be sufficiently well educated, and otherwise fitted for that purpose, and any indentures of apprenticeship duly made by them the said Guardians in manner and form required by any acts of Great Britain or of the United Kingdom of Great Britain and Ireland, now in force therein, shall be binding on all the parties in like manner as the said indentures could be affected in Great Britain or in the United Kingdom; for which purpose be it, and it is, hereby further declared to be the full meaning and intent of this act that the several laws now in force in the said United Kingdom shall be, and the same are hereby extended, so far as regards the several parties to such articles of Indenture, to this Colony.

XIV. *And be it further enacted*, That for the more effectually carrying into force the objects of this Bill the said Guardians, as hereinbefore appointed shall be authorised and empowered from time to time to draw on the Treasurer of this Island for such sums as may be required for the support, maintenance, clothing, boarding and education of the Parochial children, the payment of salaries and other contingencies required, which order so drawn, and countersigned by His Excellency the Governor, the said Treasurer is hereby authorised and directed to pay, and which sums shall be duly accounted for yearly, and submitted to the Legislature in the accounts of expenditure to be kept under the superintendance of the said Guardians.

XV. *And be it further enacted*, That a sum not exceeding thirty pounds shall be annually appropriated to the Medical care and attendance of the said Parochial Children.

XVI. *And be it also further enacted*, That so soon as the Building now occupied as a Jail, shall be vacated, by the removal of the prisoners therein to the proposed new site of the Barracks, and as soon as it may be adapted for the purpose, the same shall be appropriated to the use of the said School, and the purposes of this act be carried into full effect: But whereas some time may possibly elapse before the same can be properly fitted for the purpose, the Guardians shall in the mean time be authorised and empowered to rent some convenient place, wherein the intentions of this act, as far as is practicable, may be forthwith carried into effect, on the plans hereinbefore laid down;—but by reason of the uncertainty when the said Gaol may be ready, they shall not bind themselves to rent such place for a longer term than six months, renewable for the same term from time to time if occasion should make it necessary, and for the payment of which rent they are authorised to draw on the Treasurer, who is hereby required to pay the same, if drawn as provided in the fourteenth clause hereof.

XVII. *And be it further enacted*, That this act shall be and continue in force for the space of five years from the publication thereof, and further until the next meeting of the Legislature thereafter.

Dated at Antigua the Seventeenth Day of August, in the Year of our Lord one Thousand Eight Hundred and Thirty one, and in the Second year of His Majesty's Reign.

Nicholas Nugent, Speaker.

Passed the Assembly the Seventeenth Day of March One Thousand Eight Hundred and Thirty one.

Nathaniel Humphrys, Clerk of the Assembly.

Passed the Council the Eleventh Day of August One Thousand Eight Hundred and Thirty one.

By Command, Thomas S. Warner, Clerk of the Council.

Patrick (L. S.) Ross

Duly Published this Seventeenth Day of August, One Thousand Eight Hundred and Thirty-one.

Martin Nanton, Dep. Prov. Marshal.

Thomas Coke, *To the Benevolent Subscribers for the Support of the Missions*

Dearly beloved in the Lord,

I cannot present you with a more accurate Account of the present state of our Missions in the British Islands in the West Indies, than by laying before you extracts of several Letters, which I have lately received from the Missionaries.

EXTRACTS &C.

[From Mr. Benjamin Pearce, dated Bridge Town, Barbadoes, March 16, 1789.]

In a little time after the commencement of my labours in this Island, I formed a Society of nine members in this Town, and met them myself. I then laid a Plan as follows: I spent four nights every week in the Country, and three in Bridge-Town. Thus I continued preaching with all my might for two months, in which time my Congregations and Societies increased both in Town and Country; which compelled me to seek for a large house in the Town, but I could not procure one in any part of it. Mr. Button will remove from his house soon, and of course I shall then have no place to preach in.

These extracts were published in Thomas Coke, *To the Benevolent Subscribers for the Support of the Missions Carried on by Voluntary Contributions in the British Islands in the West-Indies for the Benefit of the Negroes and Caribbs* (London, 1789). A copy of the original is in the Drew University Library, Madison, N.J. Reprinted by permission.

My mind was very much distressed, and I could not tell what to do. I laid my affairs before my Maker in mighty prayer, and concluded I would see, whether it was possible to get a Preaching-house, but I saw such difficulties in the way as seemed to me impossible to surmount. I was sensible that no time was to be lost, and in spite of all my doubts, I set about it with all my might, and my face against every hindrance. I am now going on with my Subscriptions, and am from morning till night begging of all ranks and colours wherever I go, both in Town and Country; which gives me an opportunity of getting acquainted with the people. A spot of land was pointed out, which was every way convenient, and I ventured to purchase it in the name of the Lord. The price is one hundred and fifteen pounds currency; it is sixty-nine feet and one third deep, and about thirty-two in the clear. The whole I intend for the Chapel. I am promised a great deal of labour from Masons and Carpenters, and if I can but cover it (of which I have not the least doubt) my point will be carried. I hope to begin in a fortnight with this important building. I rent a house next to the purchase for twenty-five pounds per annum (currency,) into which I shall remove soon.

The devil rages in a horrid manner, finding his kingdom in this part of the world in such danger, which is truly the case. He has stirred up many enemies; some of them I have brought to justice, and have peace. They publish me in the Newspapers in a dreadful manner, and threaten behind my back what they will do. "If the impudent madman should build his Chapel." But I bless God, I fear them not, none of these things move me; neither does the cause of God suffer by such things, but the reverse. My congregations are larger than ever. Such crowds to and about the room at Mr. Button's where I preach, I never had before. It is truly glorious! Many of the first people in the Town came to hear, and heard with attention. It is hard work to preach to such multitudes. I believe if I had a convenient place, I should have a thousand hearers on a Sunday evening, for our doctrine is much liked. It would do your soul much good to see how the word is prevailing amongst all ranks and degrees of men both in Town and Country. I never in any place or any part of my life saw such an open door as is now before me. If I can but get up my Chapel, I shall carry all before me with the help of the Lord.

The state of my Society is as follows: in towns I have two Classes, fifty members in all, sixteen of whom are Whites, and the rest coloured; two Societies in the Country, one of eighteen, the other of fifteen members. One Richards, a soldier, is their Leader. I intend to form another next Friday of about eighteen more. How wonderfully is God working. I am very careful in taking members into Society, or I should soon have some hundreds. It is truly pleasing to hear them express themselves. I never remember to have found a people grow in the knowledge of divine things in the manner many of the Mulattoes and Blacks do.

With respect to myself, my labours are very great, and my mind is often much tried. I never was so engaged before. Great is the work of the Lord. Dear Sir, you little think or can conceive the noise and disputes, pointed sermons, and work we have amongst us. Notwithstanding the great heat of the climate, and my being exposed so much to its effects in preaching, I never enjoyed better health than at present, and indeed ever since you left me; for I have not had two hours sickness, since I came to the Island. What a blessing. My soul is happy, very happy in the enjoyment of my beloved Master. O how does he support me, give me courage, light and favour in the sight of the people. I hope, dear Sir, you will remember me and my great undertaking before the throne, and send me every possible assistance. I shall draw upon you for thirty pounds soon for the first time.

[From Mr. Baxter, dated St. Vincents', May 4, 1789.]

Last Thursday on my return from Byeta I received your letter, dated Charleston, and according to your request write you the fullest account I am capable of, of my proceedings since I left you. I have been with Mr. Gamble to visit the Leeward part of the Island. We preached on all the Estates where we stopped, and had leave to preach on more than we could supply. The Negroes on this Island are very ignorant, most of them not having been long from the Coast. Returning to Kingston we knew nowhere to call to dine: sitting down by the roadside we took the bits out of our horses' mouths, and let them graze while we applied ourselves to reading, not knowing that any person took notice of us; when a Frenchman from the top of the hill, came down and addressed Mr. Gamble, who referred him to me. I perceived him to be a messenger of love, and he gave us a kind invitation to his home. We accepted the invitation of the kind stranger, and riding up the hill, were hospitably entertained. I was at Grandsabel last Wednesday and the Caribbs were kind to me; and I intend to go out for good this week, the house being nearly ready to receive me; and then I shall visit Grandsable three times a week, and spend the rest of my time amongst the Negroes. I have got the land into a state of cultivation, and shall have it planted with cotton and coffee. I have drawn on you for one hundred pounds sterling, and draw for an hundred pounds more to-day to pay off the bills. I assure you I am frugal, and shall not draw on you again this year. I cannot send you the draught of the house and land at present, as I cannot procure a person to draw it, but will forward it as soon as I can.

I mean to set apart a day for fasting and prayer for the prosperity of the Caribb work: and hope you and all our friends will pray for us.

[From Mr. Gamble, dated Kingston, St. Vincents', May 20, 1789.]

Since you left me upon this Island, I have had several struggles with many slavish doubts and fears, that much good would not be done here. I therefore set apart a day for fasting and prayer; and ever since I have seen some fruit of my labours. Those who were in Society, began to be more on the stretch for God, and were more regular at their Classes, which gave me a greater opportunity of speaking close to them, as I meet them always. My Societies now increased daily; and those who had joined increased in the divine life every day; as they do now. And though the work is not so very rapid, there are a few coming in regularly.

We have had invitations to Tobago, though a French Island. Mr. Clark says that much good might be done there, as the Negroes are Creoles, and can talk English.

[From Mr. Clark, dated St. Vincents', April 23, 1789.]

I am now returned from the Island of Tobago, where I have been invited and tolerated. John Hamilton Esq. at whose house I chiefly resided, requests you to lend a Minister as soon as possible;

and he will provide for him, so that he shall not want any money from home.

I have also been at Barbadoes, and in company with Mr. Dent, one of the Ministers that officiates in Bridge Town, who told me that when General Matthews was in Barbadoes, he (Mr. Dent) intreated him to encourage a Mission in Grenada; with which requests he complied, so that Grenada also is open.

[From Mr. Lumb, dated St. John's Antigua, June 22, 1789.]

The work is prospering in almost every part of this Island. And we have had several happy deaths. But we cannot see the half of them who die.

[From Mr. Owens, dated Nevis, May 6, 1789.]

I hope this letter will find you in the full possession of health and happiness, pleased with the religious prospects exhibited in your travels, and grateful to heaven for all its mercies. Thanks be to God for his unspeakable gift. I am better in health, than when I wrote to you from St. Kitt's. I am never satisfied with myself, nor my performances, but am lost and astonished when I consider my Saviour's love. I am almost brought to determine with the apostle, to know nothing but Jesus Christ and him crucified.

Yesterday I had the honor to be introduced to General Matthews, by my worthy friend Mr. Ward, at whose house he is on a visit. He invited me to Grenada, and said, that I should not want a friend. Colonel Williams is also at Mr. Ward's, and presses me; and when I told him I could not go immediately, he seemed uneasy. Dear Doctor, if you can, let me go as soon as possible. Use your influence to obtain a Missionary for Nevis. I do not want to go from Nevis because the scene is gloomy but because the field at Grenada is ripe for the sickle.

[From Mr. M'Vean, dated St. John's, Antigua, May 14, 1789.]

I think the word of God goes on rapidly and prosperously in this Island, and as I am informed, in the neighbouring Islands also. Scores are flocking in, and joining continually: and the Societies seem to be very lively and diligent, more so, I think, in the Country than in Town. All seem to press forward, but hard and vile-hearted me.

[From Mr. M'Vean, dated Nevis, June 28, 1789.]

Brother M'Cornock died at Dominica about three weeks ago; and Brother Owens went there to settle his affairs, and preach to the people, and I came here to preach in his absence, and see how the building of the Chapel at Nevis is carried on, and though Brother Owens met with very bad usage here, yet the Lord has graciously made my path pleasant. I think my labours are blessed to the dear people. At my first landing I was received very kindly by one of the principal men in the Island, Mr. Ward.

The Lord has opened a wide door for this gospel in St. Eustatius, and opened the hearts of the people to beg for, and hunger after, the glad tidings of free salvation: and though they have no Preacher, yet Christ has been with them; and many a precious soul amongst them bears witness that Christ hath power to forgive sins. Glory, glory to God in the highest, the West Indies will soon bear sweet spices, even the fruits of holiness to the Lord. Brother Warrener is invited to visit St. Eustatius, he goes tomorrow, and Brother Owens is gone back to St. Kitt's, and goes with him. I expect Brother Owens here in five or six days, and then I shall immediately go to Mr. Hammet without fail, God willing. The works of Satan are daily appearing in their own colours more and more odious, in the fight of all who are under the gospel found and glory to God I think he is laying to his hand, and battering down the works of darkness, and establishing his kingdom in these islands. Religion seems to flourish in Antigua; but St. Kitt's will soon be renowned for sound and pure religion. Souls all over the island are inquiring the way to Zion, and seeking Jesus who was crucified. O I wish I had time to write to you. I am just now going to preach.

[From Mr. Hammet, dated Tortola, July 22, 1789.]

By a ship to Liverpool, I sent you a long letter not many days ago. As the packet is to sail this day, and I shall not be favoured with another conveyance prior to my going to Jamaica, I think it best to send you as circumstantial an account as I can, both of the work here, and the opening in St. Croix.

As to Tortola, I have already given you several hints about it, but shall now give you a general, as well as a particular information, lest you may want to print any extracts out of it.

As to the state of our spirituals.—We have 1500 in Society gathered in six months, forty or fifty of whom experience the pardoning love of God! and scarce a week passes away, but we add fifty new members! It appears to me as if these are the droppings before some greater shower. The people are sometimes so violently wrought on by conviction that I am obliged to adopt a plan of having the convicted taken out of doors, to admit of my going forward with my discourse. I do not think a week passes away without one at least obtaining the pardon of sins. Glory, glory to God: he doth not despise the day of small things!

Our temporals.—Our house has been fit to preach in for weeks past, though it is not altogether finished; but now it is nearly compleat. We have a small dwelling-house of two stories, with every necessary out-office. Our total expences for purchase and building, is about £1300 currency. Our debt £700 or near to it. I have drawn upon you for £100 sterling towards this island, which with frugality has supported two Ministers and three servants of the Church and house; and have also purchased a horse and furniture, and defrayed my expence to and from St. Croix: besides I have between two and three joes to pay in St. Croix for the expences of my memorial to the King of Denmark so that I can assure you, I do not possess one pound of the above money this day as I write. You will acknowledge I have not been idle in collecting from different sources £600 currency, and faithfully expending it and more on the premises in six months. The £700 we are in debt, is to be paid at £100 per annum, till the whole is paid with interest.

I informed you in one of my last letters of my visit to St. Croix. I waited on the General, who informed me I must get a memorial to the King, and have it presented to the Government Council for their furtherance. I spent nine days in that island, all which time I preached at the Rev. Dr. Knox's the Presbyterian Minister's Church, who interests himself in our cause, and translates all my business relative to the presenting our petition. I should be glad if you would send him a letter of thanks in the warmest manner for he is worthy.

By the trouble I have taken, with the assistance of my worthy friend Dr. Knox, and the trifling experience here, and at home, we shall have an establishment in St. Croix, St. Thomas's, and St. John's, three islands of great consequence to our connexion in these parts.

Dr. Knox's letter will inform you of his opinion as a man of experience on the subject: and I am apt to think it would be best to send some person of not only true piety, but good abilities as a Minister seeing it is a foreign island.

Brother M'Vean is arrived at Tortola, and I believe with a remarkable blessing to this people. Brother Brazier and he are to labour together in this island, who will (on account of the infancy of the work) have more to do than any two in the West Indies. The island will support itself, so that it will not trouble the fund for any more supplies.

[From a Lady in Jamaica, to her Son in Birmingham, dated Kingston, Feb. 24, 1789.]

As my letters have been for a long time past, chiefly of a disagreeable and melancholy kind, so I think it my duty when any thing offers that is pleasing to myself, and I have room to suppose will be in some degree so to you, to inform you of it by the earliest opportunity. Doctor Coke who is in connection with Mr. Wesley, has honoured this wicked land with a visit. He sailed the 9th instant for Charleston, after a short stay (as many of us think) of ten days; during which I had the happiness of frequently hearing him preach. For my part, I more particularly admire him, as a son of consolation: yet on proper occasions, he convinced us he could reprehend as well as console. Two of his sermons particularly have made some noise among us. In compliance with the request of some of his friends, the Doctor was so obliging as to leave the heads of one sermon, with permission to have them inserted in our public papers, and I have not the least doubt but it will have a good effect upon the people at large, and be the means of opening a door for the undisturbed reception of sincere Clergymen, whose zealous endeavours will, I trust, through God's blessing, be crowned with success, and be the happy instruments of bringing many to salvation. The second discourse of the Doctor's, which more particularly attracted the people's attention, was delivered at Port Royal: the expression espe-

cially which gave offence was a strong one, "Was Jesus Christ again
to visit a sinful world for the same purposes he once did the people
of Jamaica would cry out, "crucify him," "crucify him." A Gentleman who called in at our shop, was remarking on it, as being talked
of in Kingston and the means of drawing some of the inhabitants to
Port Royal: and I could not help applauding that which (tho' it may
seem severe) there is too much reason to believe is perfectly just.
And the Doctor must have had little penetration; had he not discovered that there was a greater necessity for the caustic and imputation
knife of a skilful surgeon, than the lenitives of a mild physician.

[From the same Lady, to her Son, dated May 28, 1789.]

If you see Dr. Coke, tell him that brother and sister Fishley[?]
Mr. Fosbrook, your father and myself wish to be remembered to
him in the most affectionate manner; we trust his labours were not
wholly in vain in this land of corruption: there are two or three
that endeavour to keep alive the remembrance of his instructions,
by sometimes repeating what our frail memories retain; indeed I
often thought he addressed himself particularly to me; his words
so searched my inmost soul. How truly welcome indeed was the
Messenger of plenty to famished wretches!

We are in daily expectation of seeing Mr. Hammet. A Captain
who arrived eleven days since, informed Mr. Bull, that the vessel
he is in bound for this place, had put into Nevis, to get some little
repairs, and would soon be here. This Captain has been one of his
hearers in Tortola, where he has had amazing success, and he must be
eminently qualified for doing good wherever he goes. But though I
trust their loss will be our gain, I cannot help compassionating their
feelings on being deprived of such a Pastor.

[From a Letter written by a Lady in the West Indies to a Merchant
in London, dated June 29, 1789.*]

The work among the Caribbs is so arduous and the toils and

---

*The Description of our work among the Caribbs in this Letter is so just, that I
thought it would by no means be improper to add the following Extract to the
foregoing.

labours are so many that those who are engaged in it, have need to
be in the greatest union with each other, that they may by mutual
prayer and sweet counsel, hold up each other's hands, amidst every
discouraging circumstance that may occur. I do believe, in this case
a work may be effected, for which succeeding generations shall re-
vere the memory of all that have any way promoted its progress,
and praise God on their behalf; as it would not only add to the Redeemer's kingdom, but be of the greatest utility to the nation to
which the isle belongs: but which, in its present state, must be lost,
if at any time attacked, in being so much like the human heart, in
having its worst enemies within. In the late war the Caribbs offered
the Marquis de Boullie, that at his word they would massacre every
subject of Great Britain that resided in the island; but he generously
deterred them, by saying that if they attempted it, he would throw
in such a force as should wholly extirpate them. Mr. Baxter's heart
is much in the work, and it is surprizing with what facility he has
learned the Indian language. The Caribbs are so fond of him that
they little regard any other. As soon as he returned from the Conference at Antigua, they flocked about him as if he was their father.
I saw several of them, among whom some are greatly civilized, and a
few can read. They discover a desire for instruction, and shew marks
of reverence, when prayer or any other religious duty is performed;
and if offered any refreshment, they will not touch it, till a blessing
is asked. There is something very noble in the spirit and manners of
those that are improved, far surpassing the Negroes in general.

[From Mr. McCornock,* to Mr. Stubbs, Silversmith, in London,
dated Roseau, Dominica, March 3, 1789.]

I arrived at Roseau the first of last January. I preach on eight
Estates and in the Fort: and have had a quiet people in the Country
to hear me, and about sixty in Society in the Country, and about
one hundred in the Town. Soon after I landed I payed my respects
to the Governor, who promised me his interest. I suppose there are
hundreds here, who never heard a Sermon since they came to the

---

*Mr. McCornock died of a fever on the 28th of June, in Dominica.

island. O pray for me, and my poor ignorant people, and strive to meet me at God's right-hand all glorious.

We have not been as successful among the Caribbs as we could wish: but as Mr. Baxter has learned the Indian language, and is esteemed and beloved by the Caribbs as a father, he will I doubt not be enabled, through the blessing of God, to christianize many of the parents, who will of course rejoice in the privilege of a christian education for their children.

I must now leave the whole at the feet of the pious, the humane and generous, who may peruse these lines. I confess, the interests of this work, particularly that part of it which relates to the myriads of poor Negroes who inhabit the British Isles in that great Archipelago, possess a large portion of my heart. I doubt not but the day will arrive, when Negro-Preachers may be found, that will carry the Gospel into the Negro land. The expences of these Missions are very great at present: and the larger the Contributions are, the more extensively may the work be carried on. I have only to add my prayers, that the Lord out of his abundant treasures may bestow an infinite reward on all those who are pleased to assist me in this labour of love.

Thomas Coke.

City-Road, London,
Aug. 26, 1789.

THE STATIONS OF THE MISSIONARIES

1. Antigua	William Warrener, John Harper.
2. St. Christopher's, Nevis, & St. Eustatius	Matthew Lumb, Thomas Owen, George Skerrit
3. Tortola	William Brazier, John M'Vean
4. Jamaica	William Hammet, John Lynn
5. St. Vincents	John Baxter, Robert Gamble, John Clarke
6. Grenada	William Meredith
7. Barbadoes	Benjamin Pearce

THE NUMBERS IN SOCIETY

1. Antigua	Whites	70
	Blacks	2730
2. St. Christopher's	Whites and Mulattoes	280
	Blacks	500
3. St. Eustatius	Whites	3
	Blacks	153
4. Nevis	Coloured People	98
5. Tortola	Coloured People	600
6. St. Vincents	Whites	16
	Blacks	140
7. Barbadoes	Whites	10
	Blacks	98
	In all,	4,693 *

*I have not inserted the numbers in Dominica, as we are so unhappy as to have no Missionary in that Island at present by reason of the death of Mr. M'Cornock. I have omitted in my Narrative to inform our friends that the Persecution in St. Eustatius is at an end through the interference of a very respectable person in England. The Society in Tortola being quite in its infancy, I have inserted only 600 members instead of 1,500.

A STATE OF THE RECEIPTS AND DISBURSEMENTS
FROM AUGUST 1788 TO AUGUST 1789

Received inclusive of £1001 advanced for
my own expenses and £561 subscribed.   £1401   1s.   6d.

Paid for the travelling expences of five
Missionaries, three from Ireland and two
from England, all of whom sailed from
Gravesend; for their clothes, linen, &c.
for a small collection of Books for each;
for their Passage; and for my own Passage
and expences.   566   11   10

Paid for Books of various kinds, part of which were to be sold, and the money appropriated to the carrying on of the work, and part to be given away to those of the Negroes who can read.	62	3	4
Lost by light gold, &c.	0	17	5
Paid for printing Addresses to the Public, &c.	3	11	2
Advanced for the support of the work in Barbadoes	50	0	0
Advanced for the work in Tortula whilst I was there and since.	90	0	0
Advanced for the support of Mr. & Mrs. Baxter, and Mr. & Mrs. Joyce, among the Caribbs.	156	2	9
Advanced for the Passages of all the Preachers who met me at the Conference in Antigua (those excepted who were stationed there,) for my own Passage in visiting twelve of the Islands; for my expences during my abode in the Islands; and small sums of money which I found it necessary to give several of the Missionaries before I parted with them.	195	12	0
For the compleating of the School and Dwelling-house among the Caribbs, and for furnishing it.	180	4	0
For various small Bills which were drawn upon me, and the money for which was applied for various necessary purposes in the Islands, with several small particulars not coming immediately under the foregoing heads.	117	5	8

Advanced for the work in Nevis.	50	0	0
Advanced in all,	1472	8	4
Received in all,	1404	1	6
Balance in my favour	£68	6s.	8d.

FINIS

Extract of a Letter from
Thomas Coke to John Wesley

Grenada, Nov. 28, 1790

Hon. and most dear Sir,

. . . .

The next day we rode to a town called *Guave*, where we took ship-ping again; and after touching at St. *Vincent's* and taking up Mr. *Lumb* and Mr. *Werrill*, arrived in *Antigua* on the 5th of December.

Here I indeed found myself at home; and spent four comfortable days in this Island. At the baptism of three adults we had a memo-rable time. One of them was so overcome, that she fell into a swoon, and all she said for some time, but with an enraptured countenance, was "Heaven! Heaven! Come! Come!" On the last evening, after I had preached, three drunken *gentlemen* (so called) attacked Mr. *Bax-ter* in a most rude manner at the door of the chapel. He made some reply, on which they seized him; and one of them cried out, "I'll murder thee, *Baxter*, I'll murder thee." Mrs. *Baxter* hearing the hor-rid expressions, seemed to be almost distracted: and many of the Negroes cried, "Mr. *Baxter*, our own Mr. *Baxter*, is murdered." Many who were in their own houses, and did not distinctly understand the cry, apprehended there was a fire: so that soon the whole town was in an uproar. Two Magistrates however with great spirit and discre-tion at last reduced every thing to order; and sent to Mr. *Baxter* to inform him, that if he would lodge an information in the morning, the rioters should be severely punished. We returned our thanks by

---

From *A Journal of the Rev. Dr. Coke's Third Tour through the West-Indies: In Two Letters to the Rev. J. Wesley* (London: G. Paramore, 1790). A copy is in Concordia Theological Seminary Library, Fort Wayne, Indiana. Reprinted by permission.

letter in the most courteous and grateful manner we were able; but informed them that we took greater pleasure in forgiving than in prosecuting, and therefore begged leave to drop our information.

The work of God deepens in this Island; and the converted Negroes give a more pointed and more scriptural account of their experience than they used to do. On Wednesday the eighth, at eleven at night we set sail for St. *Christopher's*.

The Stations of the Preachers
Antigua, John Baxter, Benjamin Pearce
The Numbers in [Antiguan] Society
Whites, 36
Mulattoes, 205
Blacks, 2113

In some of the returns the round numbers only are inserted, although there were a few more.

I am, my dear Sir, With very great respect,
Your most dutiful, obliged, and
Affectionate Son, THOMAS COKE

James Macqueen,
"The Colonial Empire of Great Britain"
Letter to Earl Grey,
First Lord of the Treasury, &c. &c.
From James Macqueen, Esq.

My Lord,

It was my intention to have laid before your Lordship, without lengthened prefatory remarks, the magnitude and importance of the trade, the commerce, the revenue, the industry, and the wealth of the whole Colonial Empire of Great Britain, and to have pointed out how the greatness and wealth of this colonial empire encreased and supported the resources, the strength, and the power of the mother country; but the appearance of a venomous Anti-colonial Manifesto, tagged in the shape and in the place of an advertisement to the end of the influential publication through which I have again the honour to address you, compels me first to expose to the scorn of your Lordship, and to the scorn and indignation of the public, that infamous and baneful system which a set of mischievous moles employ to undermine our colonial empire, and of which this manifesto forms a part.

The anti-colonial advertisement alluded to, must have cost its authors a considerable expense for insertion, exclusive of the expense for paper and printing the large number of copies required to attach to the Magazine, a proof of the importance which the moles in question attach to the circulation and the influence of Christopher North, and also of the deep wounds which his columns have inflicted on the system of calumny, mischief, injustice, and robbery.

In the month of February last, I laid before your Lordship, in the

---

Published in *Blackwoods Magazine*, November 1831, pp. 744–64.

particular cases of Mr and Mrs Moss of the Bahamas, and of Mr and Mrs Telfair of the Mauritius, specimens of the hideous falsehoods and misrepresentations which are advanced against the colonists by their enemies in this country; another, and, if possible a blacker, specimen remains to be noticed and exposed. This is to be found in their pretended history of their despicable tool, Mary Prince, compiled and published by an individual named, to use, and to retort emphatically, his own words, "that well known" Mr Pringle. This great personage, "well known" to the Colonial Office, has, in the labour of the craft by which he lives, given to the world the history of the profligate slave mentioned, for the purpose of destroying the character of two respectable individuals, her owners, Mr and Mrs Wood of Antigua. Joseph Phillips, a man in every respect fitted to support such a cause, guarantees the authenticity of this history. With the sayings, the doings, and the designs of these worthies, contemptible as they are, it is necessary that your Lordship and this country should be made as intimately and extensively acquainted as can be effected by the columns of Blackwood's Magazine.

The limits of a monthly publication restrict me to notice only the leading points of the accusations; but if I can extract, as I trust by the aid and strength of truth to be able to do, Pringle's sting, and Pringle's venom, out of Mary's tale, all her other accusations must of necessity drop off harmless and despicable.

[Then follows a seven-page diatribe against emancipationists and Mary Prince, a West Indian slave who has walked away from her owners, Mr. and Mrs. John Wood.]

Foiled in his object of obtaining proof from the Rev. Mr. Curtin of Mr and Mrs Wood's relentless cruelty, and Mary's unimpeachable veracity, Mr. Pringle has recourse to the testimony of his worthy fellow-labourer in this vineyard of iniquity, namely, Joseph Phillips. This man readily subscribes, "I can with safety declare that I see no reason to question the truth of a single fact stated by her," &c.

This anti-colonial fungus, who did not leave Antigua for building churches, has, in the language of Aldermanbury Street, (he has no correct language of his own,) been for some time past directing every species of abuse and reproach against me in this country.

Joseph's ignorance and impudence have as incautiously as gratu-
itously thrown himself in my way; and for the sake of truth and
justice, he shall at no distant day meet his deserts. In his capacity
as second secretary to the deluding society entitled, "The Society
for the Relief of Old Worn-out and Diseased Slaves," the Assembly
of Antigua, in the name of the colony he had unjustly attacked and
barely calumniated, thus speak of him in the Report of their Committee appointed to examine into his charges against the colony:—
"Previously to dismissing his evidence, your committee cannot help
remarking upon the character of this second secretary of the Society,
which unfortunately ranks equally low with that of the former one,
so much so, as scarcely to leave a worse in the whole community!!"

Time, space, and circumstances, compel me to quit this miserable
tool of anti-colonial faction and rancor, and his bosom crony, Mr. S
Thwaites: as also, to refrain from bringing before your Lordship and
the public the exposure of the calumnies and falsehoods advanced
against the colonies, by that ex-curate, Dr. Thorpe, from Jamaica;
the libels advanced against the Mauritius; and the hideous misrepresentations, and exaggerations, and falsehoods, advanced by the
Anti-slavery Reporter against the Reverend Mr. Bridges of Jamaica,
and various other similar calumnies and falsehoods; but they are all
remembered, and will not be forgotten.

By tools like Mary Prince, and Joseph Phillips, Pringle, and the
band of which Pringle is the tool and the organ, mislead and irritate
this country, browbeat the Government, and trample upon, as they
are permitted to trample upon, our most important transmarine
possessions, the value and importance of which I am bound to shew
to your Lordship and the public.

Sitting in London, and supported by the purses of credulous
fools in this country, Pringle considers that he may libel Mr and
Mrs Wood when in Antigua, or any other innocent individual in our
colonies, in security and at pleasure. He knows they live at such a distance that they cannot immediately come in contact with him—he
knows that to come to this country and to produce evidence to rebut
in a court of law such infamous falsehoods as he advances, would,
while all his expenses are defrayed out of the pockets of blockheads,
cost the injured parties an expense that would ruin the most in-

dependent families; hence his impunity in the work of slander and mischief, and hence this country is inundated with, and disgraced by, the circulation over it of the barest libels and the bitterest falsehoods against truth and justice that were ever concocted, penned, and published. Mr Wood owes it in justice to himself, however, to seek at the hands of the laws of this country redress for the cruel injuries which himself and his family have sustained. A jury of independent Englishmen, notwithstanding all the prejudices which have been artfully raised against the colonies, would give damages against his libeller; but with regard to the dastardly attack on the character of the wife of his bosom, there is but one way to seek compensation for this, and that is, to come and take Pringle by the neck, and with a good rattan or Mauritius ox whip, lash him through London, proclaiming as he goes that the chastisement is inflicted for the base calumnies and falsehoods directed against the character and the peace of the wife that he loves; and I feel confident that if he does so, not an arm, male or female, would be raised to stop or to oppose him.

The asserted opposition to religious instruction on the part of the colonies, is a string on which the anti-colonists have long harped with a pernicious effect in this country. The assertion is wholly untrue. It is not Christian instruction, but insubordination and revolt, taught under that name, which the colonists oppose, and which they are right to oppose. On this subject let us hear what the Rev. Mr Blyth, a Christian missionary in spirit and in name, and who has lately arrived from Jamaica, says in a letter addressed to the editor of "The Edinburgh Christian Instructor," and dated the 9th of June last. It is in refutation of some atrocious calumnies and falsehoods, which, on the subject of religious instruction in the colonies, had previously and lately appeared in that publication.

"During my residence in the island, I never met with any insult"—"but was uniformly treated with civility and respect; on mentioning my wish to the overseers, I readily received permission to see slaves, even if they did belong to estates where I did not instruct the negroes. I have not in a single instance detected any attempt whatever to prevent the negroes from assembling to the worship of God, either on the Sabbath, or the day I visited estates; so far from the

mill being put about to prevent the slaves from receiving instruction, I have frequently seen it stopped during the service, that every
individual might have an opportunity of attending." "It has been asserted," says Mr. Blyth, "that it is impossible for a minister of the
gospel to be faithful in the discharge of his duties, in a country where
slavery is upheld by law. This I can deny, from experience. Will he, or
any one else, who asserts it to be a moral impossibility to instruct the
black population of Jamaica till slavery is completely ameliorated, if
not totally abolished—will he, or any one who has had an opportunity of being acquainted with the state of that island (Jamaica), deny
that there are thousands of negroes in it whose religious knowledge
and conduct are consistent with the profession of Christianity which
they make?—and have not slaves as well as free people submitted to
the influence of the gospel in every age and country? Why should
Jamaica be an exception? When the age of freedom, which appears
to be approaching, shall arrive, it is difficult to conjecture whether
equal advantages shall be afforded, at the least, for the spiritual improvement of the negro race. Such are the facilities given to Presbyterian ministers, that three times their present number would find
sufficient and immediate employment; and such is the anxious wish
of the planters, and of the respectable inhabitants, to be supplied
with such clergymen, that they are already building two churches,
and talking of building others, even before they have any certain
prospect of obtaining ministers to fill them."

It is not therefore, my Lord, religious instruction that the colonists oppose. Mr. Blyth sets that point at rest, at once and for ever,
and a more monstrous stretch of arbitrary power cannot well be
conceived, than to find the Colonial Secretary of Great Britain step-
ping forward to command almost the exclusive employment of sec-
tarians (I use the term without any offensive meaning) to bestow
religious instruction on the slaves. Even on this momentous subject, like others of minor import, the master, it appears, is not to be
allowed to judge, or to interfere. So says the British Government:
that government which has left the emancipated negroes in Trinidad, formerly belonging to the West India regiments, the creatures
of its hand, and the work of its power, without religious instruction, or instructors of any description; till they are again become so

paganized, as to be cutting and carving pieces of timber into the figures of gods, before whom they bend down and worship. When General Grant laid the melancholy state of these people before the Colonial Office some months ago, he was requested to be quiet, and to say nothing about it! So much for Taylor and Co.'s attention and anxiety to bestow religious instruction upon their black population!!

The West India Colonies are particularly accused of profaning the Sabbath, by following worldly pursuits. I do not justify or extenuate these where they are followed, but remark, that the Anti-slavery Reporter may find equal profanation of the Sabbath going on every day under his own eyes in London and its neighbourhood, where shops are open, selling every thing eatable, drinkable, and wearable. At a meeting of the Magistrates of Queen's Square, [see London Courier, 2d September,] a number of butchers and bakers were fined for selling articles on Sunday. They defended themselves by stating that the practice was universal,—"that it would be impossible to pay their rent and taxes without so doing;" that they "took more money on Sunday morning than on any other day," because "the poor people would not purchase the meat on Saturday nights; many of them lived in one room with large families, and had no convenience for keeping meat without spoiling it, and therefore preferred buying their Sunday dinners on the same day."

I readily acknowledge the great power of my native country; but truth and justice are still more powerful than she is; and neither the power of her government, nor the command of her people, can alter human nature, nor make the lowest description of African savages, or the children's children of these savages, industrious, intelligent, and civilized, in a year, or in an age; nor can they accomplish all or any one of these desirable objects except by the application, for a long time, of arbitrary control, amongst such a race of men. Yet, to improve the savage, and to exalt him in the moral and political scale, the people of Great Britain have fallen upon the inconceivably ignorant, and inconceivably mischievous plan, to denounce in the senate, from the pulpit, and at the bar, the free inhabitants of the West Indies as barbarous savages, wicked beyond precedent, and debased beyond example. Thus striving, not only to reduce the master and his family to absolute beggary and despair, but by every public act and proceeding to debase him in his own eyes, and to degrade him in the eyes of his barbarous dependents, and of the whole human race!

Great Britain believes, and acts upon the belief, that the African savage whom she has transported from Africa to the islands in the Gulf of Mexico, has deteriorated, and is deteriorating, under the system of personal bondage in which he is placed. A moment's enquiry would tend to shew to the most ignorant and most prejudiced, that the fact is just the reverse. Great Britain, however, will not believe the truth; she legislates in obstinate ignorance thereof, and, consequently, she legislates wrong. Such conduct is worse than insanity. It can only produce mischief; it can only drive back the slave into a state of barbarism, and it must, if further acted upon, produce the destruction of our colonies, and the consequent humiliation of our country, and dismemberment of our empire.

I am one of those, my Lord, who, from experience, know how greatly those feelings of affection and respect for our native country are increased by being removed to the distance of many thousand miles from it, and to the midst of new scenes and things; but in proportion as those feelings are strengthened by such a separation, so deep and so strong will the resentment be in the breast of children, when they find that the parent pursues a reckless cold-blooded course, which must, by precipating destruction, burst asunder these ties. In no civilized community, but more especially in a British community, can, or ought, men for ever to submit to be calumniated, reviled, and persecuted. In commerce, and in politics, it is impossible that matters in the Colonies can go on longer without most fatal results. The consequences to this country will be, throwing altogether inside the probably destruction of human life, the loss of one hundred and forty millions sterling of British capital and property, vested in and secured over these colonies. The shock which this loss will occasion to this country, this country, great as it is, could not possibly sustain. Its immediate effects would cover towns and districts with poverty and distress, and its more remote effects would shake to their foundations her other strongest colonial and internal commercial establishments.

The immediate interference of government can alone prevent this tremendous catastrophe. Government must tell this misled country, that the West India colonists have been unjustly accused; they must tell this country that West India property, like every other property in the empire, must be protected and rendered productive; they must tell this country that the West India colonists are British subjects; that while they remain such, they must be treated as such, and protected as such; and they must tell this country that the West India colonists are no longer to be persecuted as they have been by ignorance, and by zeal without knowledge. If Great Britain will not act in this way; if she will continue to believe, as I am told she believes, that all her colonies, but more especially the West India colonies, are a burden to her; that they shame and disgrace her scepter; and that they are altogether worthless; then Great Britain can speedily relieve herself of the load, the shame, and the sin, by permitting these colonies to protect themselves in the best manner that they can, or to disunite themselves from her sceptre, and to seek protection where they can find it. The hour that compels such valuable possessions to adopt such a course, will prove one clouded with the heaviest disgrace that is to be found in the annals of Great Britain. Let me hope, that there is still sufficient strength and judgment left in the British government, and common sense and justice remaining amongst the people of Great Britain, to prevent this humiliating and destructive result.

The picture here presented to your Lordship of colonial affairs, may be supposed to be highly coloured. Others may tell your Lordship a different tale; but my long and intimate acquaintance with these possessions, and the perfect knowledge which I have of all that is at present passing amongst them, enables me, with perfect confidence, to state that the danger is neither misrepresented nor exaggerated. From every quarter in them I hear the same tale of distress and sorrow; regret and anguish; indignation and despair. The colonies are, for any useful purpose, nearly lost to Great Britain; and a short time will shew whether they are also to be lost to themselves, and to the rest of the world.

I do not for a moment mean to impute to government, that they either sanction or pursue the system of malevolent falsehood and misrepresentation which the anti-colonists have adopted; but it is a fact, as lamentable as it is undeniable, that government legislate and act in whatever concerns the colonies, as if they were fully persuaded of the truth of every accusation which the anti-colonists make. It is a fact, equally undeniable, that whenever any document which is sent from the colonies, partial and imperfect as many of these are, is demanded by the anti-colonists, that the same is readily produced; while, almost every document that comes from the colonies—however perfect it may be, which goes to refute the calumnies and falsehoods advanced by the anti-colonists, and to oppose the particular theories which government hold on colonial subjects—when demanded, is most difficult to be procured, or frequently withheld, and when produced, is frequently produced in a garbled and mutilated state. Every one about the Colonial Office is acquainted with these facts. It would be very easy for me to name documents that have been withheld or garbled; but to enter into the detail of such matters, would greatly exceed my limits. It is, moreover, painful to be compelled to observe, that scarcely in one single instance does any member of government, at any time when the anti-colonists pour forth their falsehoods and misrepresentations in Parliament, come forward to contradict them, as in duty they are bound to do; nor do the government, when the anti-colonial periodical press is spreading its false accusations and venom over the land, ever attempt to arrest the march of the pernicious system, by stating the truth through the press (a murder, a hanging-match, or cock-fight, are more important subjects!) under its influence and control; on the contrary, government continually leans to the anti-colonial side.

Under these circumstances, the defenseless colonists must think that they are despised by the mother country, and deserted by the government; and that while their ruin is pursued by the former, it is, to say the least of it, consented to by the latter. Every order and every communication that is transmitted from Downing Street to the colonies, manifestly goes upon the dangerous principle, that the slave is every thing and the master nothing, and hears the stamp of anti-colonial party and anti-colonial rancor, and tends to humiliate and to abase the master. All the measures adopted by government, are founded upon the erroneous and injurious notion, that it is impossible to be at the same time a colonist and a humane man—a colonist and a just man—or a colonist and a good man. It is impossible to conceive any state more degrading or debasing than this. The experience of all ages has shewn to mankind, that the individuals who are locally and intimately acquainted with the society and institutions of a country, are the fittest persons to legislate for that country; and every day goes to shew Great Britain, that she cannot safely legislate for possessions so many thousand miles distant from her, and with the particular interests, the habits, the character, and the pursuits of the population of which she is ignorant and unacquainted.

The anti-colonists demand and act upon measures of proscription. Government has been compelled to yield to their views. Every new law is consequently stamped with a character which wounds, which humiliates, and, in fine, which drives the colonists to despair. Thus, the order in Council, sent out last year for the government of slaves in the crown colonies, intolerant as it was, has been rendered insupportably so, by proceedings which have lately taken place in Demerara under it. The protector, and the superior courts in that colony, had it in their power, by that order, to modify the fine, for any offence committed, from £100 to £5, and from £5000 to £100, according to the circumstances of the case; but the influence of the anti-colonial party, for their influence I assert it is, has lately got instructions sent out to the protector and the superior courts, commanding them in every offence, whatever may be the degree, to exact the highest penalty, without any power of modification whatever! . . . .

As an excuse for such extraordinary conduct, we are officially told that the colonists ought to be excluded from every exercise of authority, because "the universally acknowledged principle of justice is, that no man should be a judge in a case where he is himself united by any tie of common interest with one of the parties concerned." By acting in this manner, the government do not, they say, insult the feelings, or depreciate the characters of the colonists, any more than they do the subordinate authorities established in this country, where it is not thought right in those parts of it "in which disputes between manufacturers and their workmen are of frequent occurrence, that one of the former class should act as a magistrate!" To the people of this country, the fact is notorious, that magistrates are indiscriminately appointed from, and act indiscriminately amongst, the manufacturing and agricultural population, and those chosen are properly selected on account of their local knowledge and experience. The principle, therefore, which the government applies to establish subordinate authority in the colonies, is directly at variance with the principle adopted in this country; but of the operation of which, and also of the fact, the Downing Street rulers of the colonies, it would appear from what has just been stated, are completely ignorant; nay, more, when injustice, under the mask of law, runs riot in a West India colony against the property of absent white and free British subjects, the Colonial Office turns round upon the complaining sufferer, and tells him that he suffers because proprietors do not reside in the colonies to aid in the administration of the laws! Will my Lord Howick deny the truth of that which I now state?

The most pernicious principles prevail in those departments of government connected with the colonies. These state, We know that the measures which we pursue will ruin British North America and North American merchants; but what about that?—we shall in their room have Norway and Baltic merchants! We know that the measures which we pursue will ruin the West India colonies, and the whole mercantile and shipping interests connected with them; but what about that? we shall in their stead have Brazil, Cuba, &c. trade and shipping interests, and the nation will lose nothing. These colonial dictators cannot be brought to comprehend that the loss of the whole property and capital of all the proprietors and merchants alluded to, is not only so much dead loss to the nation, but that by this loss, an equal value is placed in the hands of foreign and rival nations, which will enable them to wrest more wealth from us; and ultimately to shackle, to degrade, and to enslave us.

The blindness of Great Britain upon all these subjects is quite unaccountable. On the part of her government, it is separated from the principles of reason and all right feeling. The judgment of a schoolboy would lead that schoolboy to comprehend, that the more pains Great Britain takes to degrade and to ruin her extensive and valuable colonial possessions, the more pains foreign nations will take to exalt and to render theirs prosperous; in order that when those belonging to Great Britain are destroyed, these nations may reap all the advantages, commercial and political, which the British colonies have so long given to the parent state. Hence the extension of the African slave-trade to Cuba and the Brazils. Into the latter alone, according to official documents just published, 76,000 slaves were imported last year! The sinews of our commercial and financial strength are, in fact, and in more ways than one, drawn from us to support that trade.

If, my Lord, the emancipation of the slaves in the British colonies is to prove, commercially and politically, so great an advantage as it is asserted it will do, why does not the nation purchase the whole, take the management of the concern into their own hands, and thus enrich herself? Admitting that it would be a meritorious and right thing to enlighten and to civilize the African barbarians, planted by Great Britain in the western world, still, it is asked, why should the heavy burden, and the trouble of effecting that object, be imposed upon the West India colonist without any remuneration for his labour? Why should the colonist be called upon, without reward, to enlighten and reclaim savages for the good of the nation, while the Macauley's, "et hoc genus omne," are richly rewarded for merely trying to do the same thing in Sierra Leone? I say merely trying; for while, after a vast expense to this country, they have effected nothing, the West India colonists, without any expense to the country, but at a great expense to themselves, have effected a great deal.

The West India colonists assert, that neither the government nor this country ever will accomplish the objects which they propose by the measures and course which they pursue, and they assert this from local knowledge and experience. Let the government and the country therefore take the property in the colonies into their own hands, and then experiment upon it as they please; but till they do this, the colonists cannot be called upon to be at the risk and the expense of experiments, which we are told are undertaken for the national good. In this country, where a turnpike-road, a rail-road, or a canal, or any public edifice or thing is undertaken, or to be erected for public use, private property cannot be appropriated or invaded to do so until its value is ascertained and paid by the public, and the consequent consent of the proprietor obtained. The same principle ought to guide Britain in her conduct to her colonies; and until she acts in this manner, she has no right to call upon the colonists to become her slaves—under such circumstances, slaves they would in reality be—to attempt to carry her crude and dangerous schemes into effect.

The extent to which the minds of their countrymen are poisoned against, and alienated from the colonies, is best shewn by the opposition, coupled with revilings, which is always made to every just and rational measure which is proposed to relieve them from their undeniable and overwhelming distress. Thus the landed interest determined that foreign grain shall continue to be used in British distillation, in preference to British colonial molasses,—nay, the landed interest, and the distillers combined, have determined that neither the brewers nor distillers shall have it in their power to use the latter, even if they were inclined, and felt it their interest to do so; in like manner, and notwithstanding all the clamours which the anti-colonists and the people of this country raise against the African slave-trade, they advocate and permit the admission of Brazil sugar into great Britain to refine it for the foreign market, although the Brazilians not only maintain personal slavery, but carry on the African slave-trade to a prodigious extent! Mr. Poulett Thomson boldly told us (House of Commons, Sept. 28th), that "a very large amount of British capital was employed in producing sugar in the Brazils, and that it was for the advantage of this country that those capitalists should be allowed to bring the sugar so produced to this country in British ships!" In like manner, also, the clamourers against the West India colonies advocate the free admission of grain from Poland and Eastern Prussia, which grain is all produced by the labour of slaves! Such conduct, my Lord, is as impolitic and unwise as it is inconsistent.

The colonial possessions of Great Britain may properly be divided into two heads: first, such colonies as are commanding military and naval stations and outwards of the national citadel—such as the Ionian islands, Malta, Gibraltar, &c., where the expenditure is necessarily beyond the apparent advantages which the nation receives; secondly, the North American colonies, the West India colonies, and the Cape of Good Hope, &c. These are not only military and naval stations of the very first importance to the strength of the British empire, but also commercial and agricultural points of the greatest possible importance in the scale of commerce and finance, and from which the returns to the nation and to individuals far exceed in value the expense which is incurred. I shall place these before your Lordship in the different bearings of the question, and with the accuracy which the latest official returns that have come into my hands enable me to do.

Index